CONCENTRATE Q&A
COMPANY LAW

FREE online study and revision support available at **www.oup.com/lawrevision**

Take your learning further with:

- Multiple-choice questions with instant feedback
- Interactive glossaries and flashcards of key cases
- Tips, tricks and audio advice
- Annotated outline answers
- Diagnostic tests show you where to concentrate
- Extra questions, key facts checklists, and topic overviews

unique features

student-focused online support

CONCENTRATE
Q&A
COMPANY LAW

Imogen Moore

Associate Professor in Law
University of Bristol

THIRD EDITION

OXFORD
UNIVERSITY PRESS

OXFORD
UNIVERSITY PRESS

Great Clarendon Street, Oxford, OX2 6DP,
United Kingdom

Oxford University Press is a department of the University of Oxford.
It furthers the University's objective of excellence in research, scholarship,
and education by publishing worldwide. Oxford is a registered trade mark of
Oxford University Press in the UK and in certain other countries

© Oxford University Press 2020

The moral rights of the author have been asserted

First edition 2016
Second edition 2018

Impression: 1

All rights reserved. No part of this publication may be reproduced, stored in
a retrieval system, or transmitted, in any form or by any means, without the
prior permission in writing of Oxford University Press, or as expressly permitted
by law, by licence or under terms agreed with the appropriate reprographics
rights organization. Enquiries concerning reproduction outside the scope of the
above should be sent to the Rights Department, Oxford University Press, at the
address above

You must not circulate this work in any other form
and you must impose this same condition on any acquirer

Public sector information reproduced under Open Government Licence v3.0
(http://www.nationalarchives.gov.uk/doc/open-government-licence/open-government-licence.htm)

Published in the United States of America by Oxford University Press
198 Madison Avenue, New York, NY 10016, United States of America

British Library Cataloguing in Publication Data
Data available

Library of Congress Control Number: 2020941866

ISBN 978–0–19–885672–6

Printed in Great Britain by
Bell & Bain Ltd., Glasgow

Links to third-party websites are provided by Oxford in good faith and
for information only. Oxford disclaims any responsibility for the materials
contained in any third-party website referenced in this work.

Contents

Guide to the book

Every book in the Concentrate Q&A series contains the following features:

Are you ready to face the exam? This box at the start of each chapter identifies the key topics and cases that you need to have learned, revised, and understood before tackling the questions in each chapter.

Not sure where to begin? Clear diagram answer plans at the start of each question help you see how to structure your answer at a glance, and take you through each point step by step.

Demonstrating your knowledge of the crucial debates is a sure-fire way to impress examiners. These at-a-glance boxes help remind you of the key debates relevant to each topic, which you should discuss in your answers to get the highest marks.

What makes a great answer great? Our authors show you the thought process behind their own answers, and how you can do the same in your exam. Key sentences are highlighted and advice is given on how to structure your answer well and develop your arguments.

Each question represents a typical essay or problem question so that you know exactly what to expect in your exam.

Don't settle for a good answer—make it great! This feature gives you extra points to include in the exam if you want to gain more marks and make your answer stand out.

Don't fall into any traps! This feature points out common mistakes that students make, and which you need to avoid when answering each question.

Really push yourself and impress your examiner by going beyond what is expected. Focused further reading suggestions allow you to develop in-depth knowledge of the subject for when you are looking for the highest marks.

Guide to the online resources

Every book in the Concentrate Q&A series is supported by additional online materials to aid your study and revision: www.oup.com/uk/qanda/

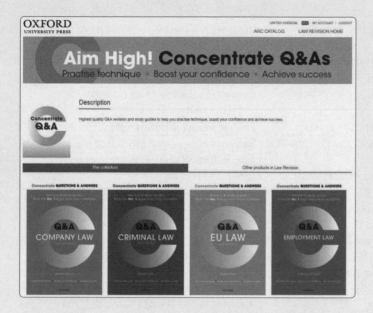

- **Extra essay and problem questions with guidance on how to approach them.**
- **Video guidance on how to put an answer plan together.**
- **Audio advice on revision and exam technique from Nigel Foster.**

Table of cases

Table of legislation

Exam Skills for Success in Company Law

1

This chapter provides some general advice on approaching exams and exam questions in company law. To get the most benefit from the advice here and in the following chapters, you should first consider your own position. In particular:

● **Know your course:** check your syllabus and focus your time and efforts on those topics. Of course your learning will benefit from exploring more widely, but do this only after you feel confident about the key topics your exam could include.

● **Know your assessment:** company law exams come in a variety of forms—number/type of questions, time available, permitted material (if any), and so on. Check the format of your own exam so you are not surprised on exam day. Past exam papers can help to familiarize you with the format and the examiner's approach, but check there have been no significant changes in course delivery.

● **Reflect on prior experience:** consider any feedback you've had from other law exams (whether implicit or explicit) and work on the skills you need to improve. An exam seeks to test your knowledge and understanding of topics and your ability to apply and analyse the law with unseen problems and issues, all within a highly pressured environment—where do your strengths and weaknesses lie?

Dealing with Questions: Essays

Essay questions appear in various forms: the most common are statements followed by an instruction such as 'discuss', or a query (eg 'to what extent is it true that . . . '), but they could encompass tasks such as writing a case note or legislative comment, or considering where law reform is needed. To do well in an essay question, remember to pull apart the question to identify the relevant issues, and focus your discussion accordingly. Whatever the phrasing of the instruction—discuss, analyse, critically assess, etc—don't be tempted to provide a general discussion or explanation of the topic.

PEA is a common acronym for an approach to essay writing: Point, Explain (or Evidence), Analysis (or Assess). Using PEA can ensure you cover all the points, explain, and provide evidence for them, and assess and analyse each point. All this is essential to doing well. But don't let it become too formulaic: PEA should be your slave and not your master. So remember the essence of PEA—you need to cover all these elements—but you can add interest by raising an argument from the start, bringing in wider and deeper critical thought, and sometimes merging the P, the E, and the A to be more concise and show your mastery of the law.

Dealing with Questions: Problems

Problem questions give a series of facts and ask you to advise one or more of the parties. You need to identify the legal issues arising, keeping an eye on all the facts. Don't just ignore facts that seem inconvenient—even if you conclude a particular point is not legally relevant, you need to indicate why (otherwise the examiner may think you missed the point). Focus on who you are advising and direct your response accordingly; this shows the examiner you are really thinking about the problem and not the topic generally.

IRAC is a well-known approach to problem questions. It stands for Issue, Rule (or Relevant Law), Apply, Conclude. (It also appears as ILAC or IPAC—Issue, Law/Point, Apply, Conclude.) Just as with PEA, IRAC is a tool and not an end in itself. IRAC ensures you have covered the things you need to cover and, particularly if you lack confidence, helps you to work steadily through the issues. IRAC is less effective if applied to a question as a whole: if you set out all the issues, followed by all the law, then the application, and then a conclusion, the discussion of the law can be quite descriptive without a focus on the facts, and the application and analysis may be limited or insufficiently linked to the facts. IRAC is more effectively used within sections, rather than the essay as a whole—use it to check that for each of the points you identified, you have clearly identified the issue and relevant law, applied the law to the facts, and concluded on that point.

Tips for Exam Success

Prepare actively: Revision needs to establish solid foundations—knowledge and understanding of the syllabus topics—but should also ensure you can analyse, criticize, and apply the law convincingly. A good student moves beyond describing the relevant law and is able to apply it; recognize problems, inconsistencies, and 'grey areas', consider its significance and effect, critique the approach of statute or the courts, consider how it could (or should) be applied in new situations, etc. Conventional revision such as reading, thinking, note-making, and mind-mapping is important, but you should also develop your skills through practice—test your knowledge and understanding against questions and other challenges and critically evaluate your own efforts. Practice can also help you cope better with time pressures and stress come the exam itself.

Learn, don't memorize: Don't be tempted to try to memorize material, particularly model answers, to reproduce in full or in part in the exam. Even if that were academically acceptable (it isn't!), it is a clear sign to the marker that you have not understood the topic and engaged with the question you have been asked. Use model or practice answers to show you different ways of explaining and analysing issues, and to help you develop your own understanding and skills by giving you a tool to critique your own work.

Answer the question: Too often students don't get the marks they expect because they discuss a topic too generally, rather than answering the question set. It is answering the question that shows the examiner you have really understood the subject, and can use (and not simply reproduce) your knowledge. Focus on the question, and explicitly identify the issues. Concentrate on these, even if this means you have to jettison some knowledge that you'd really hoped to share with the examiner. Never reproduce a prepared answer.

Be time-aware: Split your time in the exam sensibly, allocating enough time to each question. Spending too long on one question is highly unlikely to gain you sufficient extra marks to compensate for an incomplete or missed answer at the end. Similarly, don't spend too long on any answer, or on an introduction or setting out the basics—get to the main issues as quickly as you can. Taking a few minutes to plan your answer before starting to write will help enormously with this.

Make connections: The interlinking nature of topics in company law means it is very important in the exam to concentrate on the question and not jump to conclusions about what topic(s) it covers. When studying and revising, you will naturally focus on individual topics, but you should also aim to understand the subject as a whole and the connections between topics, rather than viewing each topic as entirely self-contained. Your own course of study, together with your reading, will help you grasp the principles and see the connections—mind-mapping helps here too.

Be structured: A clear structure allows you to work steadily and logically through the issues that arise, so always take a few minutes to plan your answer. There is no single 'right' way to structure a company law answer (subject to anything your lecturer says to the contrary) but remember that every answer needs a start, a middle, and an end. The start is the introduction. For an essay, this could identify the context and issues, explain your approach and/or argument, and ideally link explicitly to the question. In a problem question, keep it brief, just identifying the area of law and/or issues, so you don't get distracted by general discussion. The middle contains the main sections of your essay. Separate issues into paragraphs (and don't be afraid to use sub headings); explain and analyse each issue, linking to the question and/or applying the law to the problem, reaching interim conclusions on each point. Splitting the issues in this way helps to encourage analysis and comment as you go along, rather than waiting until the final paragraph. The end of your essay is the conclusion. This should wrap up your discussion, pulling together any threads of argument, and linking back to the question, ensuring the essay is addressed, or advice provided.

Stand out from the crowd: Examiners love to see a student really focusing on the question, critiquing (as well as confidently explaining) the law, and engaging with (not just reciting) the material, including further reading. Show off your wider appreciation of (relevant) developments in the legal and commercial worlds, topical issues, and recent news stories. Don't overplay this—your first priority must be to deal with the law—but deeper awareness and interest in the subject is valuable. You can also bring in relevant elements of legal theory and/or commercial practice, using your own course (the syllabus and the teaching) as a guide to what your examiners might expect.

Keep calm: Easier said than done, but thinking (and writing) requires a calm head. Initial panic can make questions seem incomprehensible but take a deep breath and read them again. Remember that if you've attended classes, prepared the work, undertaken the revision, and practised your skills, there is nothing you can't tackle. Ultimately an exam is there to test you, but not to trick you—enjoy the ride.

2 Companies and Corporate Personality

ARE YOU READY?

In order to attempt the questions in this chapter you will need to have covered the following topics:

- Forms of business enterprise and distinguishing features
- Consequences of incorporation
- Company formation requirements and restrictions
- Issues arising in the pre-formation period
- Corporate personality and the *Salomon* case
- Piercing or lifting the veil of incorporation
- Connections (in particular) with: directors, constitution, management and governance, corporate liability, insolvency
- Note: Coverage of some of these issues—particularly forms of business enterprise, and registration—can vary widely between courses, so please check your own syllabus

KEY DEBATES

Debate: Availability/appropriateness of business vehicles and limited liability

Do the available business vehicles adequately meet the needs of modern businesses? One issue surrounds the requirements of small businesses, and whether it is appropriate or necessary to offer limited liability with the additional formalities and restrictions that brings. Various papers, notably those by Judith Freedman and Andrew Hicks, address this point, while the introduction in 2001 of a new business vehicle with limited liability, the LLP, also gave rise to much discussion. Other developments, such as recent reforms to the older 'limited partnership', and increasing interest in developing appropriate business forms for social enterprises, are beyond the scope of most company law courses.

Debate: The nature of the company and the role of company law

What is the status of the company—a purely private contractual arrangement, or a 'concession' or privilege granted by the State? What should be the proper role of company law in supporting, enabling, and regulating companies? Although these issues can seem largely theoretical, these notions underpin much thinking on corporate regulation and topical issues such as corporate social responsibility. There can be very different perspectives on companies and company law; for example contrast Cheffins, B, *Company Law: Theory, Structure and Operation* (Oxford, 1997) and Parkinson, J, *Corporate Power and Responsibility: Issues in the Theory of Company Law* (Cambridge, 1993). The Company Law Review (see in particular *The Strategic Framework*, 1999) touched on these issues when considering company law reforms.

Debate: How far should the courts be willing to lift/pierce the veil of incorporation?

Whether and to what extent the veil of incorporation should be pierced has been a very long-running debate, and, although not in those terms, underpins *Salomon v A. Salomon & Co Ltd* itself. While some (including the courts in this jurisdiction, see *Prest v Petrodel Resources Ltd*) favour commercial certainty and a strict approach, others would prefer a more interventionist and proactive approach, particularly in relation to involuntary creditors. This debate links to the wider debate about the availability and risks of limited liability.

Q QUESTION | 1

While studying art at university, Mei has been designing and making her own greetings cards to send to friends and family. Following positive feedback she has now decided to develop this into a business and her friend Gok (a business studies graduate) is going to join her to provide business and marketing expertise. The business will need some initial capital to obtain appropriate premises and stock. Mei and Gok seek your advice on the most appropriate business form for their new enterprise and the benefits and drawbacks of that choice. They are anxious to protect their personal assets from business risk.

Advise Mei and Gok.

 CAUTION!

- Don't just describe the different types of business enterprise—the examiner wants to see that you really appreciate what the key features are and how they relate to the problem facts

- Avoid a simple list of advantages and disadvantages of incorporation

DIAGRAM ANSWER PLAN

| Identify the issues | ▪ Identify Mei and Gok's key concerns and requirements
▪ Identify the different options available |

| Relevant law | ▪ Different business vehicles: particularly partnerships, LLPs, and companies
▪ Definitions, benefits, and drawbacks for each |

| Apply the law | ▪ Apply to the facts
▪ Consider which benefits and drawbacks will be most significant and why |

| Conclude | ▪ Advise on most appropriate form |

SUGGESTED ANSWER

This essay will consider which of several possible business forms would be most appropriate for Mei and Gok, taking particular account of their wish to protect their personal assets and the need to raise capital for the business. As there is no indication that Mei and Gok want to run the business as a social enterprise, specialist vehicles such as the Community Interest Company (CIC) will not be considered.[1]

The simplest form of business vehicle is the sole trader, but as it appears that Mei and Gok will be running the business jointly, this is not an option. Unless they take steps to create a specific legal form for the business, by working together Mei and Gok would create a partnership—defined in the Partnership Act 1890 (PA 1890), s. 1(1) as 'the relation which subsists between persons carrying on a business in common with a view of profit'.[2] It is sometimes called a 'general partnership' to distinguish it from other types of partnership.

A (general) partnership comes into existence as soon as the definition is fulfilled; there is no need for registration or any formal written agreement. This means there is no cost for Mei and Gok, although they might choose to create a formal written partnership agreement anyway (particularly if they wanted to avoid the default provisions of PA 1890 on matters such as the division of profits). There is no need to disclose information, meaning no loss of business confidentiality, a further advantage. Capital could be brought in through investment by

[1] Rather than waste time going through every possible business form, explain why you are narrowing down your choices

[2] Use statutory material sparingly; you don't need more than this here

the partners, whether jointly or in different shares, or by a loan from a bank or other source. However, a partnership does not exist as a separate legal entity in England and Wales (the position is different in Scotland), and the partners remain personally liable for the business debts to the full extent of their personal wealth. This would obviously concern Mei and Gok.[3] They could be advised that the risks inherent in their proposed business would be low, and they might be able to achieve a high level of protection through adequate insurance (admittedly with cost implications) so there may be little need to protect their personal assets further,[4] but if they want the benefit of 'limited liability' then they will need to choose a different business form.

This would require the friends to take formal steps to create a business structure through registration, most sensibly either a Limited Liability Partnership (LLP), or a private limited company. The other form of partnership giving limited liability, the Limited Partnership, under the **Limited Partnerships Act 1907**, would not be suitable here[5] as all the partners will be active in the business. The friends will need to pay a registration fee, but this is not a large amount (£10 using filing software, or £40 on paper).

An LLP is a relatively new creation, formed under the **Limited Liability Partnerships Act 2000**, combining elements of the partnership (particularly internally) and the limited company. An LLP is a separate legal entity (distinct from its members, as partners in an LLP are called) and members are not liable for the LLP's debts. However, it has the same drawbacks as a company—it has to be registered (involving formality, disclosure of information, and cost), and the benefits of limited liability may be more apparent than real in practice. From the information we are given an LLP would not seem to offer Mei and Gok any advantages over a company, while not offering quite the flexibility or familiarity of the company form. Mei and Gok might wish to obtain specialist advice on the differing tax treatments[6] of LLPs and companies, but subject to that advice, a company would probably be better suited to their requirements.

There are several types of company: unlimited, limited by guarantee, and limited by shares. As this will be a normal trading business, the company limited by shares (members' liability is limited to the amount (if any) unpaid on their shares, **Companies Act 2006 (CA 2006), s. 3(2)**) is the most appropriate form for Mei and Gok. They can take either equal or different shareholdings to reflect their individual stakes in the company and will both be directors. Companies limited by shares can be private or public. Here a private limited company is most appropriate,[7] as a public company cannot trade without a minimum issued share capital of £50,000 (**CA 2006, ss. 761–3**) and is subject to more onerous regulation. The company could be re-registered as a public company (**CA 2006, ss. 90–6**) in the future should this become desirable.

---

[3] This shows that you have understood the relevance of the point you make to the information given in the question

[4] This sentence as a whole shows you have thought about the practical position as well as the more obviously 'company law' points

[5] This gives you credit for recognizing the LP, while ensuring that you do not waste time describing it when it is not a good option

[6] You won't be expected to know what the tax position is, but you can raise the point to show you understand its significance when choosing a business form

[7] This links your explanation to the question itself

A private company is cheap and simple to form and offers the advantage to Mei and Gok that their liability would be limited to their capital contribution as opposed to their being exposed to unlimited personal liability. It also provides a bit more flexibility in respect of the provision of capital.[8] Mei and Gok could provide the capital themselves, either by way of shareholder investment (in return for their shares) or by way of a loan, but would then be at risk of losing the money in the event of the business failing. They could issue shares to friends and family in return for investment, but should bear in mind more shareholders could lead to later disputes and disagreements. More likely, the capital investment would come from a loan, probably from a bank, and the business may benefit from slightly better rates because it could offer a floating charge (as well as a fixed charge) over business assets as security for the loan, whereas sole traders and (general) partnerships are not able to grant a floating charge. In reality, as well as taking security for the loan, the bank will probably require Mei and/or Gok to act as guarantor/surety for the debts of the company meaning that they would effectively lose the benefit of limited liability in respect of these debts. Research by Freedman indicates that over half of small business proprietors have given personal guarantees ('Small businesses and the corporate form: burden or privilege?' (1994) 57 MLR 55).[9] This insistence on personal guarantees from banks (and other providers of credit) means that the benefit of limited liability for Mei and Gok may not be as extensive as they might suppose.

Mei and Gok should also be aware that using a limited company does not protect their personal assets in all circumstances, particularly if they do not act responsibly if the company gets into financial difficulty. As directors, they could be made personally liable in the event of the company's insolvency, for example for wrongful trading under **Insolvency Act 1986 s. 214**, or could be disqualified from acting as directors under the **Company Directors Disqualification Act 1986 (CDDA 1986)**, which could now also lead to a compensation order being granted against them (**CDDA 1986, s. 15A**).

Another possible drawback of using the corporate form is that some company information will be available for public inspection— known as 'the price of incorporation'. However, as long as the company qualifies as a 'small' company under **CA 2006, ss. 382–3**, as seems likely here, the extent of the disclosure of its affairs would be greatly reduced, and it will be exempt from the audit requirement of **CA 2006, s. 477**. The criteria are: two out of three (tested every other year) of: turnover—not more than £10.2m; balance sheet total— not more than £5.1m; number of employees—not more than 50 (**CA 2006, ss. 382–3**). To this extent, the threat of disclosure is greatly diminished and the company can enjoy almost the same degree of

[8] Deal expressly with capital as it is raised in the question

[9] This shows both that you appreciate the reality of business life, and that you have engaged with academic work

privacy as a partnership. Companies are subject to more regulation, and thus a higher administrative burden than partnerships, but some of this administrative burden has been reduced for small companies by **CA 2006** (the reform agenda explicitly followed a 'Think Small First' approach to reduce the legislative burden on small companies[10]) so for example Mei and Gok will not need to appoint a company secretary (**s. 270(1)**) and will not need to hold Annual General Meetings (**s. 336**).

[10] This indicates that you have read more widely about the reform of company law and understand some of the policy thinking behind the legislation

For Mei and Gok a private limited company is a sensible option (and one chosen by many small businesses: there are over 3 million companies on the register, the majority of them small private companies). It is not without its drawbacks and some of the apparent benefits may prove to be limited but as their prime concern appears to be to minimize their risk, a company is the easiest way of achieving this aim, in part at least. To reduce the scope for later disagreements they should consider making specific provision in the company's articles of association (the main constitutional document of the company) and/or enter into a separate shareholder agreement to deal with the resolution of disputes between them.

LOOKING FOR EXTRA MARKS?

- Engage with some of the relevant research in the area to support your points and show your deeper understanding of the issues

- Use your broad understanding of company law to raise pertinent issues, particularly those that impact on liability and capital raising, rather than limiting yourself to points covered specifically within the lecture topic

QUESTION | 2

'Despite being viewed as the key advantage of incorporation, the benefit of limited liability may prove to be illusory and so be outweighed by the disadvantages of incorporation.'
Discuss.

CAUTION!

- Avoid a simple list of advantages and disadvantages of incorporation, this would not give you any scope for analysis and would not adequately address the question

- Don't provide a general account of 'lifting the veil'—this question is focused on limited liability in the wider context rather than veil-lifting

DIAGRAM ANSWER PLAN

> Potential advantages of incorporation—is limited liability the 'key' advantage?

▼

> Lack of benefit of limited liability in practice for many companies

▼

> Drawbacks to incorporation—weighing up benefits and disadvantages

▼

> Continuing potential for personal liability

SUGGESTED ANSWER

On registration, members of a limited company gain the advantage of limited liability—their liability is limited (for a company limited by shares) to the amount unpaid on their shares (**Companies Act 2006 (CA 2006), s. 3(2)**). Accordingly, while a member would lose their investment in the event of the company's insolvency, the rest of their personal wealth is safe, protected by the 'veil of incorporation' separating the company from its members. As a member in a small company will commonly invest only a small amount (often as little as £1), there may be little financial risk. This contrasts with the position of a sole trader or partnership where the trader/partners are personally liable for the business debts. Understandably this benefit of limited liability is often seen as the key advantage of incorporation[1] and writers such as Easterbrook and Fischel ('Limited liability and the corporation' (1985) 52 U Chi L Rev 89) have written persuasively on the broader economic rationale behind limited liability. Nonetheless, the benefits of limited liability may indeed prove illusory for members of some companies and be outweighed by disadvantages of incorporation.

Salomon v A. Salomon & Co Ltd **[1897] AC 22** established that the veil of incorporation applies just as much to 'one-man companies' as it does to the multi-member large corporations initially envisaged by Parliament, so members even of very small companies can benefit from limited liability. Although the decision has been criticized (Kahn-Freund described the decision as 'calamitous', tempting traders to incorporate when there was no business need: 'Some reflections on company law reform' (1944) 7 MLR 54),[2] the availability of limited liability to practically all who seek it is now firmly established.

[1] This shows that your initial explanation of the essential points—limited liability, the veil, risk, etc is all directed to answering the question

[2] Judicious citation of academic work can show you have read more widely and understand different points of view

It might be assumed most traders choosing to use a limited company do so largely to benefit from this protection. However, research by Freedman and Hicks indicates[3] this protection is only one of many factors influencing a trader—other factors as diverse as tax and prestige/credibility can also be highly influential (Freedman, 'Small businesses and the corporate form: burden or privilege?' (1994) 57 MLR 555; Hicks, 'Corporate form: questioning the unsung hero' [1997] JBL 306). Incorporation also brings other benefits, such as flexibility of organizational structure and increased financing options including the ability to bring in outside investors and offer floating charges. Accordingly, while limited liability may be a significant benefit of incorporation, it is not the only benefit.[4]

In any event, members of small companies in particular may not benefit fully from limited liability. The inadequate capital of many small companies may mean the company cannot borrow against the security of its own assets. Private companies have no minimum capital requirement and often have only a nominal capital (a public company in contrast must have a minimum capital of £50,000 (**CA 2006, s. 763**)). This makes it difficult for the company to obtain credit from banks and suppliers without external support. Banks commonly require additional security for any loans (Freedman's research revealed over 50 per cent of respondents had personal guarantees to the bank), and suppliers may also seek protection through third-party guarantees. This means those seeking protection through limited liability are in fact likely to be liable as guarantors for loans or lines of credit, and so face personal losses (even bankruptcy) in the event of the company's failure. The benefit of limited liability is indeed illusory in such situations[5] and as Freedman has observed, some traders may be incorporating to 'obtain the unattainable'.[6]

What is more, incorporation may have disadvantages, sometimes unforeseen. A trader might well form a company without the benefit of legal advice and fail to appreciate fully the consequences. The research of Freedman and Hicks shows the majority of entrepreneurs are not particularly aware of, or interested in, the precise legal form their business will take. But the veil of incorporation may have negative as well as positive effects. For example, in[7] *Macaura v Northern Assurance Company* **[1925] AC 619**, Macaura was unaware that his transfer of property to a company in which he was virtually the sole shareholder, meant he no longer owned the property. As a result, a policy taken out in his name over that property was not covered by the insurance since he no longer had an insurable interest in it.

A further example is *Tunstall v Steigman* **[1962] 1 QB 593** where Steigman, the landlord of a pair of shops, gave notice to the lessee of

[3] Engage with the academic articles—here you can use them to bring together the law, practice, and respected research

[4] This shows you are keeping an eye on the question but also challenging the statement

[5] Use terms from the question itself to show you are answering it

[6] Don't waste your time trying to memorize long passages, but if you can remember a few pithy comments from your reading, whether cases or articles, it can add interest and depth to your work

[7] The following paragraph and a half look at relevant cases and show how important it is to be able to summarize the relevant facts and points of law very succinctly

one on the ground (**Landlord and Tenant Act 1954, s. 30(1)(g)**) that she intended to occupy the premises for the purpose of her business. However, the court held that she had not met the requirements as the business was not to be carried on by her but by her company—which was a separate legal entity. A similar lack of awareness of the separation of the company and its proprietor meant that in *Re Lewis's Will Trusts* [1985] 1 WLR 102 Lewis' bequest of 'my freehold farm and premises' to his son failed because the farm had been transferred to a company. Although Lewis owned three-quarters of the shares in the company (his son owned the other shares) the bequest failed as the farm was owned by the company, not Lewis. Individuals may also get into difficulty through failing to recognize that the company is a separate legal person and treating the company's assets and bank accounts as mere extensions of their private assets: *Attorney-General's Reference (No. 2 of 1982)* [1984] QB 624 established that a sole shareholder of a company could nevertheless be guilty of stealing from 'his' company.

Generally, shareholders and directors are safe from the courts piercing the veil of incorporation to impose liability on them for company debts. The reluctance of the higher courts to pierce the veil as seen in *Salomon v A. Salomon & Co Ltd* has been confirmed in *Prest v Petrodel Resources Ltd* [2013] UKSC 34,[8] limiting veil-piercing to very rare situations where the evasion principle applies. However, statute may remove the protection of the veil of incorporation. Directors may find themselves liable to contribute to the assets of a company in insolvent liquidation where they have engaged in fraudulent or wrongful trading (**Insolvency Act 1986 (IA 1986), ss. 213–14**), or to meet the claims of creditors where they have misused the name of a company that had previously gone into insolvent liquidation (**IA 1986, s. 217**). Liquidators may also use the misfeasance procedure (**IA 1986, s. 212**) to recover from directors who have been breached their duties. Successful claims by a liquidator can result in large orders against directors eg *Re DKG Contractors Ltd* [1990] BCC 903; *Re Purpoint Ltd* [1991] BCC 121. In such cases the benefits of limited liability are significantly reduced.

Directors may also be found personally liable for torts committed within the company environment, depending on the circumstances. It is not common for directors to be found personally liable for negligent misstatements in the context of company activity as the courts require evidence that the director assumed personal responsibility (see *Williams v Natural Life Health Food Ltd* [1998] 1 WLR 830) but where a director does assume personal responsibility, liability can follow as in *Fairline Shipping Co v Adamson* [1974] 2 All ER 967 where the court was influenced

[8] There isn't time in this question to go into veil-piercing in depth but you can show you have the necessary understanding

by the fact that the director communicated in the first person and on personal notepaper. Directors have also been held personally liable for other torts, for example in *Standard Chartered Bank v Pakistan National Shipping Corpn (Nos. 2 and 4)* **[2002] 3 WLR 1547** the court held the managing director liable in deceit. The veil of incorporation will not protect all those behind it in respect of all their actions.

[9] Let the examiner know where you are in your structure—it shows you are still in control

In conclusion,[9] it has been seen that while limited liability is an attractive proposition for many entrepreneurs, it is not the only reason for incorporation in practice. Furthermore, its benefits are often illusory and it does not guarantee total protection from personal liability. Incorporation may result in unplanned and undesired outcomes, particularly when an entrepreneur does not fully appreciate the consequences of separate legal personality. In addition, the 'privilege' of limited liability is balanced by the need to comply with formalities and disclose information at Companies House. This increases the administrative burden through the need to file documents such as confirmation statements (previously annual returns), as well as reducing privacy. Disclosure obligations are reduced for small companies but even small additional burdens with the attendant cost of compliance and potential loss of privacy may be too much if the benefits of limited liability are not fully available. For some traders the disadvantages of incorporation could indeed outweigh the apparent benefit of limited liability.[10]

[10] It can be helpful to make a clear link back to the question at the end

LOOKING FOR EXTRA MARKS?

- Consider how the merits and drawbacks of incorporation and the effect of limited liability might differ for businesses of different sizes and types and different types of shareholder

- Recognize how some statutory provisions (or other legal mechanisms) may impose personal liability on individuals despite otherwise limited liability

Q   QUESTION | 3

Youssef and Zelda are friends who recently graduated from the University of Woolbridge and decided to set up a fashion design business. Having considered their options, they have decided to set up a company to conduct the business. They are considering calling their business either 'F U Fashion' or 'Great University Trends'.

Advise Youssef and Zelda on the steps they will need to take, and any issues or restrictions they should bear in mind, in creating and naming their company.

CAUTION!

- Avoid just describing the registration process or the name restrictions—assess the different elements and provide advice based on the facts of the question

- Don't just copy out statutory material: make sure you link relevant material to the facts

- Don't go into detail on the merits of the corporate form as the question tells us that the decision about the business form has already been made

DIAGRAM ANSWER PLAN

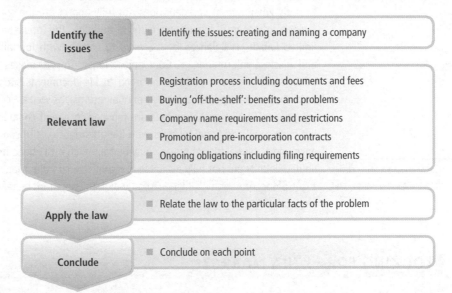

Identify the issues
- Identify the issues: creating and naming a company

Relevant law
- Registration process including documents and fees
- Buying 'off-the-shelf': benefits and problems
- Company name requirements and restrictions
- Promotion and pre-incorporation contracts
- Ongoing obligations including filing requirements

Apply the law
- Relate the law to the particular facts of the problem

Conclude
- Conclude on each point

SUGGESTED ANSWER

Youssef and Zelda should be aware that the company will (unlike a partnership) have its own separate legal personality and so they would not normally be liable for the company's debts or other liabilities (***Salomon v A. Salomon & Co Ltd* [1897] AC 22**). From the facts of the question it appears that they intend to be the only directors and shareholders of the company, but the flexibility of the company form means they could easily involve others if they wanted—whether by appointing someone as director to share management of the business, or by providing shares to people, for example family members who wish to invest without running the business. However, unlike a partnership (which can arise under the **Partnership Act 1890, s. 1(1)** without any need for formality),[1] the friends will need to observe various formalities in order to create a company.

[1] Shows, in passing, that you appreciate the difference between a company and a partnership

Creating the Company

Youssef and Zelda can choose between creating the company by registering it themselves, or purchasing a company 'off the shelf'.[2] A shelf company is one that has already been created by a company formation agent and is available for immediate purchase.

[2] Very many companies are 'purchased' rather than created from scratch by their eventual users

If they choose to register their own company (**Companies Act 2006 (CA 2006), ss. 7–13**) they will need to complete various documents and send these to the registrar of companies at Companies House (based in Cardiff for companies registered in England and Wales) either in paper form or electronically:

[3] In this and other 'bullet points' that follow, the basic information is combined with references to the facts of the problem to show the question is being addressed

- Memorandum of association[3] (**s. 8**)
  - Youssef and Zelda must subscribe their names to the memorandum—the document that forms the company. It is no longer part of the company's constitution.
- Application for registration (**s. 9(2)**)
  - This states the company's basic details including its proposed name, the address of its registered office, and that it is (in this case) a private company.
- Articles of association (**s. 9(5)(b)**)
  - Articles (the company's constitution) need not be filed if Youssef and Zelda wish to use model (standard form) articles. The current model articles are found in the **Companies (Model Articles) Regulations 2008**. If they want to have some bespoke articles, they could register these and the model articles would then fill any gaps by virtue of **s. 20**.
- Statement of capital and initial shareholdings (**ss. 9(4)(a) and 10**)
  - This states the company's share capital and shareholdings. Most small private companies (as this will be) have minimal share capital, eg the friends could have a share capital of £2 with each taking a single £1 share.
- Statement of proposed officers (**ss. 9(4)(c) and 12**)
  - It is assumed that Youssef and Zelda will be the company's first directors. They do not need particular qualifications but must be over 16 (**s. 157(1)**), which they obviously are. Their names, addresses, and consent to act should go in this document. They can use a service address to keep their residential addresses off the public register though, which might be sensible for example if their fashion business uses fur, to avoid intimidation.

[4] Recognizes the change to the law in the CA 2006

  - As it will be a private company they do not need a company secretary[4] (**s. 270(1)**).
- Statement of compliance (**s. 13**)
  - Youssef and Zelda must state that all the registration requirements have been complied with and the registrar can take this statement as evidence of compliance.

[5] Impress the examiner by showing that you are aware of wider practical points as well as the legal points

Youssef and Zelda must also pay a registration fee, which is currently £40 by post (or £10 using filing software or £12 online).[5] Same-day registration can be obtained for a higher fee. If all documents are in order the registrar registers them under **CA 2006, s. 14** and issues a Certificate of Incorporation (**CA 2006, s. 15**) which is conclusive evidence that the registration requirements have been complied with. The company comes into existence at the point of registration (**CA 2006, s. 16**).

If Youssef and Zelda did not want to prepare and send the incorporation documentation they could buy a shelf company, which is ready to use straight away. It costs more to buy a shelf company than register a company yourself, but it is not expensive (£50 is fairly standard). There are potential disadvantages to buying a company off the shelf as it will not be in exactly the form Youssef and Zelda might have chosen, so they should make changes to the articles to avoid problems later on. A shelf company will not have the desired name but the name can be changed by means of a special resolution (or other procedure specified in the articles) under **CA 2006, s. 77(1)**, or they could leave the company's name unchanged and trade under a different business name. As a company comes into existence on registration (not on purchase or change of name) they should bear in mind that their company exists prior to their purchase. This is not normally a problem but can lead to complications; for example the pre-incorporation contract provisions (**CA 2006, s. 51**)[6] do not apply where a company is already in existence at the time of the contract but under a different name (***Oshkosh B'Gosh Inc v Dan Marbel Inc Ltd* [1989] BCLC 507**).

[6] Use your knowledge of other, connected, topics to add weight to your consideration of shelf companies

Naming the Company

There are some important requirements and restrictions in the choice of name for the company (see **CA 2006, Part 5**), which also apply to business (or trading) names under **CA 2006, Part 41**. First, as a private company the company's name must end with 'limited' or 'Ltd' (or the Welsh equivalent if the company were to be registered in Wales, rather than England and Wales) (**CA 2006, s. 59**). Further, a company must not be registered if, in the opinion of the Secretary of State, use of its name would constitute an offence or be offensive (**CA 2006, s. 53**). It is possible that 'F U Fashions'[7] would be perceived as offensive: ***R v Registrar of Companies, ex parte Attorney-General* [1991] BCLC 476** revealed that the registrar had rejected 'Prostitutes Ltd' and 'Hookers Ltd' as possible names for a new company.

[7] Try to relate your knowledge of the naming restrictions to the specific names suggested

Approval of the Secretary of State is required if a company's proposed name would be likely to give the impression that the company is associated with the government, local authority, or specified public authorities (**CA 2006, s. 54**). This does not seem to be a problem in this case. The Secretary of State's approval must also be obtained if the name contains any word or expression specified in regulations under **CA 2006, s. 55**—currently the **Company, Limited Liability Partnerships and Business Names (Sensitive Words and Expressions) Regulations 2014.** This list was reduced under the government's 'Red Tape Challenge'[8] initiative to reduce the legislative burden on business but does include 'University'[9] so Youssef and Zelda would have to obtain approval if they want to use this name.

[8] Shows awareness of why the Regulations were updated

[9] It wouldn't matter if you didn't know what the list contained—you could still make an informed comment and relate it to the question, eg 'if the list contains the word "University" then …'

The company name must not be the same as, or too similar to, any other company name on the register (**CA 2006, s. 66**). To avoid this problem Youssef and Zelda can check the register of company names via the Companies House website. If the company is registered with a name that is the same as, or too similar to, another company's name then it could be directed to change it under **CA 2006, s. 67**. Or if someone objected that the company name is sufficiently similar to a name associated with them so as to be likely to mislead by suggesting a connection between them, there is an adjudication process under **CA 2006, ss. 69–74** which could also lead to a direction to change the company's name.

The company's name (whether or not a business name is used) must be disclosed at the registered office, business premises, on business communications, and websites (**CA 2006, s. 82** and the **Companies (Trading Disclosures) Regulations 2008**).

Other Issues

Youssef and Zelda should keep in mind that during the pre-formation process they can be regarded as company promoters[10] as they are taking the necessary steps to form a company with reference to a particular project (*Twycross v Grant* (1877) 2 CPD 469). As promoters they owe fiduciary duties to the company (see, eg *Erlanger v New Sombrero Phosphate Co* (1878) 3 App Cas 1218) and they must ensure that all material facts are disclosed and any profits they make personally must be accounted for to the company. They should also be aware that any contracts entered into prior to incorporation will operate as contracts with them personally under **CA 2006, s. 51** (*Phonogram Ltd v Lane* [1982] QB 938). Once the company is incorporated, it will only be bound by such contracts if the parties novate the contract and so the friends should ensure this is done following incorporation to avoid any potential personal liability.

[10] As the facts of the problem do not disclose any issues particularly relevant to promoters' duties, it is best not to go into too much detail

Once the company is registered, there are ongoing responsibilities. Annual accounts and confirmation statements (formerly annual returns) must be filed at Companies House (**CA 2006, s. 441**) unless the company is exempt, and changes to the company's constitution, directorships, membership, etc must also be notified to Companies House. Filing fees are due each time so there are ongoing financial consequences attached to the 'privilege' of forming a company.

LOOKING FOR EXTRA MARKS?

■ Show your practical knowledge—consider the possibility of buying a company 'off the shelf' as well as forming the company from scratch

■ Bring in some awareness of other connected issues, such as promoters and pre-incorporation contracts, while taking care not to go off point

■ Recognize recent developments in the law, such as the updating of the name regulations

Q | QUESTION | 4

Which of the following statements more accurately reflects the current law on lifting (or piercing) the veil of incorporation and why?

'Salomon is in the shadow. It is still alive but no longer occupies the centre of the corporate stage.'

(Schmittoff, C. M., 'Salomon in the shadow' [1976] JBL 305)

'The veil of incorporation is as opaque and impassable as an iron curtain.'

(Samuels, A., 'Lifting the veil' [1964] JBL 218)

! CAUTION!

■ The quotes are being used here as a trigger for a wider discussion, so don't be tempted simply to recite the arguments from the articles (and don't be put off the question just because you haven't read those particular articles)

■ Analyse the current law, don't just describe the cases chronologically

■ Remember to assess the impact of recent decisions—particularly those from higher courts

O DIAGRAM ANSWER PLAN

> Lifting/piercing the veil: concept, terminology, and current trend

> Groups and the 'single economic unit': explain and explore

> 'Mere facade' or 'evasion': explain and explore

> Agency, tort, and other legal principles: explain and explore

> Conclude: reconsider trend, and relate discussion to quotes

SUGGESTED ANSWER

The quotes reflect changing approaches to lifting/piercing the veil of incorporation over the years. This essay will show that, despite the attempts of some judges (notably Lord Denning) to move the principle of separate corporate personality into the shadow, the current law is much more in line with Samuels' quote than Schmittoff's,[1] particularly after recent Supreme Court decisions, most notably *Prest v Petrodel Resources Ltd* [2013] UKSC 34 (*Prest*).

The veil of incorporation is a metaphor for the separation of a company and its members. Ever since the House of Lords in *Salomon v A. Salomon & Co Ltd* [1897] AC 22 (*Salomon*) recognized the validity of Salomon's 'one-man company',[2] attempts have been made to lift this veil, whether to impose liability on those behind the veil or for some other purpose (eg attributing 'enemy alien' status: *Daimler Co Ltd v Continental Tyre and Rubber Co Ltd* [1916] 2 AC 307). The veil can be lifted by statute (*Dimbleby v National Union of Journalists* [1984] 1 WLR 427), but such provisions usually impose additional liability on individuals rather than ignoring separate personality (eg **Insolvency Act 1986, s. 214**). Accordingly this essay will focus on the approach of the courts.

Over the years different phrases have been used, sometimes indicating different categories of veil-lifting (eg Ottolenghi, 'From peeping behind the corporate veil, to ignoring it completely' (1990) 53 MLR 338). Following *Prest*, this essay will use 'piercing' the veil for occasions when the court rejects the consequences of *Salomon* and imposes liability behind the veil.[3] 'Lifting' the veil may encompass a wider range of circumstances where the veil is looked through or avoided, but the *Salomon* principle remains intact.

In general terms the trend of the courts is very much towards the Samuels statement. Suggestions that courts could lift the veil whenever justice required (eg *Re a Company* [1985] BCLC 333) were rejected in *Adams v Cape Industries plc* [1990] Ch 433 (*Adams*) as was the argument that the veil could be lifted where a company and its members form a 'single economic unit' (*DHN Food Distributors v Tower Hamlets LBC* [1976] 1 WLR 852 (*DHN*)). *Woolfson v Strathclyde Regional Council* 1978 SC (HL) 90 (*Woolfson*) stated the 'only' ground for piercing the veil is where the company is a 'mere facade concealing the true facts'. This was accepted in *Adams*, and in *Prest* but using the new terminology of 'evasion',[4] although the courts may still find ways *around* the veil, using other legal mechanisms, to achieve much the same result.

Corporate Groups

The principle of separate corporate personality applies to groups as it does to companies with human members (*The Albazero* [1977] AC 774;

---

[1] Using your introduction to set out your argument is an effective technique to encourage a critical and analytical approach

[2] This shows the examiner that you know your stuff, without wasting time setting out the detailed facts and judgment of *Salomon*

[3] At first sight this is just about terminology, but it also reveals a good awareness of *Prest*

[4] This will be dealt with in more detail later, but this reassures the examiner that you understand the 'mere facade' principle has been overtaken

Re Southard [1979] 1 WLR 1198). However, in *Littlewoods Mail Order Stores Ltd v Inland Revenue Commissioners* [1969] 1 WLR 1241 and *DHN* Lord Denning considered the economic reality—if a group was a 'single economic unit' in fact then it should be treated as such in law. Schmittoff's quote dates from this period where courts were more willing to lift the veil, pushing *Salomon* into the shadow.[5] But in *Woolfson* the House of Lords doubted this approach and *Adams* held that the veil could be lifted on the basis of 'single economic unit' only where this was the true construction of a statute or contract. This applies on occasion (eg *Beckett Investment Management Group Ltd v Hall* [2007] ICR 1539) but is very limited in scope so the veil remains largely 'opaque and impassable'.[6]

Mere Facade/Evasion

Woolfson stated the veil can only be pierced if the company is a 'mere facade concealing the true facts', with *Adams* recognizing there was 'sparse guidance' on what that means. It requires some impropriety on the part of those using the company (although not necessarily when forming the company: *Ben Hashem v Ali Shayif* [2009] 1 FLR 115). And this impropriety must be relevant—there must be a connection between the impropriety and the use of the corporate form: *Trustor AB v Smallbone (No. 2)* [2001] 1 WLR 1177. This was emphasized in *Prest* which located veil-piercing within the wider policy that 'statute must not be used as an engine of fraud', and reformulated the 'mere facade' notion as 'the evasion principle'.[7] The veil will be pierced only where the corporate form is interposed to evade an existing obligation or frustrate an existing right of enforcement, and even then only as a 'last resort'.

The motivation of the individual is important. Where the corporate form was used deliberately to evade an existing liability the veil has been pierced (eg *Jones v Lipman* [1962] 1 WLR 832; *Gilford Motor Co Ltd v Horne* [1933] Ch 935), and also where the company was used to hide misappropriated money (*Trustor AB v Smallbone (No. 2)* [2001] 1 WLR 1177) or abuse legislation (*Re Bugle Press* [1961] Ch 270), although *VTB* and *Prest* raise doubts as to whether all these are true examples of veil-piercing. Merely using separate personality to ensure liability falls onto another member of a group is not impropriety: 'the right to use a corporate structure in this manner is inherent in our corporate law': *Adams*.[8] *Ord v Belhaven Pubs Ltd* [1998] 2 BCLC 447, rejecting *Creasey v Breachwood Motors Ltd* [1993] BCLC 480, showed even transferring assets from a company after liability had arisen would not justify piercing the veil if not done with the purpose of evading that liability (the transfer was part of a group reorganization). Similarly, *VTB Capital plc v Nutritek International Corp* [2013] UKSC 5 denied

---

[5] Link back to the quotes to show you are not producing a generic response to a veil-lifting question

[6] Interim conclusions (as you deal with each point) can be very helpful to keep your eye on the question and convince the examiner that you understand the relevance of the points you make

[7] This links the *Prest* analysis with the previous categories of veil-piercing. Make sure you can briefly summarize the evasion principle

[8] Using a short quote can help to support the point being made

the veil could be lifted to impose liability on a person behind a 'dishonourable' transaction, while in *Prest* an individual's impropriety in matrimonial proceedings was not considered relevant.

Accordingly, while the courts remain able to lift the veil on this ground, the principle is applied restrictively, leaving the current law closer to the statement of Samuels than Schmittoff.

Agency, Tort, and Other Legal Principles

If a company is agent of its shareholder, liability for the company's debts will fall on the shareholder, bypassing the corporate veil (although not disturbing separate personality). The House of Lords in *Salomon* rejected the idea the company was Salomon's agent; the fact a company has a single member or is a wholly owned subsidiary is not enough to make it the agent of its member or parent company. In the past, courts have found an agency relationship between subsidiary and parent (eg *Smith, Stone & Knight v Birmingham Corpn* **[1939] 4 All ER 116**) but *Adams* made clear agency cannot be presumed from the closeness of operations between parent company and subsidiary (see also *Yukong Line Ltd of Korea v Rendsburg Investments Corpn of Liberia (No. 2)* **[1998] 1 WLR 294**). The current law shows it is very unlikely that an agency relationship will be found on the facts, leaving the veil intact.

Where a member or director has personally committed a tort then personal or joint liability could follow. However, courts are generally reluctant to impose tortious liability on those behind the veil, recognizing the potential for damage to the principle of separate personality (*Williams v Natural Life Health Foods Ltd* **[1998] 1 BCLC 689**). An important developing area is tortious liability of parent companies relating to their subsidiaries' activities. *Chandler v Cape Industries plc* **[2012] 1 WLR 3111** (*Chandler*) held responsibility does not arise by the mere fact of the corporate relationship, but on the facts the parent company had assumed a direct duty of care[9] to the subsidiary's employees. This is not piercing the veil (per Arden LJ) but may impose liability notwithstanding the veil. In *Vedanta Resources plc v Lungowe* **[2019] UKSC 20** the Supreme Court made clear that a duty of care could be owed by the parent company and this was not limited to employees nor to the factors set out in *Chandler*.

In *Prest*, despite declining to pierce the veil, the Supreme Court obtained the same result by applying trusts principles. This case was not about imposing liability on a member for the company's debts, but nonetheless indicates courts may be willing to 'lift' the veil in the wide sense by exploring the facts ('the concealment principle': *Prest*), and this may lead to the application of other legal principles through which the veil could be bypassed.

[9] You won't be expected to go into detail on tort principles, but do need to know how tort may be used to get round the problems of veil-piercing

Conclusion

The high point of veil-lifting/piercing recognized in Schmittoff's quote is long gone. Despite occasional indications of Denning-esque views (eg *Ratiu v Conway* [2005] EWCA Civ 1302) recent decisions show reluctance to depart from the principle of separate corporate personality and pierce the veil except where there is abuse of the corporate form. This is so regardless of the seriousness or moral force of the claimant's position, although the courts are willing to explore the use of other legal principles, particularly tort, to achieve the same end. Largely in line with Samuels' quote, the current law starts from the assumption that the veil is indeed an 'iron curtain'; contrary to Schmittoff's statement *Salomon* is very much 'centre stage'.[10]

[10] After summarizing the position to show that the writer's initial view has been supported, the conclusion uses the quotes themselves to link back to the question

LOOKING FOR EXTRA MARKS?

- Clearly relate the question quotes to attitudes to lifting/piercing the veil: eg a generally permissive approach (as suggested by the Schmittoff quote) or a more strict approach (Samuels)

- Engage with some additional academic writing, particularly that post-dating *Prest* as the question is about the current law, to add depth to your discussion

- Having identified what the approach of the law is, think about whether this is how it should be, or not, and why

QUESTION | 5

Amil and Barbra, a wealthy couple, are the sole shareholders and directors of Wastetrak Ltd, which runs a very profitable waste and recycling consultancy.

Wastetrak owns all 100 issued £1 shares in Grubbling Ltd, which operates several recycling centres. Amil and Barbra are the directors of Grubbling. Unfortunately Grubbling has been struggling financially this year and now owes one of its key suppliers, Pattie, £300,000. Grubbling does not have sufficient assets to meet the claim, although Wastetrak remains very successful.

Recently Wastetrak formed a new company, Rekleen Ltd, taking its single issued £1 share. The director of Rekleen is Connor, the son of Amil and Barbra. Rekleen was formed to buy and operate a further recycling centre that uses a new waste disposal process that has the potential to be highly profitable but uses potentially dangerous chemicals. The money to buy the centre was loaned to Rekleen by Wastetrak, secured over all Rekleen's assets. Unfortunately the venture has been a disaster. The chemicals have leaked, and local landowner Lamar now has a damages claim in the region of £1 million against Rekleen. Rekleen has no available assets to meet Lamar's claim.

Advise Pattie and Lamar.

CAUTION!

■ Make sure you relate your discussion to the facts throughout to show you understand the relevance of what you are saying

■ Avoid providing a chronological account of veil-lifting/piercing by focusing on the law as it currently is, not as it used to be

■ Don't spend too much time reciting either case facts or the problem facts

 DIAGRAM ANSWER PLAN

Identify the issues
■ Can Pattie make a claim against Wastetrak (or Amil/Barbra) in place of Grubbling?
■ Can Lamar make a claim against Wastetrak (or Amil/Barbra) in place of Rekleen?

Relevant law
■ Limited liability, the veil of incorporation, and corporate groups
■ Modern principles of veil-piercing
■ Veil-lifting and other ways around the veil

Apply the law
■ Identify the primary claims and the barrier to claiming against the parent company
■ Consider whether the veil can be pierced in either case
■ Consider other possible routes for imposing liability, particularly agency and tort, as appropriate

Conclude
■ Evaluate the likelihood of Pattie and/or Lamar making a successful claim against Wastetrak

 SUGGESTED ANSWER

[1] Deal with basic principles concisely and link them to the facts

Wastetrak, as shareholder of Grubbling and Rekleen, is not liable for their debts, because of the principle of separate corporate personality (***Salomon v A. Salomon & Co Ltd*** [1897] AC 22[1] (***Salomon***)), which applies also to corporate groups (***The Albazero*** [1977] AC 774). Shareholders' liability is limited to the amount unpaid on their shares (**Companies Act 2006, s. 3(2)**) so Wastetrak's maximum liability is £100 (Grubbling) and £1 (Rekleen). If the shares are fully paid, there is no further liability.

So Pattie and Lamar cannot, prima facie, claim against Wastetrak (nor Amil and Barbra), in place of Grubbling and Rekleen even though Grubbling and Rekleen do not have the resources to meet their claims. If pursued it is likely both companies would go into insolvent liquidation. This would leave nothing for Pattie and Lamar, as secured creditors such as Wastetrak take in priority to unsecured creditors whether voluntary (Pattie) or involuntary (Lamar).[2] *Salomon* shows that a shareholder may lend to 'his' company and benefit from security taken over its assets on its insolvency.

Pattie and Lamar therefore need to know whether there is any legal basis on which they could claim against Wastetrak Ltd, or Amil, Barbra, or Connor.

Pattie/Grubbling

The starting point is the *Salomon* principle—Wastetrak is protected by the 'veil of incorporation' and is not liable for Grubbling's debts. But will the companies' close connection—they operate in the same business area, they share directors, and Wastetrak will receive all Grubbling's profits—allow Pattie to lift or pierce the veil of incorporation?[3]

There is only one ground for piercing the veil: *Prest v Petrodel Resources Ltd* [2013] UKSC 34 *(Prest)*. Previously referred to as the 'mere facade concealing the true facts'[4] (*Woolfson v Strathclyde* [1978] SC (HL) (*Woolfson*); *Adams v Cape Industries* [1990] Ch 433 (*Adams*)) this is now known as the evasion principle. It can be used only as a 'last resort' (*Prest*) when no other remedy is available.

The veil will be pierced only where the company is interposed to evade an existing obligation or liability, or frustrate an existing right of enforcement. The company need not be a 'facade' and Grubbling appears not to be a facade as it operates a distinct business. There must be some 'relevant impropriety', ie some deliberate misuse of the corporate form that relates to the claim in question.

There is nothing on the facts to suggest that Grubbling has been used by Wastetrak to evade an existing liability—Wastetrak has never had any liability to Pattie. Even if Wastetrak had been using Grubbling for some improper purpose such as tax evasion, this would not be sufficient, as the impropriety would not relate to the claim (as in *Prest*). Pattie would not succeed in piercing the veil in this case.[5]

Does Pattie have any other options? In *Prest* the evasion principle was distinguished from the concealment principle, although for some this distinction is unconvincing (eg Hannigan, B, 'Wedded to *Salomon*: evasion, concealment and confusion on piercing the veil of the one-man company' (2013) 50 Irish Jurist 11). The concealment principle is 'legally banal' (Lord Sumption) but allows a court to explore behind the veil. This may reveal the basis for a legal claim that while not piercing the veil nonetheless provides a remedy for the claimant.[6]

[2] This shows you recognize the difference between voluntary and involuntary creditors, and that they are treated the same

[3] Posing a question can be quite an effective way of setting up discussion of an issue

[4] Show you understand the development of the law, without spending time discussing previous authorities (that have been overtaken to some extent) in depth

[5] State your conclusion on each point unambiguously

[6] This paragraph uses a brief reflection on the concealment principle to link into other options. You could develop this point to consider the principles more deeply, or to consider how this fits with piercing/lifting

Pattie might look at the relationship between Wastetrak and Grubbling and claim that Grubbling is Wastetrak's agent. This would make Wastetrak, as principal, liable for the debts incurred by Grubbling. In *Smith, Stone & Knight Ltd v Birmingham Corpn* [1939] 4 All ER 116 Atkinson J found an agency relationship, asking whether the subsidiary was carrying on the business as the parent's business or as its own, looking at factors such as whether the profits were treated as those of the parent and whether the parent was the 'head and brains' of the venture (see also *Re FG Films Ltd* [1953] 1 All ER 615). Yet agency was not found in *Salomon*, while *Adams* and *Yukong Line Ltd v Rendsburg Investments Corp (No. 2)* [1998] 1 WLR 294 have indicated more is required than Atkinson J's 'control' factors. Given these authorities, and the existence of two distinct businesses, it is highly unlikely that agency would be established here.

Some older cases, such as *DHN Food Distributors v Tower Hamlets LBC* [1976] 1 WLR 852, suggest the veil might be lifted within a group if the companies operate in practice as a 'single economic unit'. Depending on how connected they are, the businesses might here be viewed as constituting a single waste management enterprise governed by Amil and Barbra. But that wouldn't help Pattie as the single economic unit argument was doubted in *Woolfson* and rejected in *Adams*. Cases taking this approach were explained in *Adams* as turning on the construction of statute or contract.[7] Pattie would have to claim that her contract with Grubbling must be interpreted as binding Wastetrak as well. While a 'single economic unit' construction is possible (eg *Beckett Investment Management Group Ltd v Hall* [2007] ICR 1539), the facts of this case do not obviously support it. Such a claim against Wastetrak would fail.

Pattie would have to fall back on her primary, apparently worthless, claim against Grubbling. Wastetrak might possibly pay the debt voluntarily in order to maintain a good business reputation. If not, Pattie, as a creditor, could petition to wind up Grubbling (**Insolvency Act 1986, s. 122(1)(f)**). The liquidator, if investigations turn up relevant evidence, might establish claims against Amil and Barbra as Grubbling's directors, for example for misfeasance (**IA 1986, s. 212**) or fraudulent or wrongful trading (**IA 1986, ss. 213–14**). Successful claims would increase the amount Pattie might eventually recover but would be unlikely to result in her being paid in full.

[7] Recognize the now very limited scope to engage the 'single economic unit' argument

Lamar/Rekleen[8]

[8] In this question, as in most others, it is more effective to split your discussion by characters/complaints than by points of law

At first sight Lamar might seem to have a stronger case for veil-piercing than Pattie. Rekleen appears to have been set up deliberately to prevent potential liability from the untested process falling on Grubbling or Wastetrak. But this isn't 'evasion'. Avoiding liability is a legitimate reason for incorporation, as recognized in *Salomon* and *Adams*. The veil can be pierced only where liability is evaded, not just avoided: there must be an existing liability that the party seeks to evade through use of the corporate form (***Prest***). That is not the case here so the veil cannot be pierced.

Do the facts here support the finding of an agency relationship to render Wastetrak liable for Rekleen's activities? Wastetrak seems to have been very involved and probably has significant control over Rekleen, even with a separate director (Connor). But, as discussed previously,[9] control is not sufficient in itself and so an agency relationship is unlikely to be established on the facts. Furthermore, there seems no basis on which Lamar could argue Wastetrak is liable as part of a 'single economic unit'.

[9] Refer back rather than setting out the law again, there is too much else to cover to waste time repeating principles

Lamar's claim, unlike Pattie's, is based in tort. Tort does not pierce the veil (see Arden LJ in ***Chandler v Cape plc* [2012] EWCA Civ 525 (*Chandler*)**), but if a parent company is found to owe a duty of care to a claimant which it has breached, then the parent will be directly liable. A duty of care will arise only where 'ordinary, general, principles of the law of tort' are satisfied (Sales LJ, ***AAA and others v Unilever plc* [2018] EWCA Civ 1532**). A duty of care to the subsidiary's employees was found in ***Chandler*** because the parent had effectively taken on responsibility for health and safety matters. ***Vedanta Resources plc v Lungowe* [2019] UKSC 20** confirmed a duty of care may be owed to those directly affected by the subsidiary's actions, and its presence will depend on the extent to which the parent intervened, controlled, or supervised relevant operations of the subsidiary. Here, as in ***Chandler***, the businesses of Wastetrak and Rekleen are arguably the same to a relevant extent, and Wastetrak might be expected to have superior knowledge on relevant safety matters. Further information would be needed on the extent to which Wastetrak was involved in Rekleen's relevant activities to determine whether a direct duty of care to Lamar had arisen. If so Lamar would be able to pursue a claim against Wastetrak directly, although this would not be piercing the veil.

If Lamar is unable to establish a direct duty of care, then like Pattie he will have to pursue his claim against Rekleen, and if the company goes into insolvent liquidation, hope that the liquidator can swell Rekleen's assets through claims against Connor as director, or perhaps against Amil, Barbra, or Wastetrak as shadow directors. The security might also be potentially challengeable under the **Insolvency Act 1986, s. 239 or s. 245.**[10]

[10] The information you would need isn't provided which indicates the examiner is not expecting you to go into any detail on these insolvency legislation points

Conclusion

Pattie is very unlikely to succeed in a claim against Wastetrak. She may recover something from Grubbling's likely insolvent liquidation if the liquidator successfully pursues Amil and Barbra under relevant insolvency provisions. Lamar may have a claim against Wastetrak in tort if further facts support the finding of a direct duty of care, otherwise his recoveries will also depend on whether a liquidator can recover against Connor, or Amil, Barbra, or Wastetrak.

LOOKING FOR EXTRA MARKS?

■ Be as clear as you can be on the likely outcome on each point, making sure your conclusions follow logically from your discussion

■ Engage directly with the law as it is while showing you understand how it has got to this point—use rather than simply display your knowledge

■ Show that you are aware of different judicial approaches/concerns and academic criticisms

QUESTION | 6

'*Prest v Petrodel Resources Ltd* represents a sea-change in the attitude of the courts to lifting or piercing the veil of incorporation.'
Critically discuss this statement.

CAUTION!

■ If you are unsure about the meaning of a term or expression in a question—for example 'sea-change' in this question—then either choose another question to answer, or explain what you believe it to mean early on, so the marker can read your work in light of your understanding

■ It would be easy to present a prepared answer on **Prest** or piercing the veil but avoid this at all costs—you need to engage with the statement and develop an argument to show you have thought about the law and not just memorized it

DIAGRAM ANSWER PLAN

Prest: the evasion principle, applicability, and last resort

▼

Comparison between *Prest* and earlier approaches: evasion and the mere facade

▼

Comparison between *Prest* and earlier approaches: concealment and other grounds of veil-lifting

▼

Potential developments and significance

[1] Taking a stance from the start can help you to direct your material to the question—just make sure the discussion that follows then backs up your stance

This essay will argue that the Supreme Court decision in *Prest v Petrodel Resources Ltd* [2013] UKSC 34 (*Prest*) does not represent a 'sea-change'[1] in the courts' attitude to lifting or piercing the veil of incorporation. It confirmed both that the veil can be pierced, and the prevailing (if not always consistent) judicial reluctance to do so. Although not a sea change the decision is important in providing a restrictive statement of principle and making clear this applies in all courts and only as a 'last resort'. This may encourage claimants to use alternative legal routes, perhaps applying orthodox principles in novel ways, to seek redress. Again though this continues the prevailing attitude prior to *Prest* rather than representing a sea change.

[2] The question offers the opportunity for a little more critical analysis—not just what the law does, but whether it is a good thing

Furthermore this approach may provide little more commercial certainty[2] than a broader veil-piercing jurisdiction might have done.

In *Prest* the Supreme Court accepted there was jurisdiction to pierce the veil, removing the doubt introduced a little earlier by Lord Neuberger in *VTB Capital plc v Nutritek International Corp* [2013] UKSC 5. But the court took a very restrictive approach to its application. It defined piercing the veil as 'disregarding the separate personality of the company' (Lord Sumption) and limited its operation to circumstances where the 'evasion principle' applies. It insisted that

[3] This is a point that is sometimes overlooked in discussions of *Prest* but it is useful to include it here to show a specific impact of *Prest*

the same principles apply in all courts,[3] halting the 'independent line' (Lord Sumption) taken by some family courts eg *Nicholas v Nicholas* [1984] FLR 285; *Mubarak v Mubarak* [2001] 1 FLR 673, and held the veil could be pierced only as a last resort, where a claimant has no alternative route. Although the veil-piercing analysis in *Prest* is strictly obiter as the case was decided on the basis the assets claimed by Mrs Prest were held by the companies on resulting trust for Mr Prest,[4]

[4] This shows you understand the facts of *Prest*, without spending too much time reciting them.

it has been treated as authoritative by numerous subsequent cases in different contexts, including *Antonio Gramsci Shipping Corp v Lembergs* [2013] EWCA Civ 730 (*Lembergs*) (consent to jurisdiction); *Persad v Singh* [2017] UKPC 32 (liability under a lease); and *R v Powell & Westwood* [2016] EWCA Civ 1043 (confiscation of proceeds of crime).

[5] You'll always need to be able to explain the evasion principle. Here the answer goes on also to explain what it is not, making the link with earlier cases.

The evasion principle in *Prest* requires the company to have been interposed to evade an existing obligation or frustrate an existing right of enforcement.[5] The company need not be a facade or sham nor need it have been created for that purpose. Although the court was able to look behind the veil, this was the 'concealment principle' in operation which of itself has no effect ('legally banal': Lord Sumption). The court examined and classified earlier cases such as *Jones v Lipman* [1962] 1 WLR 832 and *Trustor AB v Smallbone (No. 2)* [2001] 1 WLR 1177 using these categories, but this reflects a focus on principles and terminology rather than a sea change in attitude, and also indicated some disagreement as to which category some cases belonged to (eg *Gilford Motor Co Ltd v Horne* **[1933] Ch 935**). Not all Justices were equally convinced by the evasion/concealment distinction (eg Lady Hale, Lord Wilson), or as keen to limit veil-piercing to evasion (eg Lord Mance, Lord Clarke) but the restrictive thrust of the judgment, particularly in key speeches from Lords Sumption and Neuberger is clear.

Although undoubtedly restrictive, this was not new: a restrictive approach is apparent in cases before *Prest*, as is the emphasis on evasion, albeit using different terminology. Key cases had already rejected the notion that the veil could be pierced or lifted simply because 'justice' so required (*Adams v Cape Industries plc* **[1990] Ch 433** (*Adams*)) although with occasional indications to the contrary (eg *Ratiu v Conway* **[2005] EWCA Civ 1302**).[6] And attempts, particularly by Lord Denning, to treat corporate groups as a single enterprise legally as well as economically (eg *Littlewoods Mail Order Stores Ltd v Inland Revenue Commissioners* **[1969] 1 WLR 1241**; *DHN Food Distributors v Tower Hamlets LBC* **[1976] 1 WLR 852**) had been doubted in *Woolfson v Strathclyde Regional Council* **1978 SC (HL) 90** (*Woolfson*) and rejected in *Adams*. The prevailing attitude of the courts was that the 'only' ground on which the veil might be pierced was where the company was a 'mere facade concealing the true facts' (*Woolfson; Adams*). Although clearly very different terminology from 'evasion', in application the principle focused on the controller's motive and the extent to which s/he intended to evade (not simply avoid: *Adams*) existing liabilities, just as the evasion principle does.[7] For example in *Ord v Belhaven Pubs Ltd* **[1998] 2 BCLC 447** the court refused to pierce the veil where assets were transferred for legitimate reasons rather than to evade liability, while in *MacDonald v Costello* **[2012] QB 244**, the claimant builders could not claim against the controllers of the development company where there was no abuse or concealment of the legal position. As *Ben Hashem v Ali Shayif* **[2009] 1 FLR 115** (*Ben Hashem)* made clear, the principle required some impropriety linked to the use of the corporate form, as *Prest* also indicates. It is therefore argued that the evasion principle is primarily a restatement and clarification of existing principle. Furthermore while *Prest* held that the same principles should be applied in all courts and veil-piercing was a last resort, these points had already been indicated in earlier cases (eg *A v A* **[2007] 2 FLR 467**; *Ben Hashem*), so *Prest* clarifies the position rather than representing a change of direction.

What about other grounds for piercing or lifting the veil? *Adams* accepted that in some circumstances agency might provide a remedy, and even more limited circumstances where interpretation of a contract, statute, or other document might justify treating a corporate group as a single unit.[8] Does *Prest* mark a sea change in this

[6] Don't just ignore cases that aren't wholly supportive of your argument, you should still acknowledge them or the marker will think you have only partial knowledge

[7] Linking the evasion principle with the former principle of the 'mere facade' is something that can be quite tricky. This part goes on to use earlier case examples to show similar considerations are being applied.

[8] There isn't enough time or space to go through other possible grounds in detail, you'll need to show you understand them without exploring them in depth

respect, by limiting veil-piercing to evasion cases? This essay argues not, because the 'concealment' principle recognizes that in appropriate cases the court is free to look behind the veil; the facts found there (or elsewhere) may lead to other legal consequences. This can be seen in *Prest* where the court concluded the companies' assets were owned beneficially by Mr Prest, achieving the same outcome as veil-piercing might have done through other means. So claims based on agency and construction of contract/statute can likewise still be utilized if they apply on the facts (although this will be unusual, see eg *Yukong Line Ltd of Korea v Rendsburg Investments Corpn of Liberia (No. 2)* **[1998] 1 WLR 294**). The *Prest* approach simply makes clear that this does not amount to 'piercing' the veil.

In light of *Prest*'s restrictive approach, claimants must have regard to further possibilities. For example tort victims may be able to recover against parent companies without piercing the veil.[9] In *Vedanta Resources plc v Lungowe* **[2019] UKSC 20** the Supreme Court recognized a parent could owe a duty of care to an employee or someone directly affected by a subsidiary's operations where the parent has taken direct responsibility for a relevant policy or controls relevant operations (see also *AAA v Unilever plc* **[2018] EWCA Civ 1532**; *Okpabi v Royal Dutch Shell plc* **[2018] EWCA Civ 191**). But this cannot be a 'sea-change' created by *Prest* because the direction of travel was already apparent, for example in *Chandler v Cape Industries plc* **[2012] 1 WLR 3111** where Arden LJ was clear this was not piercing the veil, but applying general tort principles. The restrictive attitude of *Prest* to veil-piercing may give impetus to such developments but does not itself represent a change of direction. In a similar way *Prest* showed trusts law could be used to lay claim to corporate assets rather than seeking to pierce the veil: see also *Chai v Peng* **[2017] EWHC 792 (Fam)** and *M v M* **[2013] EWHC 2534 (Fam)**. Arguably such approaches could be just as damaging to commercial certainty as the broader veil-piercing jurisdiction that *Prest* seemed to fear,[10] since such assets would not be available to meet claims of creditors despite outward appearances, but without any flexibility to adjust claims of different parties.

Prest left open some possibility for developing the veil-piercing jurisdiction beyond 'evasion' cases, but subsequent cases indicate this is highly unlikely. For example David Richards LJ in *Rossendale BC v Hurstwood Properties (A) Ltd* **[2019] 1 WLR 4567** emphasized this would be only in 'very rare and novel cases' and while not ruling out development of the doctrine, indicated it would be very difficult. This is in line with other cases (eg *Lembergs*; *Persad v Singh*), indicating *Prest* has probably effectively halted development of the veil-piercing doctrine after more than a century of discussion. The case is therefore undeniably important. It makes clear that veil-piercing

[9] Although *Prest* doesn't deal with tortious liability of parent companies, the point is relevant to the broader argument. Make sure that you explain why it is relevant though

[10] This shows engagement with the consequences of *Prest*, not just for how the law is applied, but what that might mean

is an exceptional remedy that will rarely be successfully relied upon. It effectively encourages claimants to explore other legal routes that respect legal personality and this may result in expanding established principles to cover novel situations. However, while important and not necessarily conducive to commercial certainty, this is not a sea-change in attitude, but reflective of the courts' prevailing attitude and direction of travel even before *Prest*.

LOOKING FOR EXTRA MARKS

- Engage with criticism and comment on the meaning and clarity of the evasion/concealment distinction
- Consider whether the Supreme Court's approach is an appropriate reflection of commercial necessities or a missed opportunity to balance shareholder, creditor, and other stakeholder interests

TAKING THINGS FURTHER

- Allan, G., 'To pierce or not to pierce: a doctrinal reappraisal of judicial responses to improper exploitation of the corporate form' [2018] JBL 559

  Considers the development of the veil-piercing doctrine from the early days of the registered company to Prest *and beyond, distinguishing between 'piercing', 'concealment-agency/trust', and relief through alternative avenues. For an earlier attempt to reconsider the taxonomy and terminology of veil-lifting/piercing, see* Ottolenghi, S., 'From peeping behind the corporate veil, to ignoring it completely' (1990) 53 MLR 338.

- Arvidsson, C., 'The piercing doctrine: re-examining evasion' (2019) 40 Co Law 320

  Provides a refresher on cases that have followed Prest within a discussion of evasion, corporate group structures, and allocation of risk.

- Cheng-Han, T., 'Veil-piercing—a fresh start' [2015] JBL 20

  Argues that veil-piercing is based on the privilege of incorporation having been abused and welcomes Prest as a 'significant attempt to formulate a principled approach'.

- Day, W., 'Skirting around the issue: the corporate veil after *Prest v Petrodel*' [2014] LMCLQ 269

  Recognizes the importance, particularly post-Prest, of the use of conventional legal principles to by pass the corporate veil. See also Lee, P.W., 'The enigma of veil-piercing' (2015) 26 ICCLR 28.

- Freedman, J., 'Small businesses and the corporate form: burden or privilege?' (1994) 57 MLR 555

  Explores the motivations behind the choice of particular business forms. See also Freedman, J. and Finch, V., 'The limited liability partnership: pick and mix or mix-up?' [2002] JBL 475 *on the introduction of the LLP.*

- Hannigan, B., 'Wedded to *Salomon*: evasion, concealment and confusion on piercing the veil of the one-man company' (2013) 50 Irish Jurist 11

  A typically well-written, comprehensive, and critical consideration of Prest.

■ Hicks, A., 'Corporate form: questioning the unsung hero' [1997] JBL 306

Considers and challenges the relevance and availability of limited liability to small businesses. See also Griffin, S., 'Limited liability: a necessary revolution?' (2004) 24 Co Law 99.

■ Kahn-Freund, O., 'Some reflections on company law reform' (1944) 7 MLR 54

Includes an evaluation of the Salomon *decision and considers the wider merits of providing limited liability to small businesses.*

■ Lower, M., 'What's on offer? A consideration of the legal forms available for use by small- and medium-sized enterprises in the United Kingdom' (2003) 24 Co Law 166

A quick review of the main business forms, focusing on the elements important to SMEs and considering policy issues.

■ Muchlinski, P., 'Limited liability and multinational enterprises: a case for reform?' (2010) 34 Camb J Econ 915

Considers the basis and justification of limited liability generally, and particularly in relation to corporate groups and large tort claims. See also eg Leebron, D. W., 'Limited liability, tort victims and creditors' (1991) 91 Columbia L R 1565; Hansmann, H. and Kraakman, R., 'Toward unlimited shareholder liability for corporate torts' (1991) 100 Yale LJ 1879.

■ Tjio, H., 'Lifting the veil or piercing the veil?' [2014] LMCLQ 19

A generally thoughtful explanation of Prest *and consideration of its potential impact.*

Online Resources

www.oup.com/uk/qanda/

For extra essay and problem questions on this topic, as well as advice on revision and exam technique, please visit the online resources.

The Corporate Constitution 3

ARE YOU READY?

In order to attempt the questions in this chapter you will need to have covered the following topics:

- Articles of association
- The model articles
- Alteration of the articles
- Entrenchment
- Legal effect of the articles of association—the statutory contract
- Enforceability and insider/outsider rights
- Shareholder agreements
- Connections (in particular) with: management and governance, shareholder rights, and remedies

KEY DEBATES

Debate: to what extent do the articles of association bind the parties to it?

There has been some lively academic discussion about the enforceability of the 'statutory contract' and the significance of 'insider' and 'outsider' rights but without any clear resolution. The most helpful articles are probably Wedderburn (1957) and Drury (1986), but see also Goldberg (1972), Gregory (1981), and Prentice (1980), all cited in this chapter's 'Taking Things Further' section. The debate was touched upon by the Company Law Review Steering Group but the resulting legislation left the area unchanged.

'**Section 21(1) of the Companies Act 2006** provides only one part of a much bigger picture relating to the alteration of a company's articles of association.'

Discuss.

CAUTION!

- Remember that even if a question asks you just to 'discuss' a statement, you still need to assess and analyse the issues critically

- Don't forget to move beyond the statutory provisions on alteration of the articles; you must include consideration of the 'bona fide for the benefit of the company' test

- Avoid just describing the law on alteration of the articles; think about how all the elements work together to create the 'bigger picture'

DIAGRAM ANSWER PLAN

Introduction: CA 2006, s. 21

▼

Contracting out: *Russell v Northern Bank*

▼

Entrenchment: s. 22 and alternative methods

▼

Statutory restrictions on alteration: additional contributions and class rights

▼

The 'bona fide for the benefit of the company' test: meaning and complexities

▼

Conclusion: summarize main points

SUGGESTED ANSWER

The company's articles of association are the key constitutional document of the company containing its internal regulations, and bind the company and the members: **Companies Act 2006 (CA 2006), s. 33.** Under **CA 2006, s. 21**, companies can alter their articles at any time by special resolution. This requires a 75 per cent majority of those voting (**CA 2006, s. 283**) and the written resolution procedure (**CA 2006, s. 288**) can be used. Articles can also be altered by unanimous agreement of the members, without a formal meeting or resolution (*Cane v Jones* **[1980] 1 WLR 1451**). This essay will show that although the statutory right of alteration is very important, the true picture of alteration of the articles is indeed much bigger,[1] with many statutory and common law restrictions on this right.

[1] Using the introduction to indicate the argument helps you to focus on the key issues from the start

[2] Subheadings can be useful to keep to a clear structure and deal with all the points

Contracting out of the Right to Alter[2]

Companies cannot contractually restrict themselves from exercising their statutory right of alteration. For example, in *Punt v Symons & Co Ltd* **[1903] 2 Ch 506** it was held that the company's agreement not to alter its articles to remove a restriction on the appointment of directors was unlawful. However, in *Russell v Northern Bank Development Corpn Ltd* **[1992] 1 WLR 588** the House of Lords accepted that while any such agreement was not binding on the company itself, an agreement between all the shareholders agreeing not to vote in favour of an alteration was effective and enforceable.

Entrenchment

Although a special resolution is normally sufficient to alter the company's articles, it is possible to 'entrench' an article, making it harder to alter that article. Prior to **CA 2006**,[3] it was possible to 'embed' a constitutional provision by inserting it, with protection from alteration, within the company's memorandum of association. Post-2006 a company's memorandum is no longer part of the company's constitution (it is the document that forms the company: **CA 2006, s. 8**) and so this is not an option. Provision for entrenchment within the articles of association is now possible. Under **CA 2006, s. 22(1)** a company's articles may provide that specified clauses of the articles may be amended or repealed only if conditions are met, or procedures are complied with, that are more restrictive than a special resolution. Entrenched articles therefore cannot be altered by special resolution alone, but only by following the provisions by entrenchment[4] (or by unanimous agreement of the members or order of the court: **CA 2006, s. 22(3)**) The registrar of companies must be notified of provisions for entrenchment and also of their removal: **CA 2006, s. 23**.

[3] This shows your awareness of how the position has changed and so the need for the new 'entrenchment' provisions

[4] Follow through your discussion to demonstrate the effect of the provision and make explicitly clear the relevance of the point to your argument

Companies can also effectively entrench articles by making use of weighted voting.[5] If some shares are weighted to carry more than 25 per cent of the votes on a resolution to alter a particular article, then it becomes impossible for a special resolution to be passed against the wishes of that shareholder, effectively entrenching the article. The validity of this was confirmed in *Bushell v Faith* **[1970] AC 1099**— although a company could not validly create an article depriving it

[5] Making the connection between statutory entrenchment and other devices for achieving similar effects

of the right to alter its articles by special resolution, it could give weighted voting rights that could have the same effect.

Statutory Restrictions on the Right to Alter

[6] This provides your link between sections of your essay

Even articles that are not entrenched or subject to weighted voting[6] may be subject to restrictions on alteration, or alteration may be ineffective to some extent. Alterations made after the date a person becomes a member will not bind that member so far as it requires them to take or subscribe for shares other than those held at the date of the alteration, or increases their liability to contribute to the company's share capital or otherwise pay money to the company: **CA 2006, s. 25.**

[7] As this essay is not really about class rights you cannot risk spending too much time on this point, but you can still show your good understanding of it by making a few key points very succinctly

Where the alteration of the articles constitutes a variation of class rights, the alteration cannot be made under **CA 2006, s. 21(1)**, but only in accordance with **CA 2006, s. 630.**[7] This requires alteration to be in accordance with any provision in the company's articles for the variation of those rights, or, if there is no such provision, with the agreement of a three-quarter majority of that class of shareholders (whether in writing or resolution at a separate class meeting): **Cumbrian Newspapers Group Ltd v Cumberland & Westmorland Herald Newspaper & Printing Co Ltd** [1986] BCLC 286. Although 'variation' has been construed narrowly and so not every alteration of articles concerning class rights will trigger **CA 2006, s. 630** (see **White v Bristol Aeroplane Co Ltd** [1953] Ch 65), this is nonetheless a significant restriction on the company's right to alter its articles by special resolution.

Further Restrictions: The Bona Fide Test

Arguably the most important restriction on companies' freedom to alter their articles is where the court decides the alteration is not bona fide for the benefit of the company as a whole but is an abuse of majority power. The power of the courts to police proposed alterations of the articles was established in **Allen v Gold Reefs of West Africa Ltd** [1900] 1 Ch 656. In this case the company altered its articles

[8] This is an important case so it is worth including a few salient case facts

to give a lien on shares of any member in respect of any debts or liabilities of the member to the company. At the time, the alteration only affected one member, who owed arrears of calls on his shares.[8] The court held the power of the company to alter its articles under what is now **CA 2006, s. 21(1)** had to be exercised, not only in the manner required by the law, but also bona fide for the benefit of the company as a whole. However the fact the alteration only applied to a single member at the time of alteration did not mean that it was an abuse of majority power and not for the benefit of the company as a whole.

How should the court decide whether the alteration is bona fide in the interests of the company as a whole? Early cases differed as to whether the test should be objective (**Dafen Tinplate Co Ltd v Llanelly Steel Co** [1920] 2 Ch 124) or subjective (**Sidebottom v Kershaw, Leese & Co Ltd** [1920] 1 Ch 154). In **Shuttleworth v Cox Brothers & Co Ltd** [1927] 2 KB 9 (**Shuttleworth**) the court

⁹ Think PEA: the point that the test is 'subjective' has been identified (and supported with case authority), now this part explains what that means in this context, and from here the paragraph goes on to assess how this still allows the courts to challenge the alteration

opted for the subjective test. The test is whether the shareholders believed that they were acting in the best interests of the company as a whole; it is not for the court to determine whether or not the proposed alteration was in the interests of the company.[9] A subjective test makes it hard to challenge an alteration but not impossible: **Shuttleworth** held that if an alteration is so oppressive it casts doubt on the shareholders' honesty, or so extravagant no reasonable man could consider it for the company's benefit, the alteration will not be allowed. See also *Re Charterhouse Capital Ltd* **[2015] EWCA Civ 536 (*Charterhouse*)** and *Staray Capital Ltd v Yang* **[2017] UKPC 43**: an alteration is not for the benefit of the company if no reasonable person would consider it to be such.

A particular problem is how to determine what is in the interests of the company as a whole when the proposed alteration only concerns membership matters, where the company has no separate interest. *Greenhalgh v Arderne Cinemas Ltd* **[1951] Ch 286** held in these circumstances the court should ask whether the alteration was for the benefit of 'an individual hypothetical member', and whether its effect was to discriminate between majority and minority shareholders. *Citco Banking Corporation NV v Pusser's Ltd* **[2007] BCC 205** recognized that this hypothetical member test has not been found 'entirely illuminating' but declined to disturb it. Further clarification may be forthcoming, and would be welcome (Satish 'The alteration of the articles of association' (2014) 39 Co Law 27): in *Charterhouse* the court preferred to express the test in terms of oppression, injustice, and exceeding the scope of a power.

¹⁰ Recognize the increasing importance of statutory shareholder remedies in this area

Although this area remains complex and difficult to apply, its significance is now much reduced.[10] Now where a minority shareholder alleges that there has been an alteration of the articles which constitutes an abuse by the majority of their power, the claim would normally be brought as a claim of unfair prejudice under **CA 2006, s. 994**. If a claim is brought under this section and the court decides in favour of the claimant, the court has unlimited power to make orders under **CA 2006, s. 996(1)** which include an order requiring the company not to make any, or any specified, alterations in its articles without the leave of the court: **s. 996(2)(d)**.

Conclusion

It can be seen that **CA 2006, s. 21** only provides a starting point for considering the alteration of the articles by a company. Not only can the articles be altered otherwise than by way of a special resolution; in many circumstances the company's right to alter the articles is restricted in some way, whether by statute or by the courts. Furthermore, the importance of the company's right to alter its articles contained in **CA 2006, s. 21** is reduced through court decisions allowing the use of weighted voting and shareholder agreements that effectively prevent alteration while not technically disturbing the principle of an unfettered statutory right of alteration.

LOOKING FOR EXTRA MARKS?

- Show that you recognize the links between this topic and other areas such as shareholder relations and remedies
- Explore the relevant cases in some detail, particularly in relation to the 'bona fide' test
- Engage with some consideration of academic commentary on particular areas such as alteration and entrenchment, or the bona fide test

QUESTION | 2

'By virtue of **s. 14** [now **CA 2006, s. 33**] the articles of association become, upon registration, a contract between a company and members. It is, however, a statutory contract of a special nature with its own distinctive features' (per Steyn LJ, ***Bratton Seymour Service Co Ltd v Oxborough*** [1992] BCLC 693).

Discuss.

CAUTION!

- Before attempting this question you need a really sound understanding of the topic—you need to be able to provide both breadth and depth of content
- Don't be tempted to write about the articles of association generally; focus on the nature of the articles, the 'statutory contract'
- Concentrate on the main points of interest (enforcement and alteration), but don't forget to mention other, more minor, points of similarity or difference as well

DIAGRAM ANSWER PLAN

Introduction: identify key points for discussion

The articles as a binding contact: CA 2006, s. 33

Enforceability of the statutory contract: insider and outsider rights

Alteration of the articles compared with alteration of contracts

> Inapplicability of usual contractual rules

▼

> Conclusion: assess statement overall

 SUGGESTED ANSWER

Companies Act 2006 (CA 2006), s. 33 establishes the contractual nature of the articles of association: the provisions of the 'company's constitution' (the articles) bind the company and its members as if there were covenants on both sides to observe the provisions.

¹ It is a good idea to clearly but concisely explain the key concept at the start of the essay

The articles are termed a 'statutory contract'¹ as their contractual nature derives from statute rather than the operation of conventional contract law requiring offer, acceptance, and consideration. In many ways the contract contained in the articles is of a special nature; many are highlighted in *Bratton Seymour Service Co Ltd v Oxborough*

² Even if you don't set out your full argument, your introduction can give an indication of the direction of your work

[1992] BCLC 693 itself. The most significant are² the limits on the ability of members to enforce their contractual rights, and the ability to vary the terms of the statutory contract by majority vote, but other distinctive features such as the implication of terms and the availability of contractual remedies will also be considered.

CA 2006, s. 33(1) is in equivalent terms to its predecessor, **CA 1985, s. 14** (and before that **CA 1948, s. 20**), with slight modifications, including recognizing that post-2006 the memorandum of association is no longer part of the company's constitution. It has long been established that the articles, in accordance with their contractual nature, can be enforced by the company against the members of the company, by a member against a member, and by a member against the company.

³ The rest of this paragraph deals with important cases with just enough of the facts to show the examiner that you know the cases, without wasting time

So, it has been held³ that the company can enforce compliance with an obligation to refer disputes between the company and a member to arbitration if the articles contain a valid reference to an arbitration clause (see *Hickman v Kent or Romney Marsh Sheep-Breeders' Association* [1915] 1 Ch 881), while in *Pender v Lushington* (1877) 6 Ch D 70 the plaintiff sued to enforce his right as a member to have his vote recorded. In *Rayfield v Hands* [1960] Ch 1 the court established a member could enforce against another member the obligation to acquire shares which that member wished to sell where such an obligation was contained in the articles.

⁴ Show that you are thinking about the question itself and not just producing a standard answer by using the same words as appear in the question quote

But complications arise in respect of quite which provisions of the articles are enforceable under the statutory contract, and in this regard the articles do appear special in nature compared with a traditional contract.⁴ In *Hickman v Kent or Romney Marsh Sheep-Breeders' Association*, Astbury J expressed the view that an 'outsider' given rights in his capacity as an outsider could not enforce those rights under the articles, whether or not he was or became a member (ie an 'insider'). Normal principles of contract law generally prevent an outsider from suing on a contract to which he is not party, but the statutory contract takes this a step further in denying that right even to an 'insider' if he is seeking to enforce rights in his capacity as an 'outsider'. This was applied in *Beattie v E & F Beattie Ltd* **[1938] Ch 708** to a claim brought by a director/shareholder since the claim related to his capacity as a director not as a member, while in *Eley v Positive Government Security Life Assurance Co Ltd* **(1876) 1 Ex D 88** Eley was not permitted to enforce a right contained in the company's articles that he should remain the company's solicitor. The definition of outsider rights is broad and includes remuneration rights of directors contained in the articles. In *Re New British Iron Co, ex p Beckwith* **[1898] 1 Ch 324** the court held the articles did not constitute a contract between the company and the directors (although, since the directors had accepted office on the basis of the article, the terms were incorporated as an implied term in their service contract). Similarly, *Swabey v Port Darwin Gold Mining Co* **(1889) 1 Meg 385** held the implied term was subject to prospective alteration in the normal way of any article. These latter cases show 'outsider' rights may be enforceable under contracts extrinsic to the articles, even though they are apparently not enforceable under the statutory contract itself.

The position on enforceability of the terms of the articles is further complicated by other cases, particularly *Quin & Axtens Ltd v Salmon* **[1909] AC 442.**[5] In that case, the company's two managing directors, Salmon and Axtens, were also shareholders. The company's articles gave each a veto on director resolutions relating to the acquisition of certain properties. A meeting of the directors resolved to acquire properties despite Salmon's dissent, and at a subsequent general meeting the shareholders passed similar resolutions. The House of Lords held that the shareholders' resolutions were inconsistent with the articles and restrained the company from acting on them. Was this enforcing 'outsider' rights (ie the director's veto) under the articles? Lord Wedderburn has explained the case as showing[6] that members have an enforceable right for the company to be managed in accordance with its constitution ('Shareholder rights and the rule in *Foss v Harbottle*' [1957] CLJ 194) and, provided that they sue in their 'member' capacity, can thus indirectly enforce outsider rights by enforcing their right to have all the provisions of the constitution observed. This analysis has been subjected to further refinements by Goldberg, Prentice, and Gregory[7] (see Goldberg, 'The enforcement of outsider-rights under section 20(1) of the Companies Act 1948' (1972) 35 MLR 362, Prentice, 'The enforcement of "outsider" rights' (1980) 1 Co Law 179, and Gregory, 'The section 20 contract' (1981) 44 MLR 526, although none of the arguments

[5] Make sure that you recognize the complexities of the legal position by looking at potentially contradictory cases

[6] Make good use of your wider reading by introducing academic discussion and showing you understand the key arguments

[7] If you have time you can draw out these refinements and provide a more critical assessment of the debate; where time is short you will need to indicate your understanding of the ideas but focus on particular points—here the focus has been placed on Wedderburn and Drury as they take different approaches

seem fully to reconcile the cases. Taking a slightly different perspective, Drury argued that the statutory contract should be viewed as a dynamic 'relational contract' characterized by longevity and incompleteness ('The relative nature of the shareholder's right to enforce the company contract' [1986] CLJ 219) which provides a basis for understanding why rights in the articles should not be absolutely and uniformly enforceable. It also shows an appreciation of the limits of contractual analysis in relation to the articles, further confirming the 'special' nature of the statutory contract.[8]

[8] Remember to link your discussion back to the question itself wherever you can

Another way in which the statutory contract is of a special nature, distinct from a traditional contract, relates to amendment of the contract. Unlike a standard contract,[9] the articles can be altered by means of a special resolution under **CA 2006, s. 21**, that is, by majority vote rather than agreement of all the parties. Although articles can now be entrenched (**CA 2006, s. 22**), and this entrenchment can provide for unanimity, this would be the exception rather than the rule. The court imposes restrictions on the alteration of the articles, such that they can only be altered 'bona fide in the interests of the company as a whole' (**Allen v Gold Reefs of West Africa Ltd [1900] 1 Ch 656**), but this is not equivalent to requiring the consent of all parties to the contract. Indeed, if anything it highlights the special nature of the statutory contract as it shows the parties must have the company's, and not just their own, interest in mind, unlike in a traditional contract.

[9] Draw the contrast explicitly to show you have understood the significance of your discussion

There are other ways in which the statutory contract has its own special nature and distinctive features. First, not all contractual remedies apply to the statutory contract: misrepresentation, mistake, undue influence, and duress are not applicable (**Bratton Seymour Service Co Ltd v Oxborough**). In **Scott v Frank F Scott (London) Ltd [1940] Ch 794**, the court refused to rectify the articles to make them accord with the intention of the members at the time of the company's registration. Similarly the court will not imply a term to change the articles by implication from extrinsic circumstances (**Bratton Seymour Service Co Ltd v Oxborough**). A term can be implied where necessary to give business efficacy to the language of the articles in their commercial setting (**Equitable Life Assurance Society v Hyman [2002] 1 AC 408; Marks and Spencer plc v BNP Paribas Securities Services Trust Company (Jersey) Ltd [2015] UKSC 72**) and this has sometimes been approached quite generously (**Folkes Group plc v Alexander [2002] 2 BCLC 254, Cream Holdings Ltd v Davenport [2010] EWHC 3096 (Ch)**). In **Sugarman v CJS Investments LLP [2015] 1 BCLC 1**, the Court of Appeal refused to imply a term where the article was clear and unambiguous, and even if unusual was not absurd.

In conclusion it can be seen that while **CA 2006, s. 33** gives contractual force to the articles of association, the contract is indeed of a special nature with some distinctive features.[10] The contractual nature can be justified because the hallmark of a company is that of a voluntary relationship, like a contract (see Drury, 'The relative nature of the shareholder's right to enforce the company contract'), but the contractual analysis cannot be pushed too far. Given the very significant differences it is understandable that some have criticized the 'contractual straitjacket' (*Sealy and Worthington's Text, Cases and Materials in Company Law* (11th edn, 2016)) of **CA 2006, s. 33**.

[10] Use your conclusion to link back to the question. You should also show you have engaged with the fundamental notion of a contractual relationship—so the conclusion goes on to question whether the contractual concept is justified or not

LOOKING FOR EXTRA MARKS?

- Engage with the academic work in this area: try to convince the examiner that you have really thought about the arguments and are not just repeating textbook summaries
- Explore whether a contractual analysis is justified, considering whether there are any other alternative analyses

QUESTION | 3

Grimaldi Ltd was incorporated in 2012 and its directors are Coco, Joey, and Krusty. Coco also holds the title of 'Executive Advisor'. The company's 100 shares are held equally by Coco, Joey, Krusty, Bozo, and Tumble. Grimaldi Ltd relies on the model articles, with the following additional clauses:

1.1 Any resolution of the directors relating to the purchase of new premises shall be valid only with the agreement of any director holding the title of 'Executive Advisor'

1.2 The company's sales manager shall receive an annual bonus equal to 5 per cent of the company's profits

1.3 On any resolution to alter the company's share capital, any shares voted by Bozo shall be allocated five votes per share on a poll.

At the last board meeting, Joey and Krusty voted in favour of Grimaldi Ltd purchasing new premises for the business. Coco disagreed and sought to exercise his veto over such decisions but Joey and Krusty have ignored this. The other shareholders support Joey and Krusty's decision.

All five of the shareholders believe that the company's sales manager's bonus is too high and propose altering the articles to pay him a bonus of only 2 per cent (the sales manager's contract makes no separate provision for a bonus).

Coco, Joey, and Krusty have proposed a resolution to consolidate the company's share capital into five shares, with each shareholder holding one share. Tumble is happy to support this resolution but they are concerned that Bozo is likely to demand five votes per share in accordance with the articles, which would prevent the resolution being passed.

Advise the parties.

CAUTION!

- Don't just discuss the articles of association generally—focus on the issues raised by the facts of the problem and relate your discussion to the problem
- To avoid getting confused, don't start writing until you are clear about the positions and concerns of all the parties

DIAGRAM ANSWER PLAN

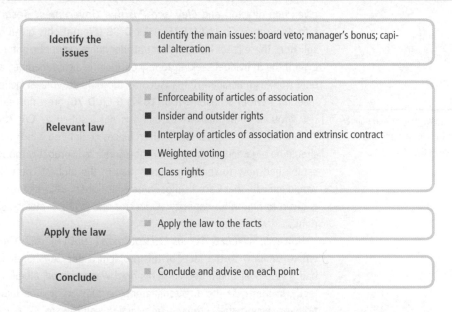

| Identify the issues | ■ Identify the main issues: board veto; manager's bonus; capital alteration |

| Relevant law | ■ Enforceability of articles of association
■ Insider and outsider rights
■ Interplay of articles of association and extrinsic contract
■ Weighted voting
■ Class rights |

| Apply the law | ■ Apply the law to the facts |

| Conclude | ■ Conclude and advise on each point |

SUGGESTED ANSWER

The model articles relevant to Grimaldi Ltd, as a private company incorporated in 2012, will be **Companies (Model Articles) Regulations 2008, Sch 1**. The issues that arise in the question largely concern the operation, alteration, and enforceability of the articles of Grimaldi Ltd, in particular the additional clauses outlined in the question.[1]

Coco's Veto

Coco's right of veto is within the articles of association, which raises questions about its enforceability. The articles are a 'statutory contract' by virtue of **CA 2006, s. 33** and its provisions bind the company and the members. This means the articles can be enforced by the members against the company, the company against the members, and the members *inter se*. For example in *Hickman v Kent or Romney Marsh Sheep-Breeders' Association* [1915] 1 Ch 881[2] a member was bound by an article that required disputes to be submitted to arbitration.

This might suggest Coco can simply enforce his veto as a matter of contract through the articles. However, in *Hickman v Kent or Romney Marsh Sheep-Breeders' Association* Astbury J stated that the articles are enforceable only so far as they relate to a member's interests in his capacity as a member: ie 'insider' rights. 'Outsider' rights, ie those that relate to an interest in some other capacity, could not be enforced under the statutory contract. This principle can be seen in operation in *Beattie v E & F Beattie Ltd* [1938] Ch 708 (rights given qua director) and *Eley and Positive Government Security Life Assurance Co Ltd* (1876) 1 Ex D 88 (*Eley*) (rights given qua solicitor). These cases indicate that outsider rights cannot be enforced even if the individual seeking to rely on them is also a member, and only true 'membership' rights (such as the right to vote at general meeting: *Pender v Lushington* (1877) 6 Ch D 70) are enforceable. It is arguable that this interpretation is not justified by **CA 2006, s. 33** itself (or its predecessors) which places no limit on which terms should be regarded as binding,[3] but the principle is probably too well established now to challenge other than in the highest court. This would indicate that Coco cannot enforce his right of veto, as the right is given to him in his capacity as director and is not a 'membership right'.

However, in *Quin & Axtens Ltd v Salmon* [1909] AC 442 (*Quin*), where similarly to the facts of this problem a director/shareholder had a veto over board decisions, his right was enforced, albeit indirectly. In that case the director/shareholder was granted an injunction restraining the company from acting contrary to its articles. Following the analysis of Lord Wedderburn in 'Shareholder rights and the rule in *Foss v Harbottle*' [1957] CLJ 194, this indicates Coco can enforce his right, provided he sues in his capacity as member, enforcing his right to ensure the company is run in accordance with the constitution, rather than in his capacity as director seeking to enforce a right of veto. Wedderburn's thesis has been variously modified and explained further by other academics,[4] and it remains difficult to predict when the courts will enforce particular provisions in the articles. As Drury has pointed out in 'The relative nature of the shareholder's right to enforce the company contract' [1986] CLJ 219, it is not possible to say that any provision of the articles is enforceable in an absolute sense as the contract is a relational one. The Company Law Review did consider reform, including a suggestion that all obligations in the articles should be enforceable unless otherwise provided, but the resulting legislation has left this issue unresolved. As this case is very close to *Quin* on the facts, Coco can be advised[5] he has a good chance of enforcing the veto, provided he acts qua member rather than qua director.

[3] This shows that you have understood some of the criticisms of Astbury J's approach

[4] If you have time you can develop the other academic arguments and consider whether the different approaches would make any difference to the present case

[5] Even where the law is not entirely clear you should make an effort to reach a conclusion

Sales Manager's Bonus

The sales manager is not a member and so is not a party to the statutory contract. He thus cannot enforce the articles directly, and even if he was a member, the right is an 'outsider' right and so enforcement would be barred (*Hickman v Kent or Romney Marsh Sheep-Breeders' Association*). Furthermore, a member (even if inclined to help the manager) is unlikely to be able to enforce the right indirectly under *Quin* as the right to a bonus does not relate to the proper functioning of the company—the case is much more like *Eley* where the 'outsider' right was not enforceable, even by a member. However, the sales manager may still be able to enforce his right to be paid a 5 per cent bonus for time already completed under *Re New British Iron Co, ex p Beckwith* [1898] 1 Ch 324. There the claimants had served the company as directors without express agreement for remuneration, but the articles provided for board remuneration (£1,000 per annum) to be divided between them as they thought fit. On the company's liquidation, they claimed arrears of directors' fees. The court held that this provision did not constitute a contract between the company and the directors for the payment of fees to the directors but held that, by accepting office on the understanding that the terms of the article applied, the article provision was impliedly incorporated in the contract of service between the company and the directors and they were entitled to payment. In *Swabey v Port Darwin Gold Mining Co* (1889) 1 Meg 385, the company's articles provided for directors to be remunerated at £200 per annum but subsequently, the company altered the articles to set remuneration at £5 per month. One director resigned and claimed for unpaid remuneration at the old rate. The Court of Appeal held in his favour on the grounds that, even though article provisions incorporated into a contract of service must be on the understanding that the articles are alterable, the alteration can only be prospective and not retrospective.

[6] After you have explained the relevant cases, don't forget to apply them to the facts

Applying these decisions to the sales manager,[6] it appears that, although the members can alter the articles to reduce the bonus to be awarded, the alteration will only have prospective effect. If the sales manager has completed a period of service prior to the alteration on the basis of the incorporation of the article provision prior to its alteration, he can sue for the bonus for that period to be calculated at the old rate.

Bozo's Voting Rights

Companies can consolidate (or subdivide) their share capital by ordinary resolution: **CA 2006, s. 618**. On the facts this resolution can only be passed if Bozo's shares are not given the additional weighting provided for in the articles. The case of *Bushell v Faith* [1970] AC 1099 shows that such a provision is valid, even where it effectively restricts the use of a statutory power (in that case the power to remove a director). Accordingly, on any poll (Bozo would be able to demand a poll: **CA 2006, s. 321**)[7] Bozo is entitled to have his votes counted in full and can defeat the resolution.

[7] This shows you have an understanding of other areas of company law

The other shareholders might seek therefore to alter the articles to remove this clause. The clause is not entrenched (**CA 2006, s. 22**) so alteration would prima facie only require a special resolution to amend or remove it (**CA 2006, s. 21**). Although alteration must be made 'bona fide for the benefit of the company as a whole', the mere fact that an alteration affects only one shareholder does not of itself breach that requirement (**Allen v Gold Reefs of West Africa Ltd [1900] 1 Ch 656**; **Staray Properties Ltd v Yang [2017] UKPC 43**). The problem for the other members is that this provision creates a class right:[8] in **Cumbrian Newspapers Group Ltd v Cumberland & Westmorland Herald Newspaper & Printing Co Ltd [1986] BCLC 286**, the weighted voting rights in **Bushell v Faith** were identified as a class right, even though not explicitly attached to a separate class of shares. This means that the clause cannot be varied (removal of the right would be a variation: **CA 2006, s. 630(6)**) unless the consent of a three-quarter majority of the class affected is obtained: **CA 2006, s. 630**.[9] As the class is made up of Bozo alone, he is unlikely to consent and so his weighted voting rights cannot be altered.

[8] When looking at alteration of the articles, always keep an eye out for class rights

[9] The model articles do not contain any provisions for the variation of class rights, so the variation must be in accordance with the three-quarter majority requirement

Conclusion[10]

[10] A conclusion is less important in a question like this as you can conclude on each point as you go along but it is still helpful—it is a check that you have covered all the issues and a final chance to raise any points (possibly practical rather than legal) relevant to the problem as a whole

Coco's right of veto over the board decision is probably enforceable following **Quin**, although the enforceability of such 'outsider' rights is a complex area where it is difficult to predict the court's approach. The sales manager cannot prevent the members from altering the articles to change the bonus for the future, but he can claim the bonus at the higher rate for years completed, provided the court is satisfied that the term was incorporated into an extrinsic contract with the company. As for the proposed consolidation of share capital, Bozo's vote should be weighted in accordance with the articles which will prevent the resolution being passed, and his right to weighted votes on this matter cannot be altered without his consent.

LOOKING FOR EXTRA MARKS?

- Concentrate on the particular issues raised but support this with strong knowledge and understanding of the fundamental principles

- In a problem question you can use academic work to show you have read more widely and understand there are debates and disagreements on points of law, but you might want to avoid detailed discussion of more theoretical points

QUESTION | 4

Critically evaluate the use of shareholder agreements as a supplement to a company's constitution.

CAUTION!

- You could structure this answer in terms of advantages and disadvantages of shareholder agreements, but it would be tempting to be very descriptive. By examining different issues instead, it is easier to be more analytical

- Remember that you'll need a good understanding of the articles of association as well as shareholder agreements to do well in this question

DIAGRAM ANSWER PLAN

Introduction: key areas for discussion

▼

Shareholder agreements and the constitution

▼

Parties: who is bound?

▼

Formalities, registration, privacy

▼

Enforcement of terms

▼

Alteration of terms

▼

Conclusion: evaluate benefits in different circumstances

SUGGESTED ANSWER

Shareholder agreements may be entered into when the company is formed or subsequently. They are usually formal contracts and are often used, particularly in small private companies, to modify or supplement the company's constitution (contained in the articles of association) to provide additional rights or protections for shareholders. By considering their nature, enforcement, and alteration, this essay will show shareholder agreements offer a useful tool for supplementation of the constitution but are not universally advantageous.[1]

[1] It can be effective to indicate both the areas you are going to cover and the thrust of your argument

Contract and Constitution

Shareholder agreements are governed by contract law, providing some certainty regarding the applicable legal rules. This is advantageous compared with the articles where, although a 'statutory contract' by virtue of **Companies Act 2006 (CA 2006), s. 33**, contract law does not fully apply. For example mistake, misrepresentation, duress, undue influence, rectification, and implication of terms do not normally apply to the articles (***Bratton Seymour Service Co Ltd v Oxborough* [1992] BCLC 693**). In contrast,[2] in *Antonio v Antonio* **[2010] EWHC 1199** the court accepted a shareholder agreement could be set aside for duress.

[2] To make your points about shareholder agreements clearly, it can be helpful to distinguish them from the articles of association explicitly

Although normally seen as just a supplement to the constitution, shareholder agreements can become part of the constitution.[3] Under the unanimous consent rule (or '*Duomatic* principle': *Re Duomatic Ltd* [1969] 2 Ch 365) unanimous agreement/consent of the shareholders is equivalent to a resolution of the company. The assent of *all* registered members is required: *Randhawa v Turpin* **[2017] EWCA Civ 1201**. *Cane v Jones* **[1980] 1 WLR 1451** established this can alter the articles, even though statute requires a special resolution (**CA 2006, s. 21**). The *Duomatic* principle has been criticized (Grantham argues it wrongly conflates the company and the members: 'The unanimous consent rule in company law' [1993] CLJ 245) but is recognized in **CA 2006, s. 281(4)**, and **CA 2006, s. 17** extends the constitution to include such agreements.

[3] The separation of contract and constitution is not complete so show you understand how one can lead into the other

Parties: Who Is Bound?

Shareholder agreements can be between all or only some shareholders. To be fully effective it should include all shareholders, making shareholder agreements of most use to small companies.[4]

[4] Recognize practical limitations on the use of shareholder agreements

Shareholder agreements bind the parties to them, which will normally be the members only. The articles bind the members and the company, and the members *inter se* (***Hickman v Kent or Romney Marsh Sheep-Breeders' Association* [1915] 1 Ch 881**; *Rayfield* *v Hands* **[1960] Ch 1**). Shareholder agreements could include the company as a party, but this risks the company wrongfully restricting its statutory powers, as in *Russell v Northern Bank Development Corpn Ltd* **[1992] 1 WLR 588**. Here the shareholders and company agreed not to increase share capital without the consent of all parties, and a shareholder objected when the board subsequently proposed an increase. The House of Lords accepted the agreement was binding but on the shareholders only, not the company as this would restrict the company's statutory right to increase capital. Although the company was not bound, the effect was the same while the original shareholders remained in place, leading to some criticism (Ferran, 'The decision of the House of Lords in *Russell v Northern Bank Development Corporation Limited*' [1994] CLJ 343).[5]

[5] Support and deepen your discussion with recognition of academic comment or criticism. You could usefully expand consideration of *Russell* here if you had time

A disadvantage of shareholder agreements compared with the articles is that shareholder agreements will not bind new members to whom shares have been allotted, nor will obligations run with the shares to bind someone acquiring shares from existing shareholders (*Greenhalgh v Mallard* **[1943] 2 All ER 234**). If new members are to be bound by shareholder agreements, they must agree to be bound.

Formalities, Registration, and Privacy

The articles must follow statutory requirements: contained in a single document, divided into paragraphs numbered consecutively (**CA 2006, s. 18(3)**), and must be registered on formation unless the company uses model articles (**CA 2006, s. 18(2)**, **Companies (Model Articles) Regulations 2008 (SI 2008/3229)**). If a company does not register its own articles, or to the extent its articles do not exclude or modify the model articles, then model articles take effect (**CA 2006, s. 20**). This facilitates the efficient creation of companies by ensuring those wishing to form a company do not need to start from scratch in creating a constitution.[6] It is not a service offered in relation to shareholder agreements—the legislature does not offer 'standard form' shareholder agreements.

[6] This touches on the purposes behind company law, and in particular the role of law as a facilitator

Unlike the articles, for shareholder agreements there are no prescribed requirements and they need not be in writing. The court has been prepared to find an oral shareholder agreement, and even imply additional terms into that agreement: in *Pennell Securities Ltd v Venida Investments Ltd* **(25 July 1974)** (*Pennell Securities*) (unreported but discussed in Burridge, S., 'Wrongful Rights Issues' (1981) 44 MLR 40) the court found the parties had impliedly agreed to maintain a particular share split and not increase share capital without consent.

Registration of the articles means they (and any alterations, which must be notified to the registrar: **CA 2006, s. 26**) are available for

[7] Think PEA—having made the point about registration, explain the consequence of this, and then draw this further into an assessment of why this might matter

public inspection at Companies House. As shareholder agreements do not need to be registered they offer greater privacy than terms in the articles, making them useful for matters the parties prefer to keep confidential.[7]

Alteration

Unlike the articles, the terms of a shareholder agreement cannot be altered by majority vote (special resolution: **CA 2006, s. 21**). This offers greater protection to minority shareholders who are party to the agreement than a clause in the articles.

[8] The point about alteration is an important one and you will get marks just for identifying it, but you can gain marks by evaluating its significance and showing you have a sufficiently deep understanding of the issues to question its importance

However, this difference may not be as significant as first appears.[8] If a term of the articles creates a class right then any variation needs the consent of a three-quarter majority of the class (or compliance with any provisions of the articles for variation of class rights): **CA 2006, s. 630**, offering some protection against alteration. Or an article could be entrenched under **CA 2006, s. 22**, providing protection against alteration by the majority without need for a shareholder agreement. Alternatively rights could be entrenched by the use of weighted voting as in *Bushell v Faith* **[1970] AC 1099**. Entrenchment means protection is available to new members as well, as protection is not limited to those who are party to the shareholder agreement.

Enforcement

As a contract, shareholder agreements are, in principle, enforceable as of right. The court may even restrict a shareholder's vote: in *Greenwell v Porter* **[1902] 1 Ch 530** an injunction was granted restraining shareholders from opposing re-election of a director they had agreed to vote for. Even where an agreement purports to oust legal rules, *Fulham Football Club (1987) Ltd v Richards* **[2011] EWCA Civ 855** indicates it will normally be enforced, provided it does not interfere with third-party rights or is contrary to public policy, an approach welcomed by Cheung ('Shareholders' Agreements—shareholders' contractual freedom in company law' [2012] JBL 504).

[9] If you have more time you could expand this to show that the position on 'outsider rights' is more complex than this, but make sure you don't lose sight of the focus which is shareholder agreements rather than the articles generally

By way of contrast, company law remedies are usually discretionary. Even a clear breach of articles may not be directly enforceable by a shareholder. Under the rule in *Foss v Harbottle* **(1843) 2 Hare 461** 'mere irregularities' cannot be litigated by a shareholder (*Macdougall v Gardiner* **(1875) 1 Ch D 13**). Further, in *Hickman v Kent or Romney Marsh Sheep-Breeders' Association* Astbury J indicated only 'insider' rights can be enforced by members;[9] rights given in an 'outsider' capacity cannot be enforced, even by a member, a distinction that would not apply to terms of a shareholder agreement.

Agreements and Shareholder Remedies

Shareholder agreements can be important in resolving shareholder disputes, particularly where articles do not provide for dispute resolution or an exit route. Shareholder agreements may offer some protection to a minority shareholder, whether through enforcing the agreement directly, or in support of a claim under statutory shareholder remedies.

[10] Many topics interlink in company law, so take advantage of your broad understanding to show you recognize this, while keeping your discussion relevant to the question asked

The existence of a shareholder agreement may be relevant to a claim of unfair prejudice[10] (**CA 2006, s. 994**) or just and equitable winding up (**Insolvency Act 1986, s. 122(1)(g)**). Although the first strand of 'unfairness' identified by Lord Hoffmann in *O'Neill v Phillips* **[1999] 1 WLR 1092** was through breach of a binding agreement, breach of a shareholder agreement will not necessarily amount to unfair prejudice: *Sikorski v Sikorski* **[2012] EWHC 1613**. The interplay of shareholder agreements and shareholder remedies (both under just and equitable winding up and unfair prejudice) can be seen in cases such as *Re A & B C Chewing Gum Ltd* **[1975] 1 All ER 1017**, and *Pennell Securities*. *Westcoast (Holdings) Ltd v Wharf Land Subsidiary (No. 1) Ltd* **[2012] EWCA Civ 1003** shows the importance of clear drafting if an agreement is to be relied upon in a dispute.

Conclusion

Shareholder agreements, particularly those encompassing all shareholders, provide a useful tool to supplement the constitution. Their importance is recognized in some jurisdictions (eg Canada) by giving them statutory force, but while not the case here, they remain significant in regulating shareholder relations, protecting minorities, and restricting directorial action, particularly in smaller companies and in areas such as joint ventures and management buy-outs. They have advantages over the articles in offering additional certainty and privacy, but will only cover shareholders for the time being and provisions need to be drafted carefully to be effective.

LOOKING FOR EXTRA MARKS?

■ Explain and engage with different judicial and academic approaches on relevant points

■ Provide detailed analysis of important decisions such as *Russell v Northern Bank* and be prepared to critique them within the context of the question

■ Draw links with topics such as shareholder remedies and the unanimous consent rule to show your deeper understanding of the issues

TAKING THINGS FURTHER

■ Cheung, R., 'The use of statutory shareholder agreements and entrenched articles in reserving minority shareholders' rights: a comparative analysis' (2008) 29 Co Law 234

Considers whether entrenched articles can offer similar protection to shareholders to that offered by the North American statutory unanimous shareholder agreement.

■ Cheung, R., 'Shareholders' Agreements—shareholders' contractual freedom in company law' [2012] JBL 504

Explores the approach of the courts to enforcing shareholder agreements—how far should private shareholder agreements be permitted to trump legal rules? Identifies an increasing trend in respecting freedom in private contracting.

■ Drury, R. R., 'The relative nature of the shareholder's right to enforce the company contract' (1986) 45 CLJ 219

Compares the statutory contract with commercial 'relational contracts' to explore the relative enforceability of its provisions. Also contains a useful summary of the other main academic arguments on the nature of the statutory contract.

■ Ferran, E., 'The decision of the House of Lords in Russell v Northern Bank Development Corporation Limited' (1994) 53 CLJ 343

Critically examines whether companies should be prevented from fettering their statutory powers through contract, and the distinction (with 'little to commend it') drawn in Russell *between that and effective fettering of a company's powers through shareholder agreements.*

■ Grantham, R., 'The unanimous consent rule in company law' (1993) 52 CLJ 245

A critical evaluation of the unanimous consent rule, examining and challenging the rule from different perspectives.

■ Rixon, F. G., 'Competing interests and conflicting principles: an examination of the power of alteration of articles of association' (1986) 49 MLR 446

Assesses the ability of a shareholder to challenge an alteration of the articles, both directly (providing a detailed examination of the Allen v Gold Reefs *test) and through the unfair prejudice remedy.*

■ Satish, S., 'The alteration of the articles of association: tracing the trajectory from Allen to Citco' (2014) 39 Co Law 27

Summary of the development of the 'bona fide for the benefit of the company' test. How far do Charterhouse *(2015) and* Staray *(2017) address some of the issues highlighted here?*

■ Savirimuthu, J., 'Thoughts on Russell—killing private companies with kindness' (1993) 14 Co Law 137

A case note on Russell v Northern Bank Development Corp Ltd, *criticizing the House of Lords' reasoning. Contrast Savirimuthu's view of whether the company and the members should be viewed as separate entities, with that of Grantham (1993), and see also Ferran (1994). A more positive view on the case can be seen in Sealy, L. S., 'Shareholders' agreements—an endorsement and a warning from the House of Lords' (1992) 51 CLJ 437.*

■ Wedderburn, K. W., 'Shareholder rights and the rule in *Foss v Harbottle*' (1957) 15 CLJ 194

Considers the enforceability of the articles of association: seeks to reconcile important cases in the area, and draws the connection with shareholder remedies. See further Goldberg, G. D., 'The enforcement of outsider rights under s. 20(1) Companies Act 1948' (1972) 35 MLR 362 and (1985) 48 MLR 158; Gregory, R., 'The section 20 contract' (1981) 44 MLR 526; Prentice, G. N., 'The enforcement of outsider rights' (1980) 1 Co Law 179.

Online Resources
www.oup.com/uk/qanda/

For extra essay and problem questions on this topic, as well as advice on revision and exam technique, please visit the online resources.

4 Shares and Shareholders

ARE YOU READY?

In order to attempt the questions in this chapter you will need to have covered the following topics:

- Definitions and characteristics of a share
- Differences between types of share
- Allotment of shares
- Rights of pre-emption
- Variation of class rights
- Connections with (in particular): the constitution, capital, directors' duties, shareholder remedies

KEY DEBATES

Debate: the nature and characteristics of a share

The complexity of the share allows writers to focus on different elements to raise different issues or support particular approaches. It links into other areas of company law such as the nature of the company's constitution; shareholder primacy and stakeholding; shareholder remedies; and issues of corporate management, governance, and responsibility.

Debate: respective rights of shareholders of different classes and variation of those rights

In exercising the duty to promote the success of the company directors must have regard to the need to act fairly between shareholders (**CA 2006, s. 172(1)(f)**) but with different classes of share, shareholders will have different rights, and these rights will need to be balanced in the company's interest. The courts have consistently limited the statutory protection given to shareholders in respect of variation of their class rights, leading to some criticism.

'The complex nature of a share makes it difficult to define concisely and comprehensively.'

Critically discuss the above statement.

CAUTION!

- Different classes of share will have different features, but don't just describe them, use the features as a way of illustrating the complexity of a share
- Although the question is potentially quite broad, don't drift too much into peripheral issues such as share allotment or transfer as this will tempt you away from deeper discussion about the nature of a share

DIAGRAM ANSWER PLAN

Introduction: recognizing the problem

▼

Types of share and shareholder

▼

Characteristics of a share: the *Borland's Trustee* description

▼

Characteristics of a share: Sealy & Worthington's three factors

▼

Conclusion: reflect on problem of definition

SUGGESTED ANSWER

Shares are fundamental to company law (the vast majority of companies are limited by shares) but are difficult to define comprehensively and concisely. Not only are there different types of share, shares' features differ in importance depending on the interests of the shareholder.[1] Shareholders may be as diverse as an owner-manager in a one-person company, or an investor holding shares in multiple

[1] This identifies the main theme of the discussion from the start

companies, and the nature of a share looks very different from those different perspectives. Accordingly, while the general notion of a share is tolerably clear, finding a workable and meaningful definition is difficult. This essay will examine definitions and features of shares to address why it is difficult to define.

A share measures a shareholder's interest in the company—the shareholder's proportional share in a company's share capital and (assuming the articles of association provide for one vote per share) proportional voting power. Shares must have a nominal value under **Companies Act 2006 (CA 2006), s. 542(1)** (usually a small amount, eg £1). But this is not the 'value' of the share, which is worth what someone is willing to pay for it, or, in the event of winding up, the proportional share of the company's assets less its liabilities.

Most shares are ordinary shares, the residual category of shares. If a company has only one class of shares, these are ordinary shares, and every company must have at least one ordinary share. These usually carry a right to a variable dividend (declared lawfully in accordance with **CA 2006** and the articles) and a right to share in the company's net assets on winding up. The other main type of share is preference shares. These typically carry rights to a fixed (and usually cumulative: *Webb v Earle* **[1875] LR 20 Eq 556**)[2] dividend and a preferential right to return on capital on winding up. These rights are described as 'preferential' as they have priority over the rights of ordinary shareholders; they are not 'better' than ordinary shares as 'preferential' might suggest, simply different.[3]

Companies may issue any number of different classes of share provided the articles allow, potentially carrying different nominal values (even in different currencies: *Re Scandinavian Bank Group plc* **[1988] Ch 87**) and different rights (including redeemable shares: **s. 684**). Any rights that attach to a particular class of shares, but not generally, are regarded as 'class rights' (see *Cumbrian Newspapers Group Ltd v Cumberland & Westmoreland Herald Newspapers and Printing Co Ltd* **[1987] Ch 1**) and provisions exist to protect shareholders in respect of variations to these rights (**ss. 630–5**). Shares can even be used to promote broader commercial or social aims,[4] eg abolishing 'bearer shares' to enhance transparency (**CA 2006, s. 779**), or encouraging employee ownership.

A share is personal, not real property, whatever assets the company holds (*Bligh v Brent* **(1837) 2 Y&C 268; CA 2006, s. 541**). It does not give its holder any share in the company's property (*Short v Treasury Commissioners* **[1948] AC 534**); the company as a separate entity owns its assets (*Macaura v Northern Assurance Co* **[1925] AC 619**).[5] The member's share is in the company's share

[2] By adding in a few points in passing you can demonstrate the depth of your knowledge to the examiner without wasting time

[3] It is important to show you understand that 'preferential' doesn't necessarily mean 'better'

[4] This recognizes that shares have wider significance than just their importance to the individual or company

[5] An important link between the topic of corporate personality and this topic, but it doesn't need much elaboration here

capital (**s. 540(1)**) and is transferable in accordance with the articles (**s. 544(1)**).

The classic analysis of a share comes from ***Borland's Trustee v Steel Brothers & Co Ltd* [1901] 1 Ch 279**: 'the interest of a shareholder in the company measured by a sum of money, for the purpose of liability in the first place, and of interest in the second, but also consisting of a series of mutual covenants entered into by all the shareholders *inter se* in accordance with [**CA 2006 s. 33**]'[6] (Farwell J). This is a partial description rather than a complete definition (Pennington, 'Can shares in companies be defined?' (1989) 10 Co Law 140), but the features identified by Farwell J should be further explored.

First, Farwell J recognizes that the interest of a shareholder is 'in' the company. This indicates how the shareholders are part of the company—unlike a creditor, whose interests are 'against' the company. A share thus creates something beyond a purely contractual interest.

Secondly, a share is an interest measured by a sum of money, but is not itself a sum of money. The nominal value is measured in monetary terms, but this provides a proportional measurement rather than a statement of monetary value. Farwell J mentions the share having elements of both liability and interest. Liability arises from the taking up of the shares—a shareholder is liable to pay for the shares, either on issue or on later call, but beyond that a shareholder has no further financial liability (shareholders are not liable for the company's debts: ***Salomon v A. Salomon & Co Ltd* [1897] AC 22**). In terms of interest, the shareholder's financial interest or return on his investment (whether by distribution of dividends or return of capital) is measured by reference to his proportional share.

The reference to 'mutual covenants' relates to the rights of shareholders under the articles—commonly known as the 'statutory contract' under what is now **CA 2006, s. 33**.[7] This deeming provision creates a contract between the company and the shareholders (and the shareholders *inter se*). This relationship is not identical to a traditional contract (***Bratton Seymour Service Co Ltd v Oxborough* [1992] BCLC 693**); for example contractual remedies of rescission and mistake are not available, and not all provisions of the articles are directly enforceable by members (***Hickman v Kent or Romney Marsh Sheepbreeders' Association* [1915] 1 Ch 881**: only membership, or 'insider', rights can be enforced). Nonetheless this statutory contract indicates the voluntary and binding nature of the relationship and the importance of the provisions of the articles. A shareholder will have further rights and obligations arising from the provisions of the **CA 2006**.

[6] It is great if you can remember a few particularly pertinent quotes but don't worry if you can't recall this word for word, you can just set down the essential points it raises and then work through them

[7] When revising make sure you highlight areas where you need to link topics to provide proper analysis of a point

A share is essentially a bundle of different rights and obligations. This is supported by Sealy and Worthington's Text, Cases and Materials in Company Law (11th edn, Oxford, 2016)[8] which identifies three key features. The first is a reflection of the shareholder's financial stake in the company; it indicates the member's level of financial interest and liability—the share measures the amount a shareholder might have to contribute to a company's capital, and provides the proportional measurement for financial returns. Secondly, a share is a measure of the shareholder's interest in the company as an association of members—a share gives its holder rights as a member of an association, including voting rights, as set out by the articles. Thirdly, a share is a species of property in its own right. This aspect is not included in Farwell J's analysis (but is reflected in **CA 2006, s. 541**)—a share is an item of property and thus capable of being bought, sold, charged, and split into legal and beneficial interests. The three elements are memorably described by Worthington as 'property, power and entitlement' ('Shares and shareholders: property, power and entitlement—Part I' (2001) 22 Co Law 258).

[9] This paragraph connects back to the main theme (identified at the start), and applies the discussion on a share's features to examples of different shareholders to show that the concepts are fully understood

Clearly the importance of these features will differ according to the type of share and reasons for holding it.[9] As a shareholder in a small private company, the second element—rights in the association—is likely to be most important. For a holder of preference shares the first element—the financial return by way of a fixed dividend payment—is likely to be most important. For investors in a listed public company, the third element is more important as financial gains are often made through purchase and sale of shares rather than dividend payments, and voting rights are largely irrelevant (as each shareholding is a tiny proportion of the company's shares).

It is similarly difficult to define shares by way of contrast with other investments in companies such as debentures (loans, usually secured on a company's assets). While in essence the concepts are very different, in practice, they can become blurred. For example, preference shares providing for a fixed return and no voting rights in many ways look more like a loan than a share (and are treated in some ways as such by the courts, eg **Scottish Insurance Corporation Ltd v Wilsons & Clyde Coal Co Ltd** [1949] 1 All ER 1068).

Pennington concludes shares are 'a species of intangible movable property which comprise a collection of rights and obligations relating to an interest in a company of an economic and proprietary character, but not constituting a debt'. This definition is not one many shareholders would find illuminating (and was described by Ireland as 'clear as mud': 'Corporate schizophrenia: the institutional origins of corporate social irresponsibility' (2018)), but may be the closest we can come to being both 'concise and comprehensive',[10] recognizing that a more meaningful definition depends on who is the shareholder.

[10] Take a final opportunity to show the question has been expressly considered

LOOKING FOR EXTRA MARKS?

- Provide further examples of how the important elements of a share differ according to the type of share and position of the shareholder
- Engage further with the cases and key academic work in this area
- Link to other topics such as the statutory contract created by the articles of association, or the rights of shareholders more generally

QUESTION | 2

Rosa owns 50 of the 1,000 issued shares in Holt Ltd, which has only one class of share. She also owns 40 preference shares in Jeffords Ltd which has an issued share capital consisting of 900 ordinary shares and 100 preference shares. The preference shares are preferential as to dividend (12 per cent) and return of capital.

Rosa has learned that the directors of Holt Ltd have decided to allot a significant number of shares to Charles. Rosa is unhappy as this allotment will dilute her shareholding and she has not been offered the opportunity to buy any further shares.

Rosa has also been informed that Jeffords Ltd has surplus capital and is proposing a capital reduction that will result in the preference shareholders being bought out and their shares cancelled. Rosa does not want to be bought out: she is getting a good return and believes the company has a strong future.

Advise Rosa.

CAUTION!

- Separate the issues and work though them step by step to avoid getting muddled
- Incorporate and use the relevant statutory provisions; don't just recite them

DIAGRAM ANSWER PLAN

| Identify the issues | ■ Validity of the proposed allotment of shares
■ Validity of the proposal to reduce capital by cancelling preference shares |

| Relevant law | ■ Power to allot shares
■ Proper purpose doctrine
■ Pre-emption rights
■ Position of preference shareholders
■ Reduction of capital |

| Apply the law | ■ Allotment and pre-emption in private company with one class of share
■ Restrictions on directors in allotting shares
■ Reduction of capital in private company
■ Variation of class rights |

| Conclude | ■ Are the proposals lawful?
■ Is there anything Rosa can do? |

SUGGESTED ANSWER

As Holt Ltd has only one class of share, these will be ordinary shares. Jeffords Ltd has two classes of share, with preference shares giving priority over ordinary shareholders in one or more areas. Rosa is entitled[1] to a fixed dividend of 12 per cent which must be paid before ordinary shareholders receive a dividend and is probably cumulative (**Webb v Earle** [1875] LR 20 Eq 556), but she will not be entitled to share in further profits: **Will v United Lankat Plantations Ltd** [1914] AC 11. She also has priority in return of capital, meaning she would get her capital back before ordinary shareholders in the event of the company's winding up, although would not be entitled to share in any further surplus (**Scottish Insurance Corpn Ltd v Wilsons and Clyde Coal Co Ltd** [1949] 1 All ER 1068). It will be assumed that every share in both companies carries one vote since in the absence of a provision as to preference, all shares are treated equally (**Birch v Cropper** (1889) 14 App Cas 25).

Holt Ltd

Directors can generally only allot shares if authorized by a resolution or the articles (**CA 2006, s. 551**). However, **CA 2006, s. 550** gives

[1] It is not essential to set out what each element of the shareholdings means, but it enables you to show your broader knowledge and that you have really thought about R's position

[2] Link to the facts to ensure you demonstrate the relevance of your statutory material

directors of a private company with one class of shares, such as Holt Ltd,[2] the power to allot shares without express authorization unless prohibited by the articles. The question does not indicate any prohibition in the articles so it seems the directors can allot without authorization under **s. 550**. Even if the articles did require authorization Rosa would not be able to block this without significant support as she has only 5 per cent of the shares.[3]

[3] It is worth doing some very simple maths in questions such as this, so that you can work out who can do what in the company

The directors of Holt Ltd thus have the power to allot shares, but they must 'only exercise powers for the purposes for which they are conferred': **CA 2006, s. 171(b)**. If they do not then the allotment would be invalid. The duty applies over the full range of directors' powers (*Eclairs Group Ltd v JKX Oil plc* **[2015] UKSC 71**) and has often been invoked in relation to the allotment of shares (eg *Hogg v Cramphorn Ltd* **[1967] Ch 254**; *Bamford v Bamford* **[1970] Ch 212**). The reasons for the allotment would have to be examined, but provided the 'substantial purpose' (*Howard Smith Ltd v Ampol Petroleum Ltd* **[1974] AC 821**) is within the proper scope of the power then even if there are secondary purposes that are outside its scope, the directors will not be in breach of duty. To invalidate the allotment, Rosa would need to show[4] that the directors' substantial purpose was not a 'proper' one such as raising capital, for example if they were allotting the shares primarily in order to reduce her influence or encourage her to sell up. If that were the case then the directors would be in breach of **s. 171(b)** even if they were acting in good faith in what they felt was best for the company (**CA 2006, s. 172**), as in cases such as *Punt v Symons & Co Ltd* **[1903] 2 Ch 506**. However as there is no evidence of any ulterior purpose, let alone of the substantial purpose being improper, it seems unlikely that Rosa can challenge the allotment on this basis.

[4] You aren't given any facts about the directors' motivations so you clearly aren't expected to examine this point in depth—just indicate what would be relevant

Rosa's further concern provides an alternative possible route for challenge. She has not been offered the chance to purchase more shares to maintain her proportional shareholding. Existing shareholders are given statutory pre-emption rights (**CA 2006, ss. 560–77**)[5] in respect of an allotment of 'equity securities', which includes ordinary shares (**s. 560**). Before an allotment, **s. 561** requires a company to make an offer to each person holding ordinary shares (communicated in accordance with **s. 562**) to allot to him 'on the same or more favourable terms' a proportion of those securities matching his existing proportional shareholding. An allotment cannot be made until the period for acceptance of such an offer (at least 21 days) has expired or the company has received notice of acceptance or refusal of the offer.

[5] You'll need to have some familiarity with the statutory provisions, and ideally have the statute in front of you (if permitted), before dealing with pre-emption rights

But Rosa needs to be aware that **CA 2006, s. 561** is subject to several exceptions. Those relating to the issue of bonus shares (**s. 564**) and securities held under employee share schemes (**s. 566**) do not seem to apply here. However allotments for non-cash consideration are also excluded (**s. 565**) and this would be an easy way for the directors to avoid Rosa's pre-emption rights. Furthermore, the articles of a private company can exclude all or any of the statutory pre-emption requirements whether generally or in relation to allotments of a particular description: **s. 567**. We don't know whether this is the case for Holt Ltd but there are also ways in which pre-emption rights can be disapplied. Particularly relevant here[6] is the ability of private companies with only one class of shares to disapply the rights, giving the directors power by the articles, or by special resolution, to allot equity securities as if **s. 561** did not apply to the allotment, or applied as modified by the directors: **s. 569(1)**. Rosa would not be able to block a special resolution as she has only 5 per cent of the shares. Rights can also be disapplied where a company has a provision in its articles to that effect (**s. 567**) or where the company's articles make separate provision for pre-emption rights in relation to a class (**s. 568**), while **ss. 570–1** provide for disapplication generally or for a specific allotment where the authority to allot arises under **s. 551**. There seems little prospect of Rosa preventing the disapplication of pre-emption rights, if not already excluded or avoided.

[6] Don't work through all the situations in turn, start with and focus on the most relevant provision

Rosa should also be aware that even if the directors did allot shares in contravention of **CA 2006, ss. 561–2**, then although she would be entitled to compensation from the company and every officer who knowingly authorized or permitted the contravention (**s. 563(2)**) the allotment itself would remain valid. Overall, there seems little point in Rosa seeking to challenge the allotment directly. Rosa could potentially petition under **CA 2006, s. 994**[7] arguing the allotment is unfairly prejudicial to her interests as a member: eg *Re Coloursource Ltd* [2005] BCC 627 and *Graham v Every* [2014] EWCA Civ 191, but should be aware that the most likely remedy under **s. 994** is an order for the purchase of the petitioner's shares, which she may not want.

[7] Show your wider understanding by indicating other avenues that a claimant might be able to pursue, without getting distracted

Jeffords Ltd

Companies can lawfully reduce their capital in accordance with the statutory scheme: **CA 2006, ss. 641–9**. From the facts it appears that Jeffords Ltd wants to 'repay paid-up capital in excess of the company's wants' under **s. 641(4)(b)(ii)**. As a private company Jeffords Ltd simply needs to pass a special resolution, supported by a solvency statement (**s. 642**), and Rosa would not be able to block a special resolution as she has only 4 per cent of the shares in Jeffords Ltd.[8] Does the fact the preference shareholders would be bought out change this position?

[8] This shows the examiner that you are really thinking about the facts and engaging with the question

The proposal will remove the preference shareholders from the company and so bring their rights to an end. This might appear to be a variation of class rights since variation includes abrogation of class rights (**s. 630(6)**). A variation of class rights can take place only in accordance with the articles or with the consent of a three-quarter majority of the class (**s. 630(2)**) which would mean Rosa (holding 40 per cent of the class) could most likely prevent it. However the courts have interpreted 'variation' narrowly (see *White v Bristol Aeroplane Co Ltd* [1953] Ch 65) and have held that paying off preference shareholders, in line with the rights of the class on winding up, is not a variation of capital. So in *House of Fraser plc v ACGE Investment Ltd* [1987] AC 387 it was held[9] that early repayment of preference shareholders and cancellation of their shares on a reduction of capital was not a variation or abrogation but 'gives effect to that right [to priority of repayment]' with the 'necessary consequence' that other rights attached to the shares then come to an end (Lord Keith). This vulnerability to early repayment is simply a characteristic of preference shares: *Re Saltdean Estate Co Ltd* [1968] 3 All ER 829. Although articles can provide that such a reduction is deemed to be a variation (*Re Northern Engineering Industries plc* [1994] 2 BCLC 704) as far as the facts indicate, this is not the case for Jeffords Ltd.

Accordingly Rosa cannot require Jeffords Ltd to secure the agreement of the preference shareholders: the company can go ahead with the reduction of capital provided it complies with **ss. 641–4**. Rosa could possibly claim the company's actions are unfairly prejudicial under **s. 994**, as actions of the company can be unfair even if lawful, particularly if in breach of some promise or understanding (*O'Neill v Phillips* [1999] 1 WLR 1092) but there is currently insufficient evidence[10] to recommend she pursue such a petition.

 [9] It is worth a bit of detail here as the case is particularly significant for these problem facts

[10] This shows you understand what would need to be demonstrated (and can think across different topics), while acknowledging that is not the focus of the question

 LOOKING FOR EXTRA MARKS?

- Keep linking your discussion of the law to the facts of the problem; doing this moves your answer from being just a relevant description of the law, to a clear application showing understanding as well as knowledge
- Provide a bit more depth on particularly relevant cases
- Add some awareness of legal reform/development (eg the ability to disapply pre-emption rights) or academic critique (eg of the courts' approach to 'variation')

Q **QUESTION** **3**

Moby Ltd has 200 issued shares, each of £1 nominal value: 100 ordinary shares and 100 5 per cent preference shares. All shares carry full voting rights. Ahab is the holder of 20 of the 100 issued preference shares. All other preference shareholders apart from Ahab also hold ordinary shares.

The articles of association state that Ahab has the right to veto any director's appointment while he retains a shareholding in the company.

At a recent general meeting at which all shareholders were present and voted, Moby Ltd passed two resolutions: (i) under authority given in its articles, to subdivide the ordinary shares, each into 10 shares of 10 pence nominal value, and (ii) altering the articles to remove Ahab's right to appoint a director. Furthermore, at a separate class meeting, a resolution has been passed removing the right of preference shareholders to receive their dividends cumulatively. Ahab voted against all resolutions (the only shareholder voting against).

Advise Ahab.

CAUTION!

- Identify the complaints at the start so that you focus on the problem facts and reduce the temptation to provide a general discussion on the topic

- Deal with each complaint separately to ensure you identify all the issues and reach a conclusion; if the same point arises in more than one complaint you can refer back to your earlier discussion rather than repeat yourself

DIAGRAM ANSWER PLAN

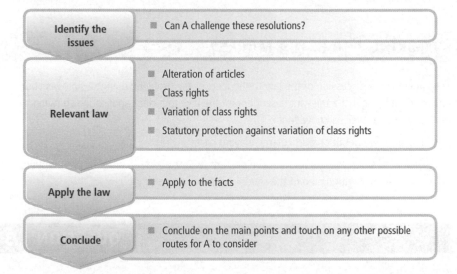

Identify the issues	■ Can A challenge these resolutions?
Relevant law	■ Alteration of articles ■ Class rights ■ Variation of class rights ■ Statutory protection against variation of class rights
Apply the law	■ Apply to the facts
Conclude	■ Conclude on the main points and touch on any other possible routes for A to consider

SUGGESTED ANSWER

Various rights connected with Ahab's shares have been disturbed. The subdivision of shares has diluted the overall voting power of his shares (from 10 per cent to 2 per cent) while his veto over director appointments and his right to receive preference dividends cumulatively have been removed.[1] Ahab's legal position will differ according to whether these changes constitute 'variations of class rights' or not, as if they are, protection is offered under **Companies Act 2006 (CA 2006), ss. 630–40**. Ahab's three complaints will be considered in turn.

[1] It can be helpful to identify the complaints, but it is important to do this very concisely to avoid wasting time repeating the question facts

Subdivision

Companies can subdivide shares provided there is authority in the articles under **CA 2006, s. 618**, which Moby Ltd has. But if the subdivision is a variation of Ahab's class rights, the resolution would be invalid as not satisfying **CA 2006, ss. 630–40** (in essence requiring separate agreement of the class affected).

The right to vote is a valuable feature of a share and the subdivision of ordinary shares has significantly reduced the relative voting power of Ahab's shares. But this would not trigger **ss. 630–40**, as the courts have interpreted 'variation' very narrowly, effectively distinguishing between direct and indirect variation of shareholders' rights.

The classic authority is **White v Bristol Aeroplane Co [1953] Ch 65** which held that issuing additional preference and ordinary shares to the ordinary shareholders did not 'vary' the rights of existing preference shareholders, distinguishing between a change in the right, and the 'enjoyment' of that right (see also **Re John Smith's Tadcaster Brewery [1953] Ch 308**). Particularly pertinent to Ahab's case is **Greenhalgh v Arderne Cinemas Ltd [1946] 1 All ER 512**,[2] where the company subdivided one class of shares, giving much greater proportional voting power to members of that class. This was held not to vary the rights of the other class of shareholders (as each shareholder still had the same right, namely one vote per share), it merely affected the enjoyment of that right.

[2] Shows you have recognized which case is most relevant

While this approach has received justifiable criticism (eg Reynolds, 'Shareholders' class rights: a new approach [1996] JBL 554), the case law is well established.[3] It therefore has to be concluded that Ahab cannot challenge the resolution as a variation of class rights. Other routes for redress will be considered later.

[3] There is less scope in problem questions for engaging with academic work; but you can still make some use of your further reading

Right of Veto

The company has sought to remove Ahab's right of veto through a resolution in general meeting. Provided proper notice was given (**CA 2006, s. 238(6)**), this will be a special resolution (not less than 75 per cent: **s. 238(1)**) as we are told that all members were present and voting and only Ahab voted against. Accordingly, the requirements of **CA 2006, s. 21** for alteration of the articles were met.[4] Alteration of the articles must also be 'bona fide for the benefit of the company' (**Allen v Gold Reefs of West Africa Ltd [1900] 1 Ch 656**), but this is a subjective test and a challenge is unlikely to succeed, unless the change was so 'oppressive' that it casts doubt on the majority's good faith (**Shuttleworth v Cox Brothers & Co Ltd [1927] 2 KB 9**).

However, a special resolution will be insufficient if Ahab's right of veto is a 'class right', as removing the right would be a 'variation' and not simply an interference with its enjoyment (variation includes 'abrogation': **CA 2006, s. 630(6)**). Class rights are conventionally those rights that explicitly attach to a class of shares, such as the right to a stated dividend. This would not obviously include the right of veto given to an individual shareholder but not attached to a class of shares. However, in **Cumbrian Newspapers Group Ltd v Cumberland & Westmoreland Herald Newspapers and Printing Co Ltd [1987] Ch 1**, 'class right' was extended to include rights given to an individual in their capacity as shareholder. The court held that the right to appoint a director while the shareholder held a certain proportion of shares was a class right, and gave as a further example the weighted voting right in **Bushell v Faith [1970] AC 1099**.

[5] Make clear where you are applying the law

Following this authority,[5] the right to veto would be a class right, with Ahab the only member of that class. Under **CA 2006, s. 630** variation must be in accordance with any procedure in the company's constitution (we will assume Moby Ltd has no specific provision as there is none in the model articles), or follow the statutory requirements. That requires consent in writing from the holders of at least three-quarters in nominal value of the issued shares of that class, or a special resolution passed at a separate class meeting: **s. 630(4)**. Ahab has not consented to the change and so the resolution is invalid.

Cumulative Dividends

The right to receive preference dividends cumulatively will be a class right, as it attaches to the class of shares. It is valuable as it means that once a dividend is declared, the company has to make up unpaid dividends to preference shareholders from earlier years prior to paying dividends to ordinary shareholders.

As a class right it cannot be varied through the normal statutory provisions for altering the articles (special resolution under

[6] It is fine to refer back to previous discussion if a point recurs, just always make sure to deal with any material differences of fact when applying it

CA 2006, s. 21), but, as explained in relation to the veto point,[6] only by following any variation procedure in the company's constitution or following **CA 2006, ss. 630–40**, which requires agreement of at least three-quarters of the class. In relation to this particular right, it appears that the company has already complied with the correct procedure. Ahab is the only member voting against, indicating that 80 per cent of the preference shareholders voted in favour, meeting the requirement.

[7] Don't assume that just because the basic procedure has been followed, that is an end to the issues

The vote could be challenged[7] as members of a class must vote with regard to the interests of the class as a whole. In *British America Nickel Corpn Ltd v O'Brien* **[1927] AC 369**, the vote was invalidated because a shareholder was induced to support the resolution by the promise of additional shares, but there is no evidence of anything like that here. *Re Holders Investment Trust Ltd* **[1971] 1 WLR 583** is closer to Ahab's position. There the majority preference shareholders were also ordinary shareholders and so gained from the variation— they were found to have voted in their own interests without regard to what was best for the class. Ahab may be able to challenge the vote on this basis: the other preference shareholders will benefit from the variation as the removal of the cumulative right potentially increases profits available for distribution to ordinary shareholders.[8]

[8] Demonstrate you are really thinking about the problem: having identified a line of attack, think now about how you can argue it on the basis of the facts and your wider knowledge of the topic

There is also a final layer of protection for Ahab. Under **CA 2006, s. 633** a shareholder with no less than 15 per cent of the issued shares in the class in question who did not vote in favour of the variation can apply to the court to have the variation cancelled on the ground that his rights as a member of the class have been unfairly prejudiced. Ahab holds 20 per cent of the class and voted against the variation, so can make an application[9] (this must be within 21 days of the variation (**s. 633(4)**)), and the variation will then have no effect unless and until it is confirmed by the court (**s. 633(3)**)). There is a dearth of authority on the interpretation of 'unfair prejudice' in relation to this provision, but it can be argued that it should follow the jurisprudence on **CA 2006, s. 994**. In such cases much often depends on the circumstances in which the member joined the company which is information we do not have, but Ahab's case for 'unfairness' is clearly supported by his being the only shareholder who would suffer only detriment and no benefit from the variation.

[9] Think IRAC: having identified the issue and the rule that applies, now apply it expressly and conclude appropriately

[10] A final conclusion wraps up the individual points, and also here allows you to raise other options, such as s. 994, that could easily have taken over the question if dealt with in the body of the essay

Conclusion[10]

It would be difficult to challenge the subdivision resolution as a variation of class rights, as the case law is strongly against Ahab. However, he could consider a claim under **CA 2006, s. 994** on the basis that it is unfairly prejudicial to his interests as a member. This offers a wide range of remedies under **s. 996**, the most common of which is a share purchase order.

Ahab's position on the removal of his veto is much stronger: the resolution appears invalid, as it is strongly arguable that it is a class right and so consent of the class was needed. Even if it were valid, the alteration of the article could amount to unfair prejudice under **s. 994**, depending on the circumstances of the case.

Moby Ltd has followed the correct procedure for variation of the cumulative dividend right, but Ahab can still challenge it, either claiming the vote was invalid because the majority were not acting for the benefit of the class, or applying for cancellation as unfairly prejudicing his interests as a member of the class. While Ahab's chances of success seem quite high, if he is considering bringing a claim under **s. 994** in respect of his other complaints it might be advisable instead to add this complaint to that claim, opening up a wider range of remedies.

LOOKING FOR EXTRA MARKS

- Make relevant connections, such as with alteration of the articles and shareholder remedies
- Add concise details of relevant cases to add depth to your discussion; explicitly identify which cases are most pertinent to the facts of the question and show how you are applying them
- Don't assume that in a problem question there is no scope for deeper comment and criticism of the law; bring in your further reading and analysis where you can

TAKING THINGS FURTHER

- Ireland, P., 'Corporate schizophrenia: the institutional origins of corporate social irresponsibility' in Boeger, N. & Villiers, C., *Shaping the Corporate Landscape* (Hart, 2018): available at https://research-information.bris.ac.uk/files/144068670/Corporate_Schizophrenia_draft.pdf

  An interesting and wide-ranging look at the nature of a share and the interests of a shareholder through the lens of the development of the modern company.

- Milman, D., 'The company share: evolution and regulation' (2018) 405 Co LN 1

  A concise consideration of recent developments relating to shares and share ownership, covering a number of related topics.

- Pennington, R., 'Can shares in companies be defined?' (1989) 10 Co Law 140

  A helpful exploration of the nature of shares, particularly in the context of the historical development of companies and shareholding.

- Pickering, M. A., 'The problem of the preference share' (1963) 26 MLR 499

  Examines class rights and the 'somewhat unsatisfactory' features of preference shares. Challenges the preference share for failing to provide shareholders with certainty and protection while meeting business needs.

- Reynolds, B., 'Shareholders' class rights: a new approach' [1996] JBL 554

  Criticizes the prevailing approach to interpreting variation of class rights, arguing that class rights should be interpreted widely and indirect alteration does amount to a variation.

- Worthington, S., 'Shares and shareholders: property, power and entitlement—Parts I and II' (2001) 22 Co Law 258, 307

  Considers the nature of shares ('property, power and entitlement'), and links shareholding to wider corporate governance questions. Argues shareholders' entitlements should be limited to the right to have the company's business conducted in accordance with the law and constitution, and not extend to the enhancement of 'shareholder value', reducing the primacy of shareholders within the class of stakeholders.

Online Resources
www.oup.com/uk/qanda/

For extra essay and problem questions on this topic, as well as advice on revision and exam technique, please visit the online resources.

5 Directors' Duties

ARE YOU READY?

In order to attempt the questions in this chapter you will need to have covered the following topics:

- Directors' duties: purpose, origins, and codification
- De facto and shadow directors
- Duty to act within constitution and powers
- Duty to promote the success of the company; shareholder primacy and stakeholding
- Duty to exercise independent judgment
- Duty to exercise reasonable care, skill, and diligence
- Duty to avoid conflicts of interest
- Duty not to accept benefits from third parties
- Duty to declare interest in proposed transaction or arrangement; substantial property transactions, loans, and quasi-loans
- Consequences of breach of duty
- Ratification and relief from liability
- Connections (in particular) with: management and governance, company contracts, shareholder remedies, capital, corporate insolvency. Most courses will expect you to be able to link duties with enforcement of duties by shareholders: see further Chapters 7 and 12

 KEY DEBATES

Debate: to whom should directors owe their duties?

This debate is particularly expansive, stretching from questions such as whether individual shareholders should be owed duties by directors, to creditor interests and directors' obligations on insolvency, to notions of stakeholding and shareholder primacy. The proposals of the Company Law

(▶)

Review and the introduction of **CA 2006, s. 172**, were catalysts for a great deal of discussion on these points. The literature is extensive, with much of interest, but the work of Andrew Keay, both on creditor interests and the 'corporate objective', is both readable and stimulating.

Debate: how strict should the law be in regulating conflicts of interest?

Differing attitudes to liability for conflict of interest can be seen in both cases and academic commentary. While some argue that a strict prophylactic rule (as exemplified by older authorities) is appropriate, others argue strongly for a more nuanced and flexible approach. There is still discussion as to what level of flexibility **CA 2006, s. 175** incorporates, and whether the ability to authorize breaches goes too far.

QUESTION | 1

Taking into account **Companies Act 2006, s. 172**, is it true to say that a director owes his duties to the company alone?

CAUTION!

- For this question you will need to have an appreciation of the difference between shareholder primacy and stakeholding approaches, and the concept of 'enlightened shareholder value' from **CA 2006**

- The focus of this question is to whom duties are owed rather than **CA 2006, s. 172** itself, so don't provide a lengthy discussion of all aspects of the section (such as the 'good faith' point) that would be relevant in a more general analysis of **s. 172**

DIAGRAM ANSWER PLAN

Duties owed to the company: s. 170 and common law

▼

The position of shareholders

▼

'Having regard to' interests of other constituents

▼

The position of creditors

▼

Enforcement of s. 172 and stakeholding considerations

▼

Conclusion: limitations and impact of s. 172

SUGGESTED ANSWER

[1] Nominee directors are an interesting group when it comes to directors' duties, but there is too much else to fit into this particular essay to explore this further

Companies Act 2006 (CA 2006), s. 170(1) states that a director owes his general duties (ss. 171–7) to the company. Even nominee directors owe their duties to the company[1] rather than the person appointing them (*Hawkes v Cuddy* [2009] 2 BCLC 427).

CA 2006, s. 170(1) confirms the approach taken at common law prior to codification of directors' duties in the **CA 2006** (following the Company Law Review) but does not elaborate on the meaning of 'the company' in this context. The company is both a separate entity (*Salomon v A. Salomon & Co Ltd* [1897] AC 22) and an association of its members, while relying and impacting on myriad other stakeholders, from employees to the environment. This essay will explore whether a director owes duties only to the company and what this means, considering the impact of **CA 2006, s. 172** in this area.[2]

[2] Having established the very basic points of law that underpin the issues, it is sensible to link explicitly to the question

At common law directors had to act bona fide in what they considered to be the interests of the company (*Re Smith & Fawcett Ltd* [1942] Ch 304); the interests of the company were the interests of the shareholders as a general body (*Gaiman v National Association for Mental Health* [1971] Ch 317). In a slight change,[3] s. 172 requires a director to 'act in the way he considers, in good faith, would be most likely to promote the success of the company for the benefit of its members as a whole'. This is the fundamental duty to which directors are subject: *Item Software (UK) Ltd v Fassihi* [2004] EWCA Civ 1244. Section 172(1) recognizes the dual nature of the company— first as a separate entity that can succeed or fail, and secondly as an association of members who will benefit from the company's success. In so far as duties are owed to shareholders though, this is through the medium of the company, and not in their individual capacity.

[3] Show that you are contrasting the pre- and post-2006 law

Percival v Wright [1902] 2 Ch 421 established that directors do not owe duties to shareholders directly, whether individually or collectively. In rare cases directors may owe duties directly to shareholders: where they act as the shareholder's agent (*Allen v Hyatt* (1914) 30 TLR 444) or where the nature of the company and director–shareholder relationship is such that directors have taken on direct responsibilities to shareholders (*Coleman v Myers* [1977] 2 NZLR 225; *Re Chez Nico (Restaurants) Ltd* [1992] BCLC 192). In *Peskin v Anderson* [2001] 1 BCLC 372, former members claimed directors had owed them a duty to disclose details of a pending sale. The court confirmed a director's duty is to the company alone, other than in special relationships where directors are in 'direct and close contact' with shareholders. This position is not changed by **CA 2006, s. 172**, and *Sharp v Blank* [2017] BCC 187 and *Vald Nielsen Holding A/S v Baldorino* [2019] EWHC 1926 (Comm) have recently reiterated that duties arise only where there was some personal relationship or particular dealing between the shareholders and directors.[4]

[4] Show that you've thought about whether the position remains the same and are therefore reflecting on the question

Duties are thus owed to the company alone save in rare cases. But this does not mean the interests of others are irrelevant. **Section 172(1)** requires directors, in fulfilling the duty to promote success of the company for the benefit of its members, to have regard ('amongst other matters') to a list of factors[5] (paragraphs (a)–(f)) which includes the interests of the company's employees; the need to foster business relationships with suppliers, customers, and others; and the impact on the community and the environment. However, this is a long way from directors owing a duty to any stakeholder or other interest listed; the duty is still to the company alone. It is akin to the former **Companies Act 1985, s. 309,**[6] which required directors to have regard to employees' interests, while leaving the duty owed to the company itself.

The approach of **s. 172** was labelled 'enlightened shareholder value' (ESV) by the Company Law Review. It is fundamentally a 'shareholder primacy' approach in that companies should be run for the benefit of their members, rather than a 'stakeholder' or 'pluralist' approach (for the benefit all those with a stake in the business). ESV recognizes taking other interests into account can enhance the success of the company which will benefit shareholders, but under ESV these factors are relevant so far as they achieve that aim; they are not pursued for their own merits. It is for the directors' judgment how far those factors are relevant, if at all, in promoting the company's success for the members' benefit. Lynch thus argues **s. 172** makes no meaningful difference ('Section 172: a ground-breaking reform of directors' duties, or the Emperor's New Clothes?' (2012) 33 Co Law 196) while a study of FTSE 100 companies concluded ESV has had little impact on the sample companies' operation or reporting (Keay and Iqbal, 'The impact of enlightened shareholder value' [2019] JBL 304). The recently added requirement for directors of large companies to describe in the strategic report (**s. 414A**) how they have had regard to the factors (**s. 414CZA**) seems unlikely to make much difference.[7]

Because the duty is owed to the company, breach of **s. 172** is enforceable only through the company; groups within the **s. 172(1)** list have no right of action. Even if an action was brought in respect of a failure to take account of a **s. 172(1)** factor, it might be hard to establish any resultant loss to the company. Breach of **s. 172** is in any case difficult to establish because of its subjective nature, requiring only that directors act in the way they believe is appropriate. It is hardly surprising that the major impact of **s. 172** is thought to be educative only.

The position becomes a bit more complex with regard to creditors. Directors do not owe duties to creditors, whether individually or collectively (*Multinational Gas and Petrochemical Co v Multinational Gas and Petrochemical Services Ltd* [1983] Ch 258; *Kuwait Asia Bank EC v National Mutual Life Nominees Ltd* [1991] 1 AC 187). However, in *West Mercia Safetywear v Dodd* [1988] BCLC 250 the

[5] It can be difficult to know how far you should set out statutory material in an answer. Here you do need to establish the law, but it is much better to summarize the key elements than simply copy out from a statute book

[6] Not an essential point but it indicates some awareness of the pre-2006 position

[7] If you had time this would be a good place to explore the academic discussion in more depth

court adopted the statement in *Kinsela v Russell Kinsela Pty Ltd* [1986] 4 NSWR 722 (*Kinsela*) that where a company is insolvent directors must have regard to creditors' interests. This does not mean that a duty is owed to creditors directly (*BTI 2014 LLC v Sequana SA* [2019] EWCA Civ 112 (*Sequana*)); instead creditors' interests displace those of the members: 'It is in a practical sense their assets and not the shareholders' assets that, through the medium of the company, are under the management of the directors' (Street CJ in *Kinsela*). This is triggered by insolvency, 'doubtful solvency or ... the verge of insolvency' (*Colin Gwyer and Associates Ltd v London Wharf (Limehouse) Ltd* [2003] 2 BCLC 153), or where directors know or should know that the company is or is likely to become insolvent (*Sequana*). Further, **Insolvency Act 1986, s. 214** imposes liability on a director[8] who permits the company to continue to trade beyond the point when s/he knew or ought to have known there was no reasonable prospect of avoiding insolvent liquidation. This is enforced through the liquidator and benefits unsecured creditors generally, rather than specific creditors.

The developing state of the law relating to creditors is reflected in **s. 172(3)**. This provides that the **s. 172** duty has effect subject to 'any enactment or rule of law requiring directors, in certain circumstances, to consider or act in the interests of creditors of the company', allowing further development of these principles in the future.

To conclude, it remains the case that a director owes his duties to the company alone, other than in very limited circumstances where a direct duty to an individual shareholder arises. However, in exercising the overriding duty to act in good faith to promote the success of the company for the benefit of the members, the director must take into account all relevant matters, which will include the interests of a range of stakeholders and other considerations. **Section 172** thus provides important guidance to directors but does not give rise to a duty owed to anyone other than the company. Furthermore, since duties are enforceable by the company, any action taken in respect of any breach must be through the company, either through the directors or, more likely, the members in a derivative action under **CA 2006, ss. 260–4**. This means that even if **s. 172** is breached, action is unlikely, and even if a claim were brought successfully, any remedy would benefit the company rather than the aggrieved stakeholder.

The changes wrought by **s. 172** thus do not change the law in terms of to whom the duties are owed but reflect a more general cultural change in recognizing wider interests and responsibilities.[9] This can also be seen in the strategic report required under **CA 2006, s. 414A** (other than for small companies), and a growing emphasis on corporate social responsibility. But the increasing awareness of the importance of corporate responsibility for both social and economic gain has not yet altered the fundamental legal position that duties are owed to the company alone.[10]

[8] Be careful not to spend time going into IA 1986, s. 214 in depth—its relevance here is in its overlap with duties to creditors

[9] Quite how far s. 172 does this is a matter for debate that you could look at in more depth

[10] This finishes off the essay by tying the conclusion back to the question itself

LOOKING FOR EXTRA MARKS?

- Develop the discussions on stakeholding and corporate responsibility, engaging with the academic debates, but remember to link this back into s. 172 as the question demands. Consideration of other approaches such as Keay's 'entity maximisation and sustainability model' could also provide scope for critiquing the current legal approach

- Show an awareness of the reform process (the Company Law Review) that resulted in s. 172 arguably being more than a straightforward 'codification' of existing law, and of ongoing reform proposals

QUESTION | 2

'A director must use his or her powers only for proper purposes.'
Discuss.

CAUTION!

- Make sure you are familiar with both the new and old terminology with respect to directors' duties—here the reference to 'proper purposes' relates to what is now CA 2006, s. 171(b)

- Don't just describe the current law or its origins; you need to provide some explanation but more importantly you need to assess how the law operates and any problems/benefits

DIAGRAM ANSWER PLAN

Introduction: s. 171(b) and its origins in the 'proper purposes' rule

Relationship with other duties

The purpose for which a power is conferred

The purpose for which a power is exercised

Relevance of good faith

Conclusion: balance criticisms against merits

The 'proper purposes' doctrine is an important part of the duties imposed by law on directors. The articles of association invariably give directors power to manage the company (eg Article 3 of the Model Articles for Private Companies (**Companies (Model Articles) Regulations 2008, Sch 1**)) and leave little power in shareholders' hands.[1] To balance directors' extensive power, the law imposes duties on directors—now codified as the 'general duties of directors' in **Companies Act 2006 (CA 2006), ss. 171–7**.

[1] This briefly recognizes the link between duties, governance, and division of powers

CA 2006, s. 171(b) requires a director to 'only exercise powers for the purposes for which they are conferred'. This is based on the long-established fiduciary duty to act only for 'proper purposes'[2] or not for any ulterior purpose (eg to benefit themselves). Accordingly, when exercising a power, a director must exercise it only for its proper purpose. If they fail to do so they will be in breach of duty and the exercise of the power will be invalid, although the company in general meeting can choose to affirm the exercise of power and/or ratify the director's breach (**CA 2006, s. 239**). The duty has been applied in areas as diverse as entering into agreements (**Lee Panavision Ltd v Lee Lighting Ltd** [1992] BCLC 22) and dealing with company assets (**Extrasure Travel Insurances Ltd v Scattergood** [2003] 1 BCLC 598), and the Supreme Court indicated in **Eclairs Group Ltd v JKX Oil plc** [2015] UKSC 71 (**Eclairs Group**) that it continues to apply over the full range of directors' powers.[3]

[2] Show early on that you understand where the current law deals with the 'proper purposes' doctrine

[3] This was important as the majority of the Court of Appeal in this case had indicated the duty did not apply to the exercise of all powers in all circumstances

At common law the proper purpose duty was combined with the duty to act bona fide in the interests of the company.[4] For example, in **Re Smith and Fawcett Ltd** [1942] Ch 304 it was said directors must act: 'bona fide in what they consider—not what a court may consider—is in the interests of the company, and not for any collateral purpose' (Lord Greene MR). However, codification in the **CA 2006** has split them with the 'bona fide' duty, reformulated as the duty to promote the success of the company for the benefit of its members, found in **s. 172**. It is clear that this split does not allow a director to escape liability by saying that only one of the duties has been breached, and there are still clear links between the two duties, as will be discussed later. The duty in **s. 171(b)** also overlaps with **s. 171(a)** as a director who fails to 'act in accordance with the company's constitution' may also, depending on the purpose for which they were was exceeding their authority, be in breach of **s. 171(b)**. A director may also be at risk of breaching **s. 171(b)** when considering other directors' duties, such as **s. 175** (conflict of interest) as 'more than one of the general duties may apply in any given case' (**s. 179**).

[4] This paragraph takes the opportunity offered by needing to explain how s. 171(b) differs from the previous law to consider the extent to which s. 171(b) relates to or overlaps with other duties

Howard Smith Ltd v Ampol Petroleum Ltd [1974] AC 821 *(Howard Smith)* established that in assessing the proper purposes duty the first stage is to ascertain the nature of the power and, 'in the light of modern conditions' the limits within which it may be exercised. In *Eclairs Group*, Lord Sumption indicated that ascertaining the purpose of the power depends on an inference from the mischief of the provision, including the court's understanding of the business context.[5] The power may be specific (as in *Howard Smith*) or general (the general power of management: *CAS (Nominees) Ltd v Nottingham Forest FC plc* [2002] 1 BCLC 613) and the limits of the power will depend upon the breadth of the power itself. On this point the interrelation of **s. 171** and **s. 172** may be relevant, as if a director is to avoid breaching **s. 172** (the duty to promote the success of the company for the benefit of the members as a whole) then they must exercise powers for the ultimate purpose of promoting the success of the company as well as any more specific, narrower purpose.

The limits to the exercise of a power are not necessarily narrow. In *Howard Smith*, it was held that the power to allot shares could properly be exercised not just to raise capital for the company but also to foster business connections, ensure the requisite number of shareholders, and to reach the best commercial agreement for the company. However, it could not be exercised in order to alter the majority shareholding, even though done without any intention of personal gain on the part of the directors. In *Extrasure Travel Insurances Ltd v Scattergood*[6] the court considered that in transferring company assets to another company within the group, the directors were exercising their power to deal with the assets of the company in the course of trading. The purpose for which such a power was conferred was the broad notion of promoting the company's commercial interests, but this meant that exercising the power to enable the other company to meet its liabilities was not a proper exercise of that power.

A problem arises where a power is exercised for more than one purpose, one of which is 'proper' and one of which is not—when should this be regarded as exercising the power for the purpose for which it was conferred? In *Howard Smith*, the House of Lords determined that once the power had been identified and its limits ascertained, it was necessary to establish the 'substantial purpose' for which it was exercised, and then address whether that substantial purpose was within the previously identified limits of the power. If so, then the power was exercised properly even if there were other 'improper' purposes; if not, the directors were in breach of duty (even if they had acted in good faith, and even if there was a proper subordinate purpose). In *Eclairs Group*, the Supreme Court confirmed that the 'substantial purpose' test continues to apply under **s. 171(b)**: the statutory codification reflects the previous law (**ss. 170(3)–(4)**).[7]

[5] You could consider whether the most recent formulation is identical to, or subtly different from the earlier test

[6] In an exam you need to be sparing with case facts to leave enough time to discuss the law and address the question, but this paragraph shows sometimes case facts are essential to support the point being made

[7] This sentence fulfils two purposes—it shows your awareness of the case, and explicitly compares the old and new law

In assessing the 'substantial purpose', *Howard Smith* requires the court to engage in an objective assessment of the situation, considering the directors' subjective motives. By assessing objectively how 'critical or pressing' a particular issue might have been, the court can evaluate the assertions of directors as to the importance of this factor in their minds when exercising the power, although the directors' judgment on matters of management should be respected. Where directors are primarily motivated by aims other than the purpose for which the power was conferred, they will be in breach of duty and the exercise of power will be invalid. This can be seen in several cases, eg *Hogg v Cramphorn Ltd* [1966] 3 All ER 420 where the directors' allotment of shares was invalidated when made primarily to retain control of the company for the directors and their supporters (and see also *Punt v Symons & Co Ltd* [1903] 2 Ch 506 and *Bamford v Bamford* [1970] Ch 212). In *Eclairs Group*, Lord Sumption indicated that the critical point in determining whether the purpose is 'substantial' is whether it was causative of the power being exercised, but this point was not adopted by all the Justices.

The fact that directors have acted in good faith and in what they honestly believed to be the best interests of the company will not prevent a breach of **CA 2006, s. 171(b)**.[8] This can be seen in *Lee Panavision Ltd v Lee Lighting Ltd*, where directors were in breach of duty for committing the company to a management agreement, even though they thought it in the company's interests to do so, and similarly in *Eclairs Group*, where the bona fides of the directors was not in doubt. While good faith does not prevent a breach of duty, it may still be relevant to a director in seeking relief from liability as, if a director acted 'honestly, reasonably and ought fairly to be excused', then they may seek relief from the court under **CA 2006, s. 1157**.

In conclusion, a director must indeed exercise their powers only for the purpose for which they have been conferred, even if otherwise complying with their duties. The duty has received some criticism, notably that it allows courts to replace directors' business judgment with their own judgment (eg Sealy, 'Directors' duties revisited' (2001) 22 Co Law 79). Furthermore, directors do not have clear boundaries as it has been declared 'impossible' to 'define in advance exact limits beyond which directors must not pass' (*Howard Smith*).[9] Nonetheless, **s. 171(b)** provides an important objective protection, contrasting with the largely subjective nature of **s. 172** under which a director only needs to act in the way he considers in good faith will promote the success of the company. *Eclairs Group* shows the importance of the duty in protecting the balance of power between directors and shareholders. Accordingly, following codification of the law on directors' duties, directors must still exercise their powers only for 'proper purposes' and this is as it should be.[10]

[8] An important point that should be made expressly

[9] It is fine to make the point in your own words if you can't remember a quote in an exam

[10] The final sentence both links back to the question and reminds the examiner that you've done your best to evaluate and not simply describe the law

LOOKING FOR EXTRA MARKS?

- Although your focus must be on s. 171(b), don't look at it entirely in isolation—show that you recognize links between s. 171(b) and other aspects of directors' duties, and use this to explore the significance of the proper purpose doctrine

- Recognize how CA 2006 separated the previously 'composite' duty into two duties—s. 171(b) and s. 172. You could consider the Company Law Review approach to this if you wanted to explore this further

- Explore the cases and academic commentary to add depth to your discussion

QUESTION | 3

Gatto Ltd, a property development company, has four directors: Honey, Cherry, Florentine, and Victoria. Honey and Cherry are the children of the original founder of the business, Madeleine, who is now retired. Honey and Cherry promised Madeleine, who has a passion for local environmental issues, that they would never take any action that affects the wildlife reserve based on nearby Maryland Meadow.

Last year, the board decided that the company should pursue new developments in the local area and asked Victoria to investigate possible new development sites. She identified two possible options: (i) Holly Wood, a brownfield site (previously developed land), and (ii) Berry Park, a greenfield site (undeveloped land) situated on the edge of Maryland Meadow. Holly Wood required decontamination prior to development and so offered lower profits than development at Berry Park, but development at Berry Park would inevitably have a negative impact on the wildlife reserve. At board discussions, Honey and Cherry refused to consider Berry Park because of their promise to Madeleine, and Victoria went along with their preference. Florentine was not present at the discussions: since last year when she became director of another company, Torta Ltd, also in the construction industry, she has rarely attended Gatto Ltd's board meetings. Decontamination of the Holly Wood site has proved very expensive and Gatto Ltd is set to lose money on the development.

Advise Gatto Ltd.

CAUTION!

- Don't work through each duty in order—this wastes time and indicates to the examiner that you are struggling to identify the relevant law. Although more than one duty can (and often does) apply, you should work out the most relevant duties and start with those

- Try to balance explanation of the law with applying the law to the facts

- Read the question carefully—as you are told to advise the company, you don't need to worry about shareholder remedies

DIAGRAM ANSWER PLAN

Identify the issues	▪ Decision making—relevant considerations ▪ Non-involvement/absence ▪ Directorship of another company
Relevant law	▪ Directors' duties ▪ Fettering discretion ▪ Duty to promote the success of the company ▪ Duty of care, skill, and diligence ▪ Conflict of interest ▪ Remedies and relief for breach of duty
Apply the law	▪ Apply different duties as appropriate to the facts ▪ Consider consequences of breach
Conclude	▪ Conclude, considering merits of claim

SUGGESTED ANSWER

The general duties the directors owe to Gatto Ltd (**Companies Act 2006 (CA 2006), s. 170**) are set out in **CA 2006, ss. 171–7** and are of both fiduciary and common law origin. There have been several possible breaches of duty[1] relating to the purchase of Holly Wood and involvement with Torta Ltd. These, and the consequences of breach, will be considered, bearing in mind that more than one duty may apply at any time (**CA 2006, s. 179**).

Holly Wood

The first issue to consider in relation to the Holly Wood purchase is Honey and Cherry's promise to Madeleine, which led to their refusal to consider the other (more profitable) alternative, Berry Park. Under **CA 2006, s. 173** a director 'must exercise independent judgment',[2] which originates in the fiduciary duty on a director not to fetter his judgment. This prevents a director entering into an agreement preventing later consideration of his duties (**Boulting v Association of Cinematograph, Television and Allied Technicians [1963] 2 QB 606**), although it does not prevent a director, in the proper exercise of his powers, making a decision to bind the company to a future course of action even though this restricts future decisions (**Fulham**

[1] You could set out in the introduction which particular duties will be most relevant, but don't go into too much detail in the introduction as you risk repeating yourself later

[2] This duty doesn't come up often in problem questions, but do keep all the duties in mind when assessing the facts to make sure you don't miss any relevant ones

Football Club Ltd v Cabra Estates plc [1994] 1 BCLC 363). While Honey and Cherry have not contractually committed themselves to acting in accordance with Madeleine's wishes, by following a pre-agreed policy rather than considering the issue on its merits, they are clearly not exercising independent judgment. As this appears not to be a decision made at the time for the benefit of the company, but for family reasons, it is probable that **s. 173** has been breached. The consequences of breach[3] are the same as if the corresponding equitable principle applied (**CA 2006, s. 178**), which would include rescission of a contract made in breach of duty or equitable compensation for loss.

[3] Use your own course as a guide to how much depth you will be expected to go into on remedies

The directors may also have breached **CA 2006, s. 172**, which is the 'fundamental' duty of directors (*Item Software (UK) Ltd v Fassihi* [2005] 2 BCLC 91). It requires directors to act in the way they consider, in good faith, to be most likely to promote the success of the company for the benefit of the members as a whole. In most cases this will mean the most profitable course of action, but the potential for damage to a company's reputation will be relevant as it could harm the longer-term interests of the members.

Under **s. 172** directors are required to have regard, 'amongst other things', to a list of factors, which includes the long-term consequences of any decision (**s. 172(1)(a)**) and the 'impact of the company's operations on the community and the environment' (**s. 172(1)(d)**). This 'enlightened shareholder value' approach maintains shareholder primacy, whereby companies are run in the interests of shareholders, not other stakeholders. Accordingly directors must have regard to environmental issues only in order to promote the success of the company.[4] It appears that Cherry and Honey have breached **s. 172** if they are taking this factor into account because of the promise to Madeleine, and not because they honestly believe this to be in the best interests of the company. Victoria will also be in breach if she has failed to consider the question for herself.

[4] Don't just explain the ESV approach—apply it to the facts

Nonetheless Gatto Ltd might have difficulty in proving breach, as the duty is subjective (what the director thinks is best, not what is, objectively, best)[5] and the directors might convince the court they genuinely believed Holly Wood was best for the company. It can also be difficult to establish loss if a director properly fulfilling the duty could reasonably have reached the same decision (as could be the case if Berry Park would cause damage to the company's reputation). This effectively brings in an objective element to **s. 172**, allowing the court to judge the director's own decision against that of an 'intelligent and honest man' (*Charterbridge Corporation Ltd v Lloyds Bank Ltd* [1970] Ch 62). It would therefore be difficult to establish breach of **s. 172**.

[5] Remember the duty only requires a director to act in good faith in what they consider to be the best interests of the company

Florentine's Position

It seems that Florentine has not met the standard of care, skill, and diligence expected of a director. This requires a director to act with 'reasonable care, skill and diligence' as measured by a dual objective/subjective test—an objective minimum of the standard reasonably expected of someone in that position in that company, increased by any general knowledge, skill, or experience of the particular individual (**CA 2006, s. 174**). Although early cases indicated a director's duties were only of an 'intermittent nature' (**Re City Equitable Fire Assurance Co Ltd** [1925] Ch 407),[6] later cases show a director must pay adequate attention to the company's affairs (eg **Dorchester Finance Co Ltd v Stebbing** [1989] BCLC 498). Ongoing failures to attend meetings and take any interest in the company, as here,[7] would be a breach of duty. The other directors could also be in breach of this duty by allowing Florentine to pay no attention to the company, as all directors have ongoing monitoring and supervisory obligations (**Re Barings plc (No. 5)** [2000] 1 BCLC 523).

The origins of the duty of care, skill, and diligence in **s. 174** lie in the common law duty of care, and the consequences of breach are the same as if the corresponding common law rule applied (**CA 2006, s. 178**). This would be common law damages as compensation for loss. However it might be difficult for Gatto Ltd to establish causation and loss as it is hard to say that Berry Park would necessarily have been favoured even if Florentine had been present at the meeting. Even if the matter had been discussed properly between all four directors, Honey and Cherry's view might still have prevailed, or they might have all concluded that Holly Wood was the right option.

There is a further possibility that Florentine has breached her duty to avoid a conflict of interest (**CA 2006, s. 175**) by joining the board of Torta Ltd.[8] In **London and Mashonaland Exploration Company Ltd v New Mashonaland Exploration Co Ltd** [1891] WN 165 (**Mashonaland**), Chitty J held there was no prohibition on a director acting as a director of a rival company, but he approached this on the basis of contractual restraints and confidentiality, rather than fiduciary duties. This decision was cited with approval in **Bell v Lever Bros** [1932] AC 161, but questioned in later cases. In **Plus Group Ltd v Pyke** [2002] EWCA Civ 370, [2002] 2 BCLC 201, the Court of Appeal indicated that, in general, the holding of competing directorships would require the approval of the companies in question, but stressed the situation was 'fact specific'. The Scottish courts in **Commonwealth Oil & Gas Co Ltd v Baxter** [2009] CSIH 75 have also cast doubt on the judgment in **Mashonaland** and limited the case to its own facts.

The codification of the conflict duty in **CA 2006, s. 175** makes explicit that the duty applies equally to a conflict of duty and duty as to a conflict of interests (or interest and duty) (**s. 175(7)**). A breach of **s. 175** can thus arise if Florentine is acting for two companies, because the duties owed to two different companies will in all likelihood pull in two different directions. Accordingly, while **Mashonaland** suggests

[6] Don't be tempted to give too much description of the earlier cases and the development of the duty, there simply isn't time and it is more important to apply the law to the facts

[7] Make the link to the facts explicitly

[8] The law on breach of duty through the holding of more than one directorship is still not entirely clear so requires a reasonable amount of consideration

there would not appear to be a breach by merely joining the board of a rival company, by acting in that position Florentine is highly likely to be in breach of **s. 175**. She could avoid this by ensuring that both companies are fully aware of the position and agree to it but in this case there seems to have been neither formal authorization of the board (**s. 175(4)**), nor prior approval of the shareholders (*Sharma v Sharma* **[2013] EWCA Civ 1287**). On balance it seems likely that Florentine is in breach of duty in acting as director of Torta Ltd, and would accordingly be liable to account for any profits made from this position.

Conclusion

[9] As conclusions have been made on each point as they appeared, this final conclusion can be short and the opportunity can be taken to provide more general and pragmatic advice

To conclude,[9] there are potential breaches of **ss. 172–5** by the directors, although there could be some problems in proving breach, causation, and loss, particularly in relation to **s. 172** and **s. 174**. The directors might also seek relief under **CA 2006, s. 1157**, claiming they acted honestly and reasonably and ought fairly to be excused, although it must be doubted whether they acted reasonably on the facts, particularly as reasonableness is measured objectively: *Bairstow v Queens Moat Houses plc* **[2001] 2 BCLC 531**. Accordingly, Gatto Ltd might be better advised not to throw good money after bad in pursuing its directors, and instead should consider refreshing its management team by removing some or all of its directors by ordinary resolution under **CA 2006, s. 168**. In any event, action against the directors will be very difficult while they remain in power because of the rule in *Foss v Harbottle* **(1843) 2 Ha 461** and the difficulties for shareholders in bringing a derivative claim.[10]

[10] This shows you understand the practical difficulties of bringing a claim, even though the question doesn't call on you to address this aspect

LOOKING FOR EXTRA MARKS?

■ Remember to consider the consequences of breach (and, if relevant, avoidance of or relief from liability), using your own course as a guide to how much time to allocate to these elements of the question

■ A recognition of wider debates or connected issues, even in a problem question, will impress the examiner, but don't go too far off point

QUESTION | 4

'The formulation of the duty of skill and care in the **Companies Act 2006** shows an important change in the law's expectations of directors.'

Discuss.

CAUTION!

- It is tempting to approach the law chronologically as the simplest way of explaining the position, but this may well encourage a descriptive approach. Instead try starting with the current law, and consider the extent to which it reflects the pre-existing common law

- Remember that there had already been important developments in the common law prior to the 2006 Act

DIAGRAM ANSWER PLAN

> Introduction: context and approach

▼

> Relevant law: the dual objective/subjective test

▼

> Contrast earlier law with current law; explore reasons for development

▼

> Assessment and conclusion: does s. 174 change the position?

A   SUGGESTED ANSWER

The 'duty of skill and care' is now found within the general duties of directors in **Companies Act 2006 (CA 2006), ss. 171–7**, as the 'duty of care, skill and diligence': **s. 174**. As the general duties are based on the common law rules and equitable principles and have effect in their place (**s. 170(3)**), this would indicate there has been no change in the law in this area.[1] However **CA 2006** is not a true 'codification' of the law, as some duties have been developed (eg **s. 172**), some aspects have not been codified (eg remedies, **s. 178**), and the common law is explicitly retained as a guide to interpreting and applying the duties (**s. 170(4)**).

[1] This pulls in broader understanding of how the general duties operate while showing a focus on the question

This essay will argue that **s. 174** does not itself change the law, but merely reflects pre-2006 common law development.[2] However that development, and so **s. 174**, results from a more modern view of the role of a director and is stricter than early judicial formulations of the duty. The essay will assess the current statutory duty, and compare this with the pre-existing common law, to evaluate the significance of the statutory formulation and its merits.

[2] If you have planned your essay sufficiently to know where you are going, it can be very effective to indicate your argument within your introduction

Section 174

Under **CA 2006, s. 174** a director must exercise 'reasonable care, skill and diligence': that exercised by a 'reasonably diligent person' with both (a) the general knowledge, skill, and experience reasonably expected of someone carrying out the functions of that individual in that company, and (b) the general knowledge, skill, and experience that the individual has. The formulation is modelled on **Insolvency Act 1986 (IA 1986), s. 214(4)** which relates to the knowledge required for liability for wrongful trading,[3] and, as will be seen, had already been adopted in some common law cases before **CA 2006**.

The minimum objective standard provided in paragraph (a) cleverly[4] varies according to the nature of the company and the position of the director, ensuring the law imposes higher standards on directors with greatest responsibility, thus reflecting modern expectations on directorial behaviour, particularly in larger companies. Paragraph (b) adds a further subjective layer where a director has skills or experience beyond that expected in their position. This operates only to increase the expectations on directors in relevant cases, it does not take the standard below the objective minimum. Although the level of skill, care, and diligence thus differs according to the director and the company, judges need not set out the precise knowledge, skills, and experience expected in a particular case: *Weavering Capital (UK) Ltd v Dabhia and Platt* [2013] EWCA Civ 71, reducing the scope for appeals.

The Common Law Standard

By way of contrast[5] with the fundamentally objective nature of **s. 174**, the common law as established by Romer J in *Re City Equitable Fire Assurance Co Ltd* [1925] Ch 407 (*City Equitable*) appears to be much more subjective and imposed fairly lax expectations on directors. *City Equitable* established three principles. The first required a director only to show that degree of skill that 'may reasonably be expected from a person of his knowledge and experience'. The second held that a director was 'not bound to give continuous attention to the affairs of his company' with duties only of 'an intermittent nature'. Thirdly, directors were entitled to trust in officials to whom duties had been (justifiably) entrusted.

These propositions reflected the generous attitude of the time towards 'gentlemen-directors'. For example, in *Re Cardiff Savings Bank, Marquis of Bute's Case* [1892] 2 Ch 100 the Marquis became chairman at the age of six months and attended only one board meeting in 38 years but was not in breach of duty. *Re Brazilian Rubber Plantations and Estates Ltd* [1911] 1 Ch 425 held that directors need not 'bring any special qualifications to their business'; and need have no awareness of the nature of the company's business.

[3] Show you understand what IA 1986, s. 214(4) relates to, but don't be sidetracked into discussion of wrongful trading more generally

[4] This is a limited but very concise way of indicating some personal evaluation of the law

[5] By starting with the modern law, the discussion of the previous law now appears to be much more thoughtful and directed, as it is no longer a simple chronological account of legal development

Comparing the Standards

That might suggest **s. 174** does show a change in the law—from a lax subjective approach, to a strict objective one. However, the common view of the *City Equitable* standard has been challenged, as it does arguably incorporate an objective element based on the reasonable director.[6] More importantly, even if one accepted that the *City Equitable* standards were lax and entirely subjective, in fact the law had evolved even before **CA 2006** and so the new law is not truly a change in approach.[7]

[6] You could engage with the academic discussion on this point if you had time to do so

[7] Explicitly using the language of the question (and making interim conclusions) throughout the essay can be an effective technique to reassure the examiner that you are continuing to focus on the question

In *Norman v Theodore Goddard (A Firm)* [1991] BCLC 1028, Hoffmann J was willing to assume that the test of the director's duty of care should be based on the dual objective/subjective test imposed in respect of wrongful trading under the **Insolvency Act 1986 (IA 1986), s. 214(4)**. He restated this as the law in *Re D'Jan of London Ltd* [1994] 1 BCLC 561 *(Re D'Jan)*.

The second and third propositions of *City Equitable* had also been qualified prior to **CA 2006**. In *Re Barings plc (No 5)* [2000] 1 BCLC 523, Jonathan Parker J highlighted the 'inescapable, personal duties' of a director, holding that directors must acquire and maintain a sufficient knowledge and understanding of the company's business to enable them properly to discharge their duties as directors, and that while functions can be delegated, there is an ongoing obligation to supervise delegated functions (see also *Re Westmid Packing Services Ltd, Secretary of State for Trade and Industry v Griffiths* [1998] 2 All ER 124 *(Westmid)*). Cases such as *Dorchester Finance Co Ltd v Stebbing* [1989] BCLC 498 and *Lexi Holdings (In Administration) v Luqman and Ors* [2009] EWCA Civ 117 show that directors cannot escape liability for the consequences of another director's fraud, where their own inactivity has enabled that fraud to take place.

[8] This is an interesting area where directors' duties and liability on insolvency interlink—it could be relevant both in questions on directors' duties and in questions on corporate insolvency

A major influence in the development of the duty of skill and care at common law was disqualification of directors for unfitness[8] under **Company Directors Disqualification Act 1986 (CDDA 1986), ss. 6 and 8**, where breach of duty by the director is relevant in determining unfitness (**CDDA 1986, Sch 1**). The courts have explicitly acknowledged that the main purpose of disqualification under **CDDA 1986** is to protect the public, and part of this protection is by raising standards of conduct among directors generally: *Westmid*. In *Bishopsgate Investment Management Ltd v Maxwell* (No. 2) [1994] 1 All ER 261, Hoffmann LJ linked the evolution of directors' duties with changing public attitudes as reflected in **CDDA 1986**. In *Re Landhurst Leasing plc* [1999] 1 BCLC 286, Hart J appeared to align the standard of the duty at common law and the standard for unfitness under the **CDDA 1986** with the *Re D'Jan* test (as now accepted in **s. 174**), although it should be remembered that breach of the duty of care and skill is not a prerequisite for a finding of unfitness (eg *Cohen v Selby* [2001] 1 BCLC 176).

[9] The conclusion contains a fair amount of evaluation of the question, so this has been made clear in the sub heading

Conclusion: Development or Change?[9]

Section 174 thus reflects a developing jurisprudence, rather than itself effecting change. The choice was made to resolve any conflict between *City Equitable* and *Re D'Jan* in favour of the latter, increasing the expectations on directors in line with modern views on director responsibility and making it easier to establish liability. But it is highly probable that the courts would have favoured the later authorities in any event and continued to develop the law in this direction, even without statutory involvement. This trend had been seen in relation to all three of the basic propositions regarding a director's duty of care, skill, and diligence. The formulation in **s. 174** makes clear that incompetence, inactivity, or abrogation of responsibility (however honest, and however limited the director's own ability) are no longer acceptable, if they ever were. It brings the old common law into line with more modern concepts such as wrongful trading and disqualification, ensuring consistency of approach.

[10] This paragraph raises some points that challenge the approach of the law, providing some additional analysis to strengthen the overall response to the question

It could be argued[10] that an objective approach is potentially unfair when no qualification is expected of directors—the law permits individuals to become directors however ill-suited they might be, and even though potentially incapable of meeting the objective standards set for them. This contrasts with other professions where qualifications are required, ensuring a level of competence. However the modern approach reflects public expectations and growing awareness of the power of directors, whose decisions and competence can impact on whole communities and economies, not just shareholders. Similar attitudes can be seen in other areas of directors' duties, particularly **s. 172**, where the opportunity was taken to develop and not simply codify the law. The potential for unfairness is reduced through **s. 174**'s variable objective standard, which allows the court to set expectations at appropriate levels for different companies, and through **s. 1157** which offers the possibility of relief where a director has acted 'honestly and reasonably' even when in breach of the duty of care and skill (*Re D'Jan*). The importance of **s. 174** thus lies not in a change in the law but in ensuring modern values and practice are properly reflected and balanced in the law.

LOOKING FOR EXTRA MARKS?

- Show that you understand how the duty of care, skill, and diligence is linked with wrongful trading and disqualification
- Consider the reasons for the change in approach, and also whether the modern approach has any downsides
- Consideration of the Company Law Review deliberations can add value to discussion of directors' duties, particularly where the law has developed during the codification process

Brianna, Alvin, Dilip, and Clara are the directors of Tweedy Ltd, manufacturers of traditional cloth. A fifth director, Joella, left the company in August, having been released from her post following a period of ill health.

In October, the directors discovered that Joella is now working with one of their former customers, Megacrush plc, developing an innovative new fabric from recycled plastics. Megacrush plc had discussed this project with Tweedy Ltd in March (all the directors being present at the meetings) but the directors had concluded this would be a distraction from Tweedy Ltd's core business and so decided not the pursue the project further. It now appears that Joella commenced work on the project with Megacrush plc very soon after her departure from Tweedy Ltd in August. Industry rumours suggest the project is likely to be very profitable.

In November, the directors agreed to place a large order for computer supplies (worth £50,000) with Futurco Ltd, and this contract has now been completed. All the directors have been aware throughout that Clara and her husband are the only shareholders of Futurco Ltd.

Advise Tweedy Ltd.

CAUTION!

- It is very easy in the panic of an exam to muddle CA 2006, ss. 175 and 177 or forget about one of them. They both deal with conflicts of interest but deal with different factual matrices, and approach the issue in a different way, so keep a clear head. Remember that s. 177 concerns transactions with the company itself, and if s. 177 applies, s. 175 doesn't.

- Where you have a transaction with the company, remember to consider the possibility that it is a substantial property transaction under CA 2006, s. 190.

DIAGRAM ANSWER PLAN

Identify the issues	■ Former director working on project formerly offered to the company ■ Purchase made from company connected to directors
Relevant law	■ Duties of no conflict, no profit ■ Corporate opportunities, particularly post-resignation ■ Disclosure of interest in transactions with the company ■ Substantial property transactions ■ Liability for breach
Apply the law	■ Apply to the facts, considering the consequence of breach
Conclude	■ Conclude

SUGGESTED ANSWER

[1] A very brief summary of the key duties is all that is required in the introduction

To advise Tweedy Ltd, the fiduciary duties of 'no conflict' and 'no profit' should be considered—a director cannot (without the company's agreement) have an interest that conflicts (or may conflict) with the interests of the company, nor profit from their position.[1] These duties have traditionally been strictly applied to ensure a director is not tempted to further their own interests at the expense of the company (***Bray v Ford*** [1896] AC 44). The duties are now codified in **Companies Act 2006 (CA 2006), ss. 175–7** but the case law remains relevant in interpreting and applying them (**CA 2006, s. 170(3)–(4)**). Additional specific duties also need to be considered, particularly that relating to substantial property transactions (**CA 2006, s. 190**).

Joella

[2] Focus immediately on the current law, ie the codified duty, and bring the case law into this, rather than establishing the pre-2006 law and only then moving on to CA 2006

By working with Megacrush plc on the project discussed with Tweedy Ltd, Joella may be in breach of **CA 2006, s. 175**.[2] This section requires a director to avoid a situation in which they have a conflict of interest between their own interest and that of the company (**s. 175(1)**) and applies in particular to the exploitation of 'any property, information or opportunity' (**s. 175(2)**). Joella may be exploiting information or an opportunity of Tweedy Ltd in moving on to work with Megacrush plc.

Although Joella has left the company, the duty continues to apply even after her departure in relation to information or opportunities of which she became aware when she was a director (**s. 170(2)(a)**).

There would be no breach of **s. 175** had the directors authorized the potential conflict (**s. 175(4)**, reflecting *Queensland Mines v Hudson* **(1978) 52 ALJR 379**), but the facts do not indicate any authorization.[3] It is therefore necessary to see how the courts have applied the duty to cases such as this to determine whether Joella is in breach.

The key authority indicates a strict approach to conflicts of interest. In *Regal (Hastings) Ltd v Gulliver* [1942] 1 All ER 378 *(Regal Hastings)*, the House of Lords found directors in breach of duty even though acting in good faith and where the company could not take up the opportunity itself. This is supported by *Industrial Development Consultants Ltd v Cooley* [1972] 1 WLR 443, where (not unlike the present case)[4] a director was released from his position (claiming ill health) and then took up an opportunity that he was aware of only through his previous directorship—it was considered irrelevant that the company was highly unlikely ever to have been able to take up the opportunity itself. **Section 175(2)** now expressly states that it is immaterial whether the company could take advantage of the information or opportunity. On this basis Joella would be liable as she was only aware of the opportunity through Tweedy Ltd. Nonetheless, a softer line is present in other cases—making use of information or an opportunity post-resignation is not invariably a breach—and **s. 175(4)(a)** recognizes there is no breach if the situation cannot reasonably be regarded as likely to give rise to a conflict of interest.

Commonwealth courts in particular have taken a more flexible line, for example *Canadian Aero Service Ltd v O'Malley* (1973) 40 DLR (3d) 371 indicated liability depends on whether all the facts reveal adoption of a 'maturing business opportunity'. A similar approach was taken in the UK in *Island Export Finance Ltd v Umunna* [1986] BCLC 460. The flexible approach has been welcomed by some academics (eg Lowry and Edmunds 'The corporate opportunity doctrine: the shifting boundaries' (1998) 61 MLR 515).[5] In relation to Joella, a potentially important point is that the opportunity was apparently rejected in good faith by the company's board. In *Peso Silver Mines Ltd v Cropper* [1966] SCR 673, a director was not liable when he took up a mining opportunity that had been rejected bona fide by the company. On this basis, Joella would not be in breach.

Although English courts have largely taken a stricter approach, exemplified by *Regal Hastings* and more recent cases such as *Bhullar v Bhullar* [2003] 2 BCLC 241 and *O'Donnell v Shanahan* [2009] 2 BCLC 666, there is greater willingness to engage in a balancing exercise in cases of post-resignation conflict (as is the case here).[6] In *Balston Ltd v Headline Filters Ltd* [1990]

[3] This is a way of getting in knowledge that you want to show off, but isn't actually relevant to the question. However, you must be careful in doing this as it is very easy to spend too much time establishing law that isn't pertinent to the problem

[4] This is a simple and very quick way of linking your discussion of the law to the facts of the problem, without having to follow a strict IRAC process

[5] Recognizing academic discussion can add interest to a problem question, although there is usually not much scope for exploring the arguments in depth

[6] Indicate expressly why you are discussing a particular line of cases—the examiner may not be willing to assume you are considering the facts and understand why they are relevant

FSR 385, there was no breach in setting up a business post-resignation to supply a former customer of the director's previous company, as no competitive activity had taken place prior to departure. This more nuanced approach with greater flexibility has been welcomed by writers such as Lowry and Sloszar ('Judicial pragmatism: directors' duties and post-resignation conflicts of duty' [2008] JBL 83). As recognized explicitly in *Foster Bryant Surveying Ltd v Bryant* [2007] **BCC 804**, the area is 'highly fact sensitive' and based on common sense. Much may therefore depend on quite what steps, if any, Joella took towards working with Megacrush plc prior to her departure.[7]

If Joella were liable under **s. 175** (and was not relieved under **CA 2006, s. 1157** on the ground she acted honestly and reasonably and ought fairly to be excused), she would be liable for an account of profits. This shows the duty can operate somewhat unfairly and provide a windfall (as in *Regal Hastings*): it would effectively give Tweedy Ltd the benefit of an opportunity it would not have secured. On balance though, at least on the limited facts provided, Joella is unlikely to be liable for breach of duty, because the company rejected the opportunity in good faith before she took it up, and she appears to have left the company on genuine rather than manufactured grounds without (as far as we can tell) taking active steps to take up the opportunity prior to her departure.

Clara

The contract with Futurco Ltd reveals a conflict of interest for Clara. However, in this case **s. 175** does not apply as the conflict arises in relation to a transaction with the company (**s. 175(3)**).[8] Other duties should be considered.

Under **s. 177** a director with an interest (direct or indirect) in a proposed transaction with the company must disclose that interest to the other directors, normally at a meeting or by notice (**s. 177(2)**). However, there is no obligation to declare an interest where the other directors are already aware of it (**s. 177(6)(b)**), and this is the case here. Accordingly there was no breach of **s. 177** in failing to make a declaration prior to the transaction, neither is there any breach of **CA 2006, s. 182** in not making a declaration after the transaction has been entered into.

However, in this particular case there may still be a breach of duty. Under **CA 2006, s. 190** a company may not acquire a 'substantial non-cash asset' from a director or a person connected with a director unless this is approved by a resolution of the company's members. Futurco Ltd is connected with Clara, as she and her husband own all the shares in the company (**CA 2006, ss. 252–4**). The asset is clearly 'non-cash' (defined **s. 1163**) and will be 'substantial' if its value exceeds £100,000 (which is not the case here), or if it exceeds both £5,000 and 10 per cent of the company's asset value (**s. 191**).

[7] It is fine to indicate that you need more information to be able to reach a firm conclusion, provided you indicate the area in which the facts are deficient and what difference they would make

[8] Considering s. 175 rather than s. 177 when a director has an interest in a transaction with the company is a very common error in exams

Accordingly, whether or not Tweedy Ltd should have obtained members' approval depends on whether its asset value (by reference to its most recent statutory accounts) is above or below £500,000. If above there is no breach of **s. 190**, but if below then the failure to obtain members' approval means that the transaction is voidable at the instance of the company, and the directors (and Futurco Ltd) are liable to account for any gains made and indemnify the company for any losses resulting (**s. 195**).[9] This can have major consequences; for example, in *Re Duckwari plc* **[1999] Ch 253**, losses included those caused by a market fall in the value of the asset.

[9] As you are not given the necessary financial information you have no choice but to give both alternatives

Conclusion[10]

[10] The conclusion can be brief as the points are concluded within the main text, but it is still worthwhile to draw everything together

If the traditional strict approach to conflicts of interest is followed, Joella appears to be in breach of **s. 175**. If so, Tweedy Ltd could claim an account of profits from her. However, the more balanced approach in the post-resignation cases indicates Joella would escape liability. That conclusion would change if more damning evidence about her plans and activities prior to departure came to light.

Although Clara has an interest in the transaction between Futurco Ltd and Tweedy Ltd, there has been no breach of **s. 177** or **s. 182**. However, there may have been a breach of **s. 190** in failing to get the approval of Tweedy Ltd's members. This depends on Tweedy Ltd's asset value, as this will determine whether the acquisition was of a substantial non-cash asset. If there has been a breach of **s. 190**, then the contract is voidable (unless one of the exceptions in **s. 195** applies). In addition, Clara, the other directors, and Futurco Ltd will be liable for any gains they have made or losses the company suffers under **s. 195(3)–(4)**.

LOOKING FOR EXTRA MARKS?

- Demonstrate you are confident with both the statutory provisions and the case law, and can combine and apply them effectively
- Show an awareness of academic discussion about the duty to avoid conflicts of interest and the requirement to declare interests in transactions with the company

QUESTION 6

Fitshop Ltd, which ran a successful sports shop in Oldentown, was founded in 1995 by Mo. He was the main shareholder and only director, with his wife, Jessica, holding a single share. In 2012 Mo decided to hand over to the next generation. His daughter Anya and son-in-law Lewis became shareholders (Mo and Jessica retaining their own shares) and were appointed directors in place of Mo.

After Mo's retirement he continued to help in the shop when it was busy, and would negotiate with Fitshop's suppliers. He continued to meet with the company's accountants and afterwards would instruct Anya and Lewis on what they should do. Although Mo did not attend most board meetings, Anya and Lewis would always follow his advice on any major decision.

Last year the family was approached by Sportzworld plc, which wanted to expand into Oldentown. Sportzworld made a good offer for all the shares in Fitshop, and the family decided to sell up. Sadly, not long afterwards Anya and Lewis were killed in a car accident.

Fitshop (under its new ownership) is now threatening legal action against Mo. Fitshop claims that Mo, Anya, and Lewis were negligent when they sold Fitshop's warehouse to a neighbour a few years previously for £200,000 when its true value was nearly £300,000. Mo doesn't dispute the figures but says he set the price honestly by looking at past property values on the internet, and Anya and Lewis agreed. Jessica was not consulted but Mo says she would have agreed if asked.

Advise Mo on his potential liability.

 CAUTION!

■ Don't spend too long looking at specific directors' duties and speculating on facts that aren't there. The main focus of this question is on de facto and shadow directors and the application of duties to them

■ Remember to consider whether there are any ways liability could be avoided

DIAGRAM ANSWER PLAN

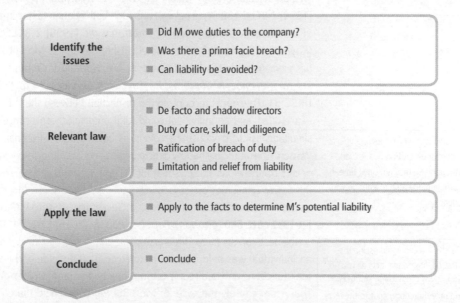

Identify the issues	■ Did M owe duties to the company? ■ Was there a prima facie breach? ■ Can liability be avoided?
Relevant law	■ De facto and shadow directors ■ Duty of care, skill, and diligence ■ Ratification of breach of duty ■ Limitation and relief from liability
Apply the law	■ Apply to the facts to determine M's potential liability
Conclude	■ Conclude

[1] It would be fine to deal with M's position first, and then the alleged breach. In some ways that would be more logical but the order used here makes it easier to relate the discussion of duties owed by de facto/shadow directors directly to the relevant duty

Fitshop's claim relies on Mo in fact owing the company duties at the time of the property sale. To advise Mo, the alleged breach of duty will be considered briefly before considering whether he in fact owed such a duty[1] by looking at whether he was a de facto or shadow director of Fitshop. The answer will then consider whether, if Mo is potentially in breach of duty, he might nonetheless avoid liability.

Breach of duty

[2] The lack of facts given on the breach would mean long discussion of the duty would be very descriptive so deal with breach concisely

The facts disclose a likely breach of **Companies Act 2006 (CA 2006), s. 174**[2] by the directors of Fitshop. Directors must exercise 'reasonable care, skill and diligence' with a minimum objective standard (**s. 174(2)(a)**) that increases if a director has particular knowledge, skill, and experience (**s. 174(2)(b)**). A reasonably diligent person in the position of Fitshop's directors should have appreciated that an expert valuation should be obtained. So failing to get a proper valuation was almost certainly a breach of this duty, causing loss to Fitshop.

[3] You could consider other duties but this would be speculative and would take time you need for the main issues arising on the facts

Other potential breaches[3] (such as **s. 172** if not acting in a way they believed would promote Fitshop's success) will not be considered as Fitshop's claim seems to be limited to negligence.

Fitshop will be unable to pursue Anya and Lewis for their likely breach of **s. 174** as they have died. The issue is therefore whether Mo was subject to **s. 174** as a de facto or shadow director.

De facto/Shadow Directorship

The concepts of de facto and shadow directorship were once considered distinct and largely mutually exclusive (**Re Hydrodam (Corby) Ltd [1994] 2 BCLC 180 (Hydrodam)**) although both relating to governance of the company (**Re Kaytech International plc [1999] 2 BCLC 351 (Kaytech)**). This could have answered Fitshop's claim, as Mo's position has elements of both. Unfortunately for Mo, **Holland v Commissioners for Revenue & Customs; Re Paycheck Services 3 Ltd [2010] UKSC 51 (Paycheck)** recognized the distinction between the concepts was eroded, and an individual could fulfil both roles, consecutively or simultaneously. Although the erosion has been criticized (Noonan and

[4] It is always worth showing your understanding of academic work, although you may not have time in a problem question to engage with it deeply

Watson, 'The nature of shadow directorship: ad hoc statutory intervention or core company principle?' [2006] JBL 763),[4] it means someone exercising power sometimes directly and sometimes indirectly, like Mo, could be both a de facto and shadow director: **Secretary of State v Chohan [2013] EWHC 680 (Chohan); Popely v Popely [2019] EWHC 1507.**

[5] To show you are addressing the question, link to the facts as you go, rather than establishing all the law and only then applying it to the facts

The test for de facto directorship originally focused on whether an individual was held out and claimed to be a director, and undertook functions only a director could properly discharge (**Hydrodam**). That is not entirely the case for Mo.[5] But **Paycheck** held there is no single test and all relevant factors should be considered, including access to proper information and taking major decisions: *Secretary of State for Trade and Industry v Tjolle* [1998] BCC 282 (*Tjolle*). In *Kaytech* the Court of Appeal asked: had the individual assumed the status and functions of a director? This seems to have been true for Mo some, but not all, of the time. Decision-making does not make an individual a de facto director, if referable to another capacity (*Smithton Ltd v Naggar* [2014] BCC 482) so Mo might argue he was acting as shareholder, or parent, although this won't protect an individual entirely: *Chohan*.

Rather than taking decisions himself, Mo more commonly advised Anya and Lewis, suggesting his position was closer to a shadow than de facto director. This is someone 'in accordance with whose directions or instructions the directors of the company are accustomed to act', excluding those giving advice in a professional capacity[6] (**CA 2006, s. 251**). Earlier cases such as *Hydrodam* required a high and sustained degree of control but later cases retreated slightly. *Secretary of State for Trade and Industry v Deverell* [2000] 2 WLR 907 (*Deverell*) held instructions/directions did not need to extend over all/most corporate activities, and could include advice; a shadow director need not be a 'puppet master' (per *Re Unisoft Group Ltd* [1994] 1 BCLC 609). So Mo's habit of instructing Anya and Lewis following meetings with the accountant, and their always following his advice on important matters could amount to shadow directorship. It doesn't matter that Mo was acting openly and didn't 'lurk in the shadows' (per *Hydrodam*): *Deverell*.

Duties Owed by Mo

If Mo is held to be a de facto or shadow director, or both, does this mean he was subject to the same duties as Anya and Lewis as de jure directors?

Duties applying to de jure directors (including the general duties under **CA 2006, ss. 171–7**) will apply to de facto directors. It can be argued that de facto directors fall within the definition of 'director' in **CA 2006, s. 250**[7] and it would be illogical for duties not to apply to those in fact acting as directors. But what if Mo is held to be a shadow director, not a de facto director, for some or all of the time? Shadow directors do not fall within **s. 250**, and in *Paycheck* the Supreme Court indicated (obiter) they are subject only to obligations explicitly extended to them, such as wrongful trading (**Insolvency Act 1986, s. 214**). However, although the law is not entirely settled (*Sukhoruchkin v Van Bekestein* [2014] EWCA Civ 399), **CA 2006, s. 170(5)**, as amended in 2015, states that the general duties apply to shadow directors 'where and to the extent that they are capable of so applying' and it now seems largely accepted that a shadow director does owe duties to the company (*Vivendi SA v Richards* [2013]

[6] It is impossible to avoid setting out the statutory provision to some extent, but summarizing it at least in part indicates more personal thought than simply copying it out

[7] 'Director' includes 'any person occupying the position of a director, by whatever name called'. This obviously includes those properly appointed but using a different title, but also arguably includes those not appointed but nonetheless fulfilling a director's role

EWHC 3006), although probably only relating to those areas where they gave directions or instructions (*Standish v Royal Bank of Scotland plc* [2019] EWHC 3116). Since Mo was clearly directly involved in the situation that gives rise to the claim against him, it follows that whether he is found to be a de facto or shadow director (or both at different times), he will most likely be found to be subject to **s. 174**.[8]

[8] Remember to follow through with your conclusion on the point

Avoiding Liability

Mo would not be liable if the breach were ratified (or authorized) by the company. Except where statute provides otherwise (eg **CA 2006, s. 175**), authorization/ratification is by the company, ie the members, not the directors.

[9] Ratification is a complicated and interesting area that you could expand on if you have time.

Not all breaches of duty are capable of ratification:[9] **CA 2006, s. 239(7)** retains the common law position. Cases indicate that negligence probably is ratifiable (*Pavlides v Jensen* [1956] Ch 565) provided it is not self-serving (*Daniels v Daniels* [1978] Ch 406). That would suggest this breach was ratifiable, although *Madoff Securities International Ltd v Raven* [2011] EWHC 3102 (Comm) indicates that only transactions in the best interests of the company can be ratified.

Even if the breach were ratifiable, it does not seem to have been ratified. This echoes *Regal (Hastings) Ltd v Gulliver* [1942] 1 All ER 378, where the breach could have been ratified but the need was not recognized, leaving the directors vulnerable. The unanimous agreement of the members is effective in place of a resolution (*Re Duomatic Ltd* [1969] 2 Ch 365) and this can be used to ratify a breach (**s. 239(6)(a)**) but it requires the assent of all members (*Randhawa v Turpin* [2017] EWCA Civ 1201). It is therefore not sufficient that Jessica would have agreed if she'd been asked. Since the breach was not ratified, Mo cannot escape liability on this basis.

Another way in which liability might be avoided is if the claim is brought too long after the breach. We are told that the sale took place 'a few years previously'. Unfortunately for Mo, this isn't likely to be long enough to prevent a claim under the **Limitation Act 1980**: the limitation period would be six years, by analogy with claims in tort.

A director may seek relief from the court in respect of a breach of duty on the basis s/he acted 'honestly and reasonably and ought fairly to be excused': **CA 2006, s. 1157.** This provision is not, on its face, open to shadow directors [10] but even if Mo could use it, he would likely have difficulty showing he acted 'reasonably'. While a negligent director can have acted reasonably (*Re D'Jan of London Ltd* [1994] 1 BCLC 561), on the facts it might be hard to convince a court that it is ever reasonable to sell valuable property without obtaining a proper valuation unless Mo has some significant further evidence.

[10] Whether the relief provision can or should apply to shadow directors is an interesting question that you could consider further

Conclusion

If Mo is found to have been a de facto and/or shadow director, he is likely to be held to have owed Fitshop a duty of care, skill, and diligence, and it seems likely this was breached. Unless he is permitted to seek relief under **s. 1157** and can show it was reasonable in the circumstances not to obtain a proper valuation, he is unlikely to avoid liability. His best hope would therefore be to convince a court that he was not a de facto or shadow director, either because his actions fall just short of both concepts or are referable to his capacity as parent, founder, consultant, or investor. The court might have some sympathy for his position in the circumstances.

LOOKING FOR EXTRA MARKS?

■ Explore whether and why it matters if the concepts of de facto director and shadow director overlap

■ Consider further whether de facto and shadow directors should be able to seek relief from liability (CA 2006, s. 1157)

■ Engage further with the problem of determining what breaches are, or should be, ratifiable

TAKING THINGS FURTHER

■ Aherne, D., 'Directors' duties, dry ink and the accessibility agenda' (2012) 128 LQR 114

An interesting article on the approach to (and limitations of) the CA 2006 codification of directors' duties: 'a sui generis codification' which attempts 'to have the best of both worlds' and engenders 'both confusion and opposition'. See also on the accessibility of the provisions, Hood, P., 'Directors' Duties under the Companies Act 2006: clarity or confusion?' (2013) 13 JCLS 1.

■ Ho, J. K. S., 'Is s. 172 of the Companies Act 2006 the guidance for CSR?' (2010) 31 Co Law 207

Considers the background to and scope of CA 2006, s. 172's 'enlightened shareholder value' approach and its value in providing guidance to companies on corporate social responsibility (CSR).

■ Keay, A., 'The duty of directors to exercise independent judgement' (2008) 29 Co Law 290

Examines the origins of CA 2006, s. 173 (the duty to exercise independent judgment), concluding that s. 173 is not identical in its ambit to the pre-2006 common law.

■ Keay, A. 'Ascertaining the corporate objective: an entity maximisation and sustainability model' (2008) 71 MLR 663

Formulates an alternative approach to stakeholding or shareholder primacy that focuses on the company as an entity in its own right with a need both for wealth maximization and survival. See also other work including, 'The ultimate objective of the company and the enforcement of the entity maximisation and sustainability model' (2010) 10 JCLS 35.

■ Keay, A., 'Good faith and directors' duty to promote the success of their company' (2011) 32 Co Law 138

An exploration of the 'most interesting and controversial' of the duties, s. 172, but, unlike most articles, focusing on the good faith element of the duty rather than enlightened shareholder value. Keay reflects on enlightened shareholder value elsewhere, including Keay, A., 'Having regard for stakeholders in practicing enlightened shareholder value' (2019) 19 OUCLJ 118 and Keay, A. and Iqbal, T., 'The impact of enlightened shareholder value' [2019] JBL 304.

■ Langford, R.T. and Ramsay, I., 'The "creditors' interests duty": when does it arise and what does it require?' (2019) 135 LQR 385

Welcomes the 'clarity' brought by Sequana *as to the point at which directors' are required to consider or act in the interests of creditors. For an earlier examination of this issue, see Keay, A., 'Directors taking into account creditors' interests' (2003) 24 Co Law 300.*

■ Lim, E., 'Directors' fiduciary duties: a new analytical framework?' (2013) 129 LQR 242

Examines conflicts of interest, in particular exploring when a situation 'cannot reasonably be regarded as likely to give rise to a conflict of interest' under s. 175(4)(a), linking this to 'scope of business' and 'maturing business opportunity' questions.

■ Lowry, J. and Sloszar, L., 'Judicial pragmatism: directors' duties and post-resignation conflicts of duty' [2008] JBL 83

Welcomes the more nuanced approach of cases such as Foster Bryant *to considering conflict of interest where a director has resigned, allowing the courts to view all the facts of the case.*

■ Lynch, E., 'Section 172: a ground-breaking reform of directors' duties, or the emperor's new clothes?' (2012) 33 Co Law 196

A critical evaluation of s. 172, viewing it as little more than a restatement of the previous legal position. Concludes it is 'all bark and no bite', but that the 'bark' may have some value in educating directors about good corporate management and social responsibility.

■ Moore, I., 'Revisiting the duty to confess: a directors' duty to disclose his own misconduct' (2016) 384 Co LN 1

Explores and challenges the somewhat controversial notion from Item Software v Fassihi *that a director may have a positive obligation to disclose his/her own breach of duty to the company.*

■ Noonan, C. and Watson, S., 'The nature of shadow directorship: ad hoc statutory intervention or core company principle?' [2006] JBL 763

Argues that shadow and de factor directorship should be conceptually and factually distinct, and a clear concept of shadow directorship is necessary to maintain a proper distinction between a director and a member. See also Yap, J. L., 'De facto directorships and corporate directorships' [2012] JBL 579, which focuses on the Paycheck *decision.*

■ Witney, S., 'Duties owed by shadow directors: closing in on the puppet masters?' [2016] JBL 311

Considers the extent to which duties are and should be owed by shadow directors. See also Moore, I., 'Duties of a shadow director: recent developments considered' (2013) 345 Co LN 1.

■ Worthington, S., 'Reforming directors' duties' (2001) 64 MLR 439

A critical review of directors' duties reform, pre-dating the Company Law Review's final report. Interesting to read these thoughtful criticisms of both general approach and specific suggestions in light of the eventual reform that appeared in CA 2006. See also Sealy, L., 'Directors' duties revisited' (2001) 22 Co Law 79 for an entertaining view of trends in directors' duties.

Online Resources

www.oup.com/uk/qanda/

For extra essay and problem questions on this topic, as well as advice on revision and exam technique, please visit the online resources.

6 Company Management and Governance

ARE YOU READY?

In order to attempt the questions in this chapter you will need to have covered the following topics:

- Role of directors in management and governance; executive and non-executive directors
- Relationship between directors and shareholders; the separation of ownership and control
- Accountability and disclosure of information
- Governance reports and codes and the principle of self-regulation
- The UK Combined Code on Corporate Governance; the 'comply or explain' principle
- The role of auditors in corporate governance
- Shareholder engagement, institutional investors, and the Stewardship Code
- Executive remuneration
- Connections (in particular) with: incorporation, directors' duties, corporate social responsibility, the constitution, shareholder rights, and remedies

KEY DEBATES

Debate: the balance of power between directors and shareholders

The separation of directors (the 'managers') from shareholders (often, but controversially, called the 'owners') encourages efficient use of resources, but also creates tensions, not least through potential misalignment between the interests of directors and shareholders. A related issue, seen in Chapter 5, is whether the traditional 'shareholder primacy' approach is appropriate for effective corporate governance.

Debate: the effectiveness of self-regulation in corporate governance

The role of the State in corporate management and governance (as in other areas of corporate life) is an important question, and the balance to be held between legal regulation, self-regulation, and full deregulation is a difficult one. The current approach of using 'soft law' through non-legally binding codes on a 'comply or explain' basis has been widely accepted, but is not without its limitations and critics.

Debate: balance on the board of directors

The right balance on the board of directors remains a topical subject, and ranges from older (but still relevant) debates surrounding the role of non-executive directors and the chair of the board, through issues such as employee representation on the board, to more recent calls for greater gender balance and diversity.

QUESTION | 1

'If powers of management are vested in the directors, they and they alone can exercise these powers.' (Greer LJ, *Shaw & Sons (Salford) Ltd v Shaw* [1935] 2 KB 113)

Discuss.

CAUTION!

- There are a lot of different but connected issues within this apparently simple question, so think carefully about how to organize your discussion
- Avoid simply setting out directors' and shareholders' powers and contrasting them—you also need to explore the wider director–shareholder relationship

DIAGRAM ANSWER PLAN

Introduction: the split of powers between directors and shareholders

Shareholders' powers: decision-making, power to direct, default power, removal of directors

Balancing the power of directors and shareholders: further thoughts

Conclusion: review quote in light of discussion

SUGGESTED ANSWER

The company's powers of management are habitually vested in directors (as indicated in the quote) by virtue of the company's articles of association.[1] This can be seen in the standard form articles (taking effect unless excluded: **Companies Act 2006 (CA 2006), s. 20**), for example **Article 3, Model Articles for Private Companies: Companies (Model Articles) Regulations 2008, Schedule 1**. Accordingly the courts have held that shareholders cannot act for the company, nor instruct the directors what to do. This can be seen in cases such as **Automatic Self-Cleansing Filter Syndicate Co v Cuninghame [1906] 2 Ch 34** where directors were not obliged to comply with a resolution of the shareholders directing a sale of the business,[2] as well as **Shaw & Sons (Salford) Ltd v Shaw [1935] 2 KB 113** itself.

So the management powers of the company are indeed in the hands of the directors alone. This reflects one of the key benefits of incorporation, the ability to bring together investors (shareholders) and expert managers (directors), while allowing the directors to operate the business largely without interference to maximize economic efficiency. But the quote does not tell the full story:[3] shareholders are not entirely without power, nor are directors' powers entirely unconstrained. There is and needs to be a balance of power between the directors and the shareholders.[4] This essay will firstly consider what powers shareholders do have and then reflect further on the relationship between shareholders and directors.

Shareholders and Decision-making

Greer LJ's statement does not mean that shareholders are excluded entirely from decision-making. Some important decisions are reserved to the company's shareholders (such as alteration of the articles (**CA 2006, s. 21**)), whether through ordinary or special resolution (**CA 2006, ss. 281–3**) although CA 2006 shifts the balance further away from shareholders by removing the need for shareholder approval in some areas, such as allotment and purchase of shares. Shareholders are generally free to vote in their own interests (**North-West Transportation Co Ltd v Beatty (1887) 12 App Cas 589**, subject to some constraints to prevent oppression of the minority[5] such as **Allen v Gold Reefs of West Africa Ltd [1900] 1 Ch 656**), but a resolution in general meeting is treated as a decision of the company itself, the general meeting being an organ of the company, rather than simply representing the shareholders. Valid decisions can also be made without a resolution, if made with unanimous consent of the shareholders (**Re Duomatic Ltd [1969] 1 All ER 161**).

---

[1] This shows immediately that you know the status of the powers being discussed

[2] Very brief case facts show you know about the case and the context in which the point of law has been developed, without taking up too much time

[3] This links explicitly to the quote, showing you are addressing the question, and also indicates a critical approach by indicating that you don't agree fully with the quote

[4] This could provide an opportunity to discuss the director–shareholder relationship in more depth, and touch on the position of other stakeholders, but don't depart too far from the question.

[5] It might be tempting to discuss this point further if you've revised it fully, but better to stick to the main director–shareholder relationship theme of the question

This pragmatic rule recognizes the power of shareholders acting unanimously, but only operates to give an alternative way of reaching valid decisions; it does not vest management powers in shareholders.[6]

6 This links the point about the unanimous consent rule to the issue in the question, otherwise it risks appearing to be just general discussion about decision-making in companies

Power to Direct

Shareholders commonly retain a right to restrain or direct the directors by special resolution, as in the standard form articles (eg **Article 4, Model Articles for Private Companies: Companies (Model Articles) Regulations 2008, Sch 1**). This is because shareholders could change the articles by special resolution under **CA 2006, s. 21** and thereby revest powers in the general meeting in any event. But in practice shareholders do not choose to restrain or direct the directors as a matter of course. Most shareholders are happy to leave management decisions to the directors, and it would normally be difficult to secure a three-quarter majority to take such a step. Furthermore, a majority shareholder who habitually directed the directors could risk being found to be a shadow director[7] (**CA 2006, s. 251**) and thus potentially liable for breaches of duty (**CA 2006, s. 170(5)**), wrongful trading (**Insolvency Act 1986, s. 214**), and disqualification (**Company Directors Disqualification Act 1986, s. 6**).

7 Connect different topics to show your understanding

Default Powers

In unusual circumstances powers otherwise vested in directors will revert to the shareholders (the company in general meeting). This 'default' power of shareholders arises only where the board is incapable or unwilling to exercise its powers. The classic example is *Barron v Potter* **[1914] 1 Ch 895** where a deadlock between the two directors meant that their powers could not be exercised. The court held that the power to appoint additional directors (conferred on the directors by the articles) reverted to the company in general meeting. Another example where the court accepted the general meeting had 'residual authority' to use the company's powers is *Alexander Ward and Co Ltd v Samyang Navigation Co Ltd* **[1975] 1 WLR 673**.

This default or residual power of the general meeting recognizes the power of shareholders to act 'as' the company where necessary, even where this means taking over powers vested in directors. However, its very limited scope means that it has no real impact on the essence of Greer LJ's statement.[8]

8 Think PEA: the point about default powers has been made, explained, and evidenced; it is then important to assess it by considering its significance in relation to the question

Removal of Directors

The most significant power of shareholders is arguably the ability to remove a director before the expiration of any term of office by ordinary resolution, notwithstanding any agreement between the director and the company: **CA 2006, s. 168**. This ensures that even though, as recognized in the title quote, management powers are vested in directors, and shareholders cannot exercise them, if a majority of shareholders are unhappy with the exercise of those powers they could choose to remove the directors responsible. Not only does this power keep shareholders in ultimate control as they choose who they want to manage the company, it also provides further incentive for directors to act in shareholders' interests to keep their own position secure.

Despite the importance of this power, in practice its use is limited. Although the articles cannot override **s. 168** to require more than an ordinary resolution, it is possible for directors to entrench their positions using devices such as weighted voting (**Bushell v Faith** [1970] **AC 1099**). Even without such restrictions, shareholders may lack sufficient information to allow them to question management behaviour and in many companies, particularly larger ones, it can be difficult to engage sufficient numbers of shareholders to secure the necessary 50 per cent majority of those voting to remove a director. In addition, special notice must be given (**CA 2006, s. 168(2)**) and a written resolution cannot be used (**CA 2006, s. 288(2)**). Accordingly, while shareholders do technically retain ultimate power over the management of a company (albeit not over day-to-day decisions) which might call Greer LJ's statement into question, in practice a company's management is usually free to act without much fear of challenge.

The Balance of Power

[9] This sentence looks back to the preceding discussion to show the examiner how the answer fits together

It has been seen that shareholders' powers are limited and do not normally encompass management powers.[9] The shareholders could choose to change this balance of power, by altering the articles by special resolution, **CA 2006, s. 21**, if the majority saw fit. However, the standard form article remains because this split between shareholders and directors is viewed as the most efficient and effective way of running a company and excessive shareholder interference could be a recipe for economic disaster.

But there are disadvantages in placing powers disproportionately in the hands of directors. This goes to the heart of the separation of ownership and control within the corporate structure, most notably recognized by Berle and Means in 'The modern corporation and private property' (1932) but much discussed ever since. Separation can give rise to problems of corporate governance as human self-interest means that directors may use their powers for their own benefit while shareholders lack the information and resource to restrain this—often called the 'agency' problem.[10] Although directors are constrained by legal principles such as directors' duties (**CA 2006, ss. 171–7**), these are difficult to enforce, particularly without effective shareholder oversight. This is often lacking, particularly in larger companies with dispersed shareholdings. Similarly, corporate governance principles in the UK Corporate Governance Code (which applies to listed public companies) are of limited effectiveness without an engaged shareholder body to challenge the board over instances of non-compliance. Even if shareholders

[10] This part of the essay shows how issues of 'company management' overlap significantly with the wider notion of corporate governance

do become dissatisfied with directors' management decisions, the temptation at least in public companies is for shareholders simply to exit by selling their shareholding rather than stay and exercise the powers they do have, reducing further any constraint on director power.

Conclusion

While the quote is right that powers of management are in the hands of directors, and shareholders do not normally have the right to exercise them, this does not mean shareholders are without power. However, the powers of shareholders are limited, and even more importantly, shareholders are often inhibited in exercising them. In most cases the separation of powers accords with the wishes of all those in the company but can potentially lead to the interests of the shareholders (and other stakeholders) being neglected in favour of the interests of the directors themselves. It is therefore important, if a company is to be run effectively in the interests of its primary (and arguably other) stakeholders, for shareholders to use the powers they have. The key is thus maintaining the delicate balance of power within the company, while recognizing that day-to-day management powers are indeed rightly vested in the directors.

LOOKING FOR EXTRA MARKS?

- Make the connection between principles of company management and wider notions of corporate governance

- Explore the problem of shareholder engagement and the notion of the separation of ownership and control; this could develop further into discussion of shareholder primacy and stakeholding/pluralism

- Recognize that these issues are of limited relevance to very many companies: in small private companies the directors and shareholders are very often the same people.

QUESTION | 2

Critically assess the role of the UK Corporate Governance Code in encouraging and enforcing good corporate governance in the UK.

CAUTION!

- You will need to explore how the Code works ('comply and explain') as well as what it requires

- The origins and purpose of the Code are relevant to provide context, but avoid giving a purely historical account of the corporate governance regime

■ Make sure you evaluate the effectiveness of the Code in ensuring good corporate governance and don't just explain what it does

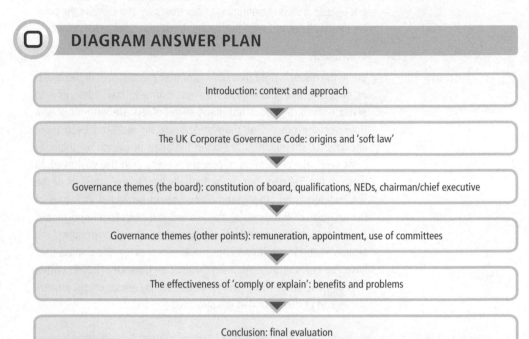

DIAGRAM ANSWER PLAN

Introduction: context and approach

▼

The UK Corporate Governance Code: origins and 'soft law'

▼

Governance themes (the board): constitution of board, qualifications, NEDs, chairman/chief executive

▼

Governance themes (other points): remuneration, appointment, use of committees

▼

The effectiveness of 'comply or explain': benefits and problems

▼

Conclusion: final evaluation

SUGGESTED ANSWER

The UK Corporate Governance Code (the Code), published by the Financial Reporting Council (FRC) (the independent regulator for corporate reporting and governance), is a code of best practice applying to listed public companies. This essay will consider the Code's origins, principles, and operation to assess how far it encourages and enforces good corporate governance.[1]

The Code originated as the Code of Best Practice (or 'Cadbury Code') following the Cadbury Report (Report of the Cadbury Committee on the Financial Aspects of Corporate Governance, 1992). Cadbury focused on a strong and balanced board, ensuring chief executives were not without challenge. This was to be achieved in particular through using independent non-executive directors, separating the roles of chair and chief executive, and using sub-committees on appointment, remuneration, and audit—all still very important today.[2]

In 1995 the Cadbury Code was supplemented by the Greenbury Code (Code of Best Practice for Directors' Remuneration) and in 1998 the Hampel Committee consolidated the two codes, with further recommendations, into the 'Combined Code'. Further reports, including Higgs on non-executive directors (2003), led to several revisions.

[1] Use your introduction to tell the examiner what you are going to do, and show that you are thinking about the question itself

[2] There is a risk that discussion on the origins of the Code becomes too descriptive; by making even brief pertinent comments you can show you are not just reciting knowledge

In 2010, following the Walker report on banking governance, and review by the FRC, the Combined Code was updated and renamed the UK Corporate Governance Code. There have been further revisions since, taking account of reports such as Davies (2011) on women on boards, Kay (2012) on long-term decision-making, and Parker (2017) on ethnic diversity on boards, with a new Code issued in 2018. The FRC also initiated The Stewardship Code in 2010 (latest revision 2020) to encourage more active engagement by institutional investors.

The Code is an example of 'soft law'.[3] It does not have the force of statute, but works on a 'comply or explain' basis: companies are obliged (under Stock Exchange Listing Rules) to make a compliance statement and explain to shareholders in the annual report if they are not compliant and why. Failure to do so is a breach of the Listing Rules, which may lead to penalties. As statute provides little on governance (other than on meetings, resolutions, and service contracts), the Code is very important in the corporate governance of listed companies.

The Code indicates best practice in a number of areas, many of which first appeared in essence in the Cadbury Code. The Code as revised in 2018 is in five sections—Board Leadership and Company Purpose; Division of Responsibilities; Composition, Succession and Evaluation; Audit, Risk and Financial Control; and Remuneration— each consisting of Principles and more detailed Provisions. Some significant aspects of the Code will now be explored to demonstrate how it encourages good corporate governance.[4]

In terms of board constitution, the Code does not specify any particular number nor qualifications required of directors. This is consistent with the underlying law: statute only imposes a minimum age qualification of 16 (**Companies Act 2006 (CA 2006), s. 157**) and while the Institute of Directors offers a 'Chartered Director' qualification, this is optional.[5] The board should have a combination of skills, experience, and knowledge and, reflecting concerns about unrepresentative boards and 'group-think', the Code requires consideration of diversity on the board, not just of gender, but also of social and ethnic backgrounds and cognitive and personal strengths.[6] There has been improvement in gender diversity following the Davies Report (2011). The initial target of 25 per cent representation of women on FTSE 100 boards was met in 2015; and the raised target of 33 per cent (Hampton-Alexander Review (2016)) met in 2020. Regarding ethnic diversity, the Parker Review (2017) found a majority of FTSE 100 boards had no 'person of colour' (the review's terminology) and set an objective of at least one 'director of colour' in each FTSE board by 2021. The FRC's annual review of the Code (January 2020) noted only limited reporting by companies of diversity beyond gender, which might indicate slow progress on this.

Independent non-executive directors (NEDs) are viewed as key to good corporate governance, providing an important check on the activities of executive directors. The Code expects at least half the board to

[3] Think PEA: this paragraph makes the point about soft law, explains what this means, and then assesses the importance of the Code despite its non-legally binding status— further assessment of the merits of the system comes later on

[4] This shows the examiner that you are still thinking about the question and not just working through the provisions of the Code

[5] There isn't always much scope for conventional legal authority in essays on corporate governance, but by bringing in a bit of your legal and practical knowledge where appropriate, you can provide support and contrast for the points you make

[6] Show your awareness of topical issues in corporate governance

consist of independent NEDs and recognizes the 'prime role' of NEDs in appointing and removing executive directors and holding them to account. Independence (considering employment or other business, financial, or family links with the company, and also length of time on the board) is essential, although independence is determined by the board itself which provides some scope for manoeuvre. A senior independent director should be appointed so NEDs and shareholders can express any concerns through him/her. The Code emphasizes that the roles of chair and chief executive should be held by different people: this provides balance and prevents powers becoming concentrated in one individual. The 2018 Code has removed 'Relations with Shareholders' as a separate section and now requires 'effective engagement' with 'shareholders and stakeholders', including the means for employees to raise concerns in confidence. Directors must report on how stakeholder interests and the **s. 172** factors have been complied with. In order to enhance shareholder engagement with corporate governance, institutional investors are expected to comply (on a similar 'apply and explain' basis) with the FRC's Stewardship Code, revised in 2020 with more rigorous requirements.[7]

[7] Link the Code with other developments such as the Stewardship Code

Director remuneration has been a concern for many decades and remains a separate section of the Code. The Code expects remuneration policies and practices to be designed to promote 'long-term sustainable success'. Remuneration policy and pay levels should be set (following a formal and transparent procedure) by a remuneration committee made up entirely of NEDs which must now also review workforce remuneration and policies, and take this into account when setting executive remuneration. The Code directs the committee to consider clarity, simplicity, risk, predictability, proportionality, and alignment to culture when setting remuneration policies and practice, and the annual report must state how these factors have been addressed.

[8] It is not enough just to consider the main principles of the Code; it is necessary to assess potential barriers to the achievement of the Code's aims in order to address the question

However admirable its principles, the Code is valuable only if it actually encourages and enforces good corporate governance.[8] As there are no direct penalties for failure to comply (the Listing Rules require statements on compliance, not compliance as such), the Code's ability to encourage and enforce good corporate governance could be doubted. Companies do sometimes ignore its principles and the FRC's annual report (January 2020) makes clear that 'full strict compliance has never been the aim'. However, the Code is largely followed: 95 per cent of the companies reviewed comply with all bar one or two provisions (Corporate Governance Review 2019, Grant Thornton). It seems 'comply or explain' imposes just enough pressure[9] while retaining flexibility, and the FRC and successive governments have continued to conclude that it remains the most appropriate way of raising standards.

[9] You could develop this point further to consider how far companies provide real and meaningful explanations for non-compliance, and whether this matters

The system has the benefit of flexibility, both by allowing alterations to the Code to reflect changes in practice and by allowing businesses freedom to operate within guidelines rather than rigid limits. By focusing on principles rather than strict rules the Code encourages compliance with the spirit of the rules rather than just a box-ticking exercise. Further, involving experts in drawing up the Code ensures provisions better reflect real practices so the principles are generally accepted by those it regulates in a way that statutory regulation could never expect. However, there are obvious concerns where those making the rules are the people who will benefit most from a relaxed system.

The current system is not without its critics. It has not prevented a series of corporate failures and significant public disquiet with corporate activities, although it is not clear these would have been avoided even with a legally binding Code. Despite the limits of the Code in preventing corporate failure and promoting public confidence (particularly in relation to excessive pay), the government has not seen fit to legislate wholesale on corporate governance although there has been minor regulatory interference, for example the introduction of the advisory vote on pay policy. The 'comply and explain' system has been adopted in many other jurisdictions. This suggests that while the Code needs continual review, it is not without merit; or perhaps governments find they achieve more through cooperation with business.

[10] Use your conclusion to pull together the main strands of your argument and balance some of the positive and negative points that can be made

To conclude,[10] good corporate governance is essential if investors are to have confidence in UK companies and so needs to be encouraged and enforced. The Code is obviously an important part of this and provides an essential guide to good practice. The Code and its predecessors can take much credit for improvements in corporate governance since 1992, and this now extends beyond public companies. Many large private companies choose to follow similar principles to the Code, for example through the voluntary 'Wates Principles', which is likely to increase given the obligation to report on corporate governance arrangements added by **Companies (Miscellaneous Reporting) Regulations 2018**. That is not to suggest the Code is without failings, as corporate failures and continuing debates over excessive remuneration have shown. Revisions to the Code and increased publicity for non-compliance may help but the system itself is inherently limited in what it can achieve.

LOOKING FOR EXTRA MARKS?

■ Consider what provisions of the Code have greater or lesser levels of non-compliance, or where explanations for non-compliance are lacking (look for example at FRC annual reports); you could go on to consider why this might be and what it could indicate about the provisions themselves or the Code's effectiveness

■ Link your discussion to your wider awareness of corporate governance matters—this could be by making reference to events in the corporate sphere or to recent reviews or reforms

QUESTION | 3

Evaluate the roles of shareholders and auditors in achieving good corporate governance in listed companies.

CAUTION!

- Split your time carefully to ensure you cover both shareholders and auditors in sufficient depth
- As well as explaining the role that shareholders and auditors should play in corporate governance, think about the factors that might inhibit the proper fulfilment of those roles
- Remember to consider the particular role of institutional investors when considering the role of shareholders

DIAGRAM ANSWER PLAN

Introduction: corporate governance and different roles

▼

Shareholders (general): removal of directors, (dis)engagement, availability of information

▼

Institutional investors and the Stewardship Code

▼

Auditor: audit requirement, audit committee, independence

▼

Conclusion: final evaluation

SUGGESTED ANSWER

[1] Take a critical approach to the question from the start by assessing what 'good' corporate governance means

Corporate governance is 'the system by which companies are directed and controlled' (Cadbury Report, 1992). Good corporate governance[1] should ensure directors do not operate the company for their own benefit rather than the company's members. This potential problem arises from the long-recognized (Berle and Means, 'The modern corporation and private property', 1932) separation of ownership (the members) and control (the directors) in large companies. For listed companies, the UK Corporate Governance Code (the Code) provides principles of best practice for corporate governance, with the Listing Rules requiring companies to 'comply or explain'. This essay will examine the roles of shareholder and auditor to evaluate how and whether they can encourage good corporate governance.[2]

[2] As well as setting the scene, use your introduction to explain what you are going to do and link explicitly to the question—this reassures the examiner

Shareholders

The company's constitution invariably gives the board of directors the power to manage the company on a day-to-day basis (**Article 3, Model Articles for Private Companies**: **Companies (Model Articles) Regulations 2008, Sch 1**) and members have no power to instruct the directors how to act or overrule their decisions (*Automatic Self-Cleansing Filter Syndicate Co Ltd v Cuninghame* **[1906] 2 Ch 34**). Statute reserves some limited matters to shareholders, including changes to the constitution (**Companies Act 2006 (CA 2006), s. 21**), but shareholders have little involvement in running the company. However, shareholders still have an important role to play in corporate governance even with their limited powers, and since they are the ultimate beneficiaries of good corporate governance they need to accept responsibility in enforcing it.

[3] This paragraph identifies the power of shareholders, but also identifies barriers to its use—both legal and practical

Shareholders can dismiss directors[3] by ordinary resolution before expiry of a term of office (**CA 2006, s. 168**), notwithstanding any provisions in a director's service contract. It is highly unlikely that entrenching mechanisms such as that used in *Bushell v Faith* **[1970] AC 1099** would be permitted by the Stock Exchange, so directors in listed companies are always at risk of dismissal without need to show cause. However, shareholders would have to be very determined to go through the special notice process of **ss. 168–9**, and removing a director before expiration of their term of office is likely to trigger generous compensation under their service contract (or damages for breach of contract), which may be a substantial disincentive for shareholders wishing to remove a director (as well as reducing the incentive for a director to keep shareholders happy, by cushioning the pain of any removal). Furthermore, even a sizeable portion of unhappy shareholders will struggle to get sufficient votes to pass even an ordinary resolution—particularly when faced with the problem of disengaged shareholders and the use of proxy votes.[4]

[4] This part of the sentence is important structurally, to link the preceding discussion (barriers to exercising shareholder powers) with the discussion that follows (looking more explicitly at engaging shareholders)

The role of shareholders in good corporate governance is limited through lack of engagement. Giving shareholders more powers (eg votes on remuneration policy, **s. 439A Companies Act 2006**) or improving communication channels (eg electronic communications, **ss. 1143–8**) is meaningless for disinterested shareholders.[5] The Code requires a company to consult with shareholders and report back when more than 20 per cent of votes are cast against a director-recommended resolution but that requires shareholders to have engaged. Most shareholders in listed companies hold their shares as

[5] This recognizes that best efforts to empower shareholders are inevitably limited

an investment, and often have little interest in the company itself or its governance. Many hold their shares through intermediaries, holding only beneficial rather than legal ownership, and attempts to enfranchise them (**CA 2006, Part 9**) have had little effect. Even if individual shareholders can and choose to vote, they may just give proxy votes to the chair—something that further entrenches the power of the board. Very few individual shareholders take the trouble and expense to attend meetings and question the board.

The general lack of engagement of individual shareholders is unsurprising as such a shareholder will typically hold only a tiny proportion of the shares. Since a shareholder's vote would be unlikely to make a difference, shareholders are disinclined to participate in governance, trusting to other shareholders to resolve any issues (the 'free rider' problem)[6], or simply trusting the executive to keep making profits. Even if a shareholder is inclined to take an active role they face the problem of asymmetric provision of information— directors have all the information about the company while shareholders have very little. While disclosure and transparency are important elements of statute and the Code, its use to a non-expert individual shareholder is often limited. The problems faced by individual shareholders mean that if shareholder engagement is to be effective, much rests on those shareholders with more expertise and proportionately larger stakes in the company—institutional investors[7] such as pension funds and unit trusts.

Institutional investors have traditionally been seen as taking too passive a role, rarely challenging the actions of the board and with a tendency to 'rubber stamp' the board's resolutions. The Myners Report (2001) recommended more active and constructive involvement in corporate governance, and the Walker Report (2009) similarly sought greater engagement on the part of institutional shareholders and fund managers. The Code expects the chair to engage with major shareholders outside general meetings and ensure the board has 'a clear understanding' of shareholder views. Additionally the UK Stewardship Code, first created in 2010 by the FRC following recommendations of the Walker Report (2009), 'sets high stewardship standards for asset owners and asset managers' with the aim of creating 'long-term value' and 'sustainable benefits' (UK Stewardship Code, 2020). The Stewardship Code operates on an 'apply and explain' basis. It requires institutional investors to produce a Stewardship Report that explains their culture, values, and investment beliefs and how these guide their stewardship and strategy and how they have monitored and engaged with companies. The Stewardship Code clearly recognizes the importance of institutional shareholder engagement but its impact in practice seems limited, see eg Reisberg, 'The UK Stewardship Code: on the road to nowhere' (2015) 15 JCLS 217.[8]

[6] This shows an awareness of wider theories and could be explained and developed a bit further, depending on time available and the emphasis put on such matters in your own course

[7] Explains why institutional investors are particularly important in corporate governance and so justifies their inclusion as a distinct issue in the answer

[8] You could explore academic articles further here to support your point

Despite occasional reports of increased shareholder activism, as in the 'Shareholder Spring' of 2012, Reisberg indicates the Steward-ship Code has resulted in little change in engagement by institutional investors. Even if institutional investors do use their influence, this is more likely to be through private communication with the board rather than in public, which while potentially more effective, does not provide the visible lead that might encourage other small investors to engage.

Auditor

Company accounts must be audited unless the company is exempt by virtue of being a small private company or a dormant company: **CA 2006, s. 475**. This audit is effectively a certification of the validity of the accounts—an independent check on the company finances. The Brydon report on the equality and effectiveness of audit (2019) describes the purpose of audit as 'to help establish and maintain deserved confidence in a company, in its directors and ... information'. Accordingly the auditor's role is crucial for financial accountability and corporate governance more generally,[9] and section 4 of the Code is dedicated to 'Audit, Risk and Internal Control'.

[9] Remember to link your discussion about the auditor with the issue of good corporate governance, rather than just describing the role

Auditors must report on the annual accounts to the members under **CA 2006, s. 495** stating whether the annual accounts have been prop-erly prepared and give a 'true and fair view'. They also state whether the directors' report is consistent with the accounts. Although this is an important protection for shareholders, auditors cannot provide a guarantee of accuracy. Auditors have been criticized for failing to spot serious financial irregularities (eg recently in the collapses of Carillion and Patisserie Valerie), and the Brydon report tellingly recommends introducing 'suspicion' into the qualities of auditing.

Overseeing the audit process is the audit committee, which should consist of independent non-executive directors, reducing the influ-ence management might otherwise have over the audit process. The committee monitors both the company's internal audit function and the external audit process, and makes recommendations on the appointment of external auditors. Its work should be described in the annual report, and the Brydon report has recommended shareholders be given the opportunity at general meeting to question the commit-tee chair and auditor.

Concerns about the auditor's role largely relate to independence and the stranglehold the large accountancy firms have over accoun-tancy and audit work in listed companies. It is rare for companies to change their audit firm, and very few use firms outside the 'Big Four'. There are fears that a cosy relationship can exist between audit firms and directors, with audit firms reluctant to highlight unfavourable information, or overly willing to accept an executive's explanation, in order to retain business. The Code requires the annual report to explain how auditor 'independence and objectivity' are safeguarded when the auditor also provides non-audit services. Going further, the CMA report on the audit market (2019) has recommended firms be required to separate audit and consultancy, and recommends steps to assist other firms to break into the audit market.

Conclusion

It can be seen that the roles of both shareholders (particularly institutional investors) and auditors are critical to proper corporate governance, but that there are limits on the extent to which they can fulfil these roles. This means the checks and balances on the activities of directors are not as effective as they could be, and without further reform even more rests on other governance structures such as independent non-executive directors.[10]

[10] This allows you to show that you know about other key corporate governance points but that you recognize that this essay is not the place for discussing them

LOOKING FOR EXTRA MARKS?

- Link your discussion to key underlying themes such as the shareholder primacy approach
- Consider how the roles of shareholders and auditors work together to achieve good corporate governance (as well as being significant in their own right)
- Reflect on whether there are other equally (or more) important factors in achieving good corporate governance

QUESTION | 4

Priti has recently been approached by commercial agents acting for a large public company looking to appoint a new non-executive director. Priti has experience of running her own business a number of years ago, and more recently has been working at a very high level in the public sector, but has not previously held any directorial role in a public company.

Priti is interested in taking on the role but has been concerned by recent publicity about excessive executive remuneration. She seeks your advice on how executive pay is controlled in the UK, and her role in relation to this as a non-executive director.

Advise Priti.

CAUTION!

- Don't forget to consider and assess relevant cases and legal provisions as well as the Code
- Make sure you examine the role of the non-executive director specifically in the context of executive remuneration as well as providing more general advice

DIAGRAM ANSWER PLAN

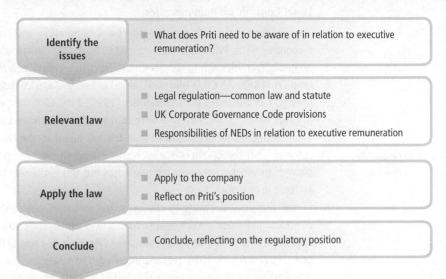

| Identify the issues | ■ What does Priti need to be aware of in relation to executive remuneration? |

| Relevant law | ■ Legal regulation—common law and statute
■ UK Corporate Governance Code provisions
■ Responsibilities of NEDs in relation to executive remuneration |

| Apply the law | ■ Apply to the company
■ Reflect on Priti's position |

| Conclude | ■ Conclude, reflecting on the regulatory position |

 SUGGESTED ANSWER

It is understandable that Priti has concerns: executive pay has caused public disquiet in the UK for a long time. Recent evidence of growing pay ratios (the difference between highest earners and average pay) in large companies has stoked this further. But this should not deter Priti from acting as a non-executive director (NED), as NEDs can and should play a significant role in controlling executive remuneration.[1] Her involvement would be particularly welcome[2] as the need to address gender imbalance and diversity on company boards has come to the fore following the Davies Report (2011), Hampton-Alexander Review (2016), and Parker Review (2017). Although the 33 per cent target for women on boards (Hampton-Alexander report, 2019) by the end of 2020 has been met, there is still plenty more to be done for gender and ethnic diversity on boards. There is also growing awareness of the need to appoint beyond 'the City', including from the public sector where Priti is working, to improve diversity and ensure the right 'combination of skills, experience and knowledge' on a board, as required by the UK Corporate Governance Code (the Code).

To advise Priti, it will be necessary to look at the common law, statute, and the UK Corporate Governance Code (the Code). Even if this company is not listed (not all public companies have a Stock Exchange listing) so is not obliged to follow the Code, it will still need to report on corporate governance following the **Companies (Miscellaneous Reporting) Regulations 2018**,[3] and since

[1] Make the link between Priti's position and concerns, NEDs, and remuneration

[2] This section picks up on facts of the problem to show broader appreciation of topical issues

[3] Recognize recent developments to show your knowledge is up to date. You could develop this discussion if you had time

the Code establishes principles of good practice Priti should still want to follow it.

Legal Controls on Remuneration

The law does not closely regulate director remuneration, and barely recognizes NEDs. Priti might be surprised to learn that directors have no outright entitlement to remuneration (*Hutton v West Cork Railway Co* (1883) 23 Ch D 654) and are reliant on the articles making provision. In *Guinness plc v Saunders* [1990] 2 AC 663, the House of Lords held that payment to a director was void when agreed to by a committee of the board rather than the full board as the articles required. Priti should check the company complies[4] with the provisions of its articles in paying remuneration, but this is unlikely to be an issue in practice.

[4] Remember to link your discussion to the advice you need to give

It is rare for the courts to challenge remuneration payments to directors, and these exceptional circumstances are unlikely to arise in a large public company. For example, in *Re Halt Garage (1964) Ltd* [1982] 3 All ER 1016 'remuneration' paid to a director who was not working for the company was rejected as a distribution out of capital (she was also a shareholder) rather than genuine remuneration. In disqualification cases the courts have held that payment of generous remuneration to directors while creditors are going unpaid may be evidence of unfitness (**Company Directors Disqualification Act 1986, ss. 6 and 8**). In setting pay, directors must consider what the company can afford and not just the 'going rate' (*Secretary of State for Trade and Industry v Van Hengel* [1995] 1 BCLC 545). Priti should be aware of this, particularly if the company's finances take a downturn.

There is some, limited, statutory regulation of executive pay. **Companies Act 2006 (CA 2006), ss. 188–9** limits contracts to two years unless approved by the members. It is designed to stop companies granting long contracts which entrench directors' positions by making it prohibitively expensive to dismiss them. (The Code indicates a one-year maximum period.) Payments on loss of office other than pursuant to a contractual obligation must be approved by members (**CA 2006, ss. 215–22**), while **ss. 227–30** require directors' service contracts to be available for inspection by members, and aggregate directors' remuneration must be disclosed in the annual accounts (**s. 412**). Quoted companies must also produce a remuneration report (**s. 420**), including details of individual directors' pay and, since 2019, the pay ratio between the chief executive's total remuneration and average worker's remuneration, intended to deter high pay awards.

Priti will be aware of recent debates over whether shareholders should have a vote on executive pay policy or awards. From 2013, **CA 2006, s. 439A** requires quoted companies to obtain shareholder approval of director remuneration policy, although voting on its practice is advisory only. However, a lack of engagement by share-holders in larger companies means these votes may often just be a 'rubber stamp'[5] and with the shareholders' 'say on pay' so limited, the position of NEDs such as Priti in setting controls on pay is particularly important.

'Soft Law' Regulation: the Code

The Code seeks to place some controls on executive remuneration in quoted companies, although increased statutory involvement indicates its lack of success in curbing executive pay. Under the Code, NEDs are at the heart of pay control.

The Code sets out best practice for corporate governance and has a section dedicated to 'Remuneration'. The Code does not have the force of law, but takes effect through the Listing Rules which require companies to 'comply or explain' or risk a penalty.[6] Under the Code, remuneration policies and practices 'should be designed to support strategy and promote long-term sustainable success' with executive remuneration 'aligned to the company purpose and values'.

The importance of NEDs generally was recognized in the Cadbury Report of 1992,[7] and the role has increased since. Independent NEDs provide a company with complementary expertise and experience that should inform corporate decision-making and improve strategy and profitability. As they are not involved full-time in running the company—so Priti will be able to continue with her public sector work if this is compatible—they are able to provide independent judgment and a check on the executive directors. Assuming the company currently complies with the Code, Priti will find there is a remuneration committee to set remuneration policy and pay, made up entirely of independent NEDs to provide a more transparent and less conflicted process than if executives set their own pay. The remuneration committee now also reviews workforce remuneration and related policies and should take this into account when setting executive pay. She may well find herself on the remuneration committee when appointed, but under the Code would need to have served on a remuneration committee for at least 12 months before being eligible to be chair of the committee.

It would be naive for Priti to assume NEDs have solved all remuneration problems. Arguably NEDs are not sufficiently independent[8] to exercise real control over remuneration. Although the Code requires independence in the sense of an absence of family/business links and a limit on the time a NED can stay with a company and still be viewed as independent (currently nine years), NEDs are often drawn from the same 'talent pool' of established executive directors. This may result in a commonality of interest and outlook and so a lack of true independence. It is promising that Priti's experience lies outside the City, as she may therefore be more willing to question and challenge the

[5] This reflects evidence of the High Pay Centre, among others, that approval is invariably given, and often with very little dissent

[6] Briefly explain the function and operation of the Code, but don't spend too much time on this as the question isn't about the Code as such

[7] This shows you understand that NEDs have been a critical part of corporate governance from the early days of the Code. The paragraph goes on to consider the current position and link this to Priti's position

[8] This paragraph questions the independence of NEDs by looking not just at the obvious concept of 'independence' as defined by the Code but also other more subtle problems of independence

status quo, and should be encouraged to do so in order to fulfil her role effectively. She should be alert to the need to retain that independence even after she has become familiar with the role, and perhaps takes on roles in other companies (many NEDs have further executive or non-executive roles elsewhere).

As a NED Priti will be part-time, which limits how fully attuned she can be to the business and operation of a company. The time spent by NEDs was a concern of the Walker Report (2009)[9] which recommended a significant increase in the time NEDs should devote to their role; the Code requires companies to consider other demands on directors' time when making appointments. Priti must ensure she has sufficient knowledge of the business to fulfil her role effectively and challenge the views of others while not losing her independence.

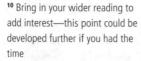

[9] Link particular points to the relevant Report to show an appreciation of the development of principles

Conclusion

Regulation of executive pay clearly has its limits. Transparency is not always positive—it may even have the effect of increasing pay awards as was seen in the years following Cadbury. And if shareholders are too passive to take action even where they do have information and statutory powers, then new powers may have little effect (predicted by Cheffins and Thomas, 'Should shareholders have a greater say over executive pay? Learning from the US experience' (2001) 1 JCLS 277).[10] Transparency may be most useful in creating negative publicity and external pressures, as with the 'pay ratio' requirement, which may not be positive for the company as a whole.

[10] Bring in your wider reading to add interest—this point could be developed further if you had the time

This makes the role of someone like Priti, as a NED, particularly important. She can help to maintain a dialogue with shareholders, and provide an informed but independent check on pay within the company. The ability of NEDs to provide this check should not be exaggerated, see eg Hellinx, 'Steeplechase in the boardroom' (2017) 38 Co Law 15—there are real difficulties in creating effective controls on executive remuneration—but increasing the representation of directors with diverse life and work experiences is an important way forward.

LOOKING FOR EXTRA MARKS?

■ Show a good understanding of how law, self-regulation, and other factors work together in this area

■ Make sure you reflect on recent developments and debates

■ Show an awareness of topical issues (bringing in examples if you can) in order to demonstrate your wider engagement with the subject

TAKING THINGS FURTHER

■ Bartlett, S. and Chandler, R., 'The private shareholder, corporate governance, and the role of the annual report' [1999] JBL 415

Examines the limitations on providing information to shareholders as a tool of corporate governance, recognizing information asymmetry between private and institutional investors (as well as between directors and shareholders).

■ Gutierrez, M. and Saez, M., 'Deconstructing independent directors' (2013) 13 JCLS 63

Casts doubt on the effectiveness of independent directors, particularly in relation to companies with concentrated (rather than dispersed) ownership structures. Also considers problems in identifying and selecting an effective independent director.

■ Hellinx, E,. 'Steeplechase in the boardroom: the obstacles for non-executive directors to fulfil their role in public companies' (2017) 38 Co Law 15

Argues the role of non-executive director is not impossible but is 'increasingly difficult' and efforts should be spent on removing the various impediments identified, including the tension between different aspects of the role, and a lack of incentive to operate effectively. See also Sweeney-Baird, M., 'The role of the non-executive director in modern corporate governance' (2006) 27 Co Law 67.

■ Keay, A., 'Company directors behaving poorly: disciplinary options for shareholders' [2007] JBL 204

Explores the options (legal and practical) shareholders may have against directors, and particularly helpful in identifying some of the practical constraints faced by shareholders.

■ Moore, M., 'The end of "comply or explain" in UK corporate governance?' (2009) 60 NILQ 85

An interesting explanation and analysis of the history and practice of the principle of 'comply or explain'. Addresses the argument that the Code had become too rigid and prescriptive.

■ Ndzi, E., 'UK shareholder voting on directors' remuneration: has binding vote made any difference?' (2017) 38 Co Law 139

Examines the position before and after the introduction of the binding vote on remuneration policy, explores the large levels of abstentions on pay votes, and considers drivers of executive pay more generally. See also Cheffins, B. and Thomas, R., 'Should shareholders have a greater say over executive pay? Learning from the US experience' (2001) 1 JCLS 277, doubting whether shareholders would be likely to exercise additional powers over executive pay.

■ Pedamon, C., 'Corporate social responsibility: a new approach to promoting integrity and responsibility' (2010) 31 Co Law 172

Links the recent financial crisis to issues of business ethics and integrity, thus providing fuel for thought on connections between corporate governance and CSR more generally.

■ Petrin, M., 'Executive compensation in the UK: past, present and future' (2015) 36 Co Law 196

An easy-to-read review of the regulation of executive remuneration. Includes an explanation and evaluation of the 2013 reforms, concluding they are 'weak at best'.

■ Reisberg, A., 'The UK Stewardship Code: on the road to nowhere' (2015) 15 JCLS 217

A highly critical analysis of the Stewardship Code (predating the 2018 revision): 'a weak code, at the heart of which lies an amorphous concept'. See also Roach, L., 'The UK Stewardship Code' (2011) 11 JCLS 463 for another critical consideration.

■ Villiers, C., 'Executive pay: a socially-oriented distributive justice framework' (2016) 37 Co Law 139

Proposes a different approach to executive pay based on distributive justice in light of the failure of linking pay and performance, and of shareholder control. See further, 'Controlling executive pay: institutional investors or distributive justice?' (2010) 10 JCLS 309, and 'Executive pay: beyond control?' (1995) 14 LS 260.

■ Wheeler, S., 'Non-executive directors and corporate governance' (2009) 60 NILQ 51

Considers the role of NEDs in corporate governance and their effectiveness, touching on issues such as the finite pool of potential NEDs and the 'circularity' of accountability.

Online Resources

www.oup.com/uk/qanda/

For extra essay and problem questions on this topic, as well as advice on revision and exam technique, please visit the online resources.

Minority Shareholder Remedies

7

ARE YOU READY?

In order to attempt the questions in this chapter you will need to have covered the following topics:

● The rule in *Foss v Harbottle*: proper claimant and majority rule principles

● Exceptions to the rule in *Foss v Harbottle*

● Derivative claims

● Personal claims, including reflective loss

● Just and equitable winding up

● Unfairly prejudicial conduct

● Legal and practical position of a minority shareholder within a company

● Connections (in particular) with: directors' duties, company management, corporate governance, shares, the constitution, shareholder agreements

KEY DEBATES

Debate: the nature of shareholders' rights and remedies

The ability of a minority shareholder to bring proceedings notwithstanding the rule in *Foss v Harbottle* has been the topic of a number of classic articles, sometimes linking to the statutory contract. Further connected debates have considered the difference between corporate and personal wrongs, and whether a shareholder can ever claim personally for 'reflective' loss.

Debate: derivative claims and the 2006 statutory changes

The complexity of derivative claims has long resulted in plenty of academic comment, often highly critical of the courts' approach. Proposals for a statutory derivative claim triggered further debates over the value and scope of such claims, with particular concerns that it would increase shareholder activism to undesirable levels when combined with a statutory statement of directors' duties.

▶

Debate: the meaning and scope of 'unfairness' and 'just and equitable'

Quite what 'unfairness' should encompass within the 'unfair prejudice' remedy, and how flexible or bounded it should be, has been an ongoing question, only partially resolved by *O'Neill v Phillips*. A related issue is what impact this has on the just and equitable winding up jurisdiction and the derivative claim, and how far these remedies overlap or remain distinct.

QUESTION | 1

'Although an improvement on the preceding law, the statutory derivative claim introduced in the **Companies Act 2006** still offers only very limited value to a minority shareholder unhappy with the management of the company.'

Discuss.

! CAUTION!

- You need to be aware of the differences between the statutory derivative claim and the former common law derivative claim
- Don't spend too much time setting the scene generally on shareholder remedies as this will be too descriptive; you need to focus on derivative claims
- In order to assess its 'value', think about various elements of the remedy, including the requirements of the claims, the problems a minority shareholder may face in bringing a claim, and the remedy a successful claim would attract

DIAGRAM ANSWER PLAN

Introduction: derivative claims

Requirements of claim; contrast with common law

Procedural requirements; contrast with common law

Other considerations: remedies and costs

Conclusion: assessing the value of the statutory derivative claim

The statutory derivative claim (**Companies Act 2006 (CA 2006), ss. 260–4**) is indeed an improvement on the preceding law. However, the improvement is not hugely significant[1] and claims remain unattractive for shareholders wanting to remedy problems with the company's management. To assess the improvements and value of the statutory derivative claim, this essay will explain its origins, and compare the pre- and post-2006 law,[2] looking in particular at the requirements (substantive and procedural), remedy, and costs.

[1] Immediately indicating the line of argument can be effective to grab the examiner's attention

[2] Comparison is essential, but structure this within themes, rather than setting out the pre-2006 law followed by the post-2006 law, otherwise the essay will be very descriptive

Derivative Claims—Statute and Common Law

The derivative claim is a true exception to the rule in *Foss v Harbottle* **(1843) 2 Hare 461** that the proper claimant in an action in respect of a wrong to a company is the company (the rule also encompasses the majority rule principle: where a wrong may be made binding by a simple majority, no individual member can maintain an action in respect of it, *Edwards v Halliwell* **[1950] 2 All ER 1064**). The rule reflects the separate personality of the company, and prevents multiplicity of claims, futile claims, and harassment of management by minority shareholders, but may lead to injustice where the wrongdoers are in control of the company.[3] Because of this last point, shareholders may bring derivative claims on behalf of the company in limited circumstances.

[3] This brings in background understanding (the justifications for the rule in *Foss v Harbottle*) but still keeps the focus on derivative claims

Derivative claims were a common law creation (requiring 'fraud on the minority') but were placed on a statutory footing in **CA 2006** following proposals by the Law Commission ('Shareholder Remedies', Law Com No. 246, 1997) who sought to simplify and modernize the law and improve its accessibility, supported by the Company Law Review Steering Group ('Developing the Framework', 2000). The statutory claim supersedes the common law, other than for multiple derivative claims where the claimant is a shareholder in the company's parent company under the same 'wrongdoer control' (*Universal Project Management Ltd v Fort Gilkicker Ltd* **[2013] EWHC 348**; *Abouraya v Sigmund* **[2014] EWHC 277**), and claims against foreign companies (*Novatrust Ltd v Kea Investments Ltd* **[2014] EWHC 4061**). In these (unusual) situations the statute offers shareholders no improvement at all.[4]

[4] Multiple derivative claims aren't directly relevant to the question but it would be misleading to state that the statutory claim entirely supersedes the common law

Basis of Claim

Under **CA 2006, s. 260(1)** a derivative claim is brought by a member in respect of a cause of action vested in the company, seeking relief on behalf of the company. The cause of action must arise from an actual or proposed act or omission involving negligence, default, breach of duty, or breach of trust by a director (**s. 260(3)**) whether the cause of action arose before or after the claimant became a member of the company (**s. 260(4)**). This latter point emphasizes that this is a corporate, not a personal remedy. This is slightly wider than before,[5] as at common law 'fraud' covered most breaches of duty but did not cover negligence (***Pavlides v Jensen* [1956] 2 All ER 518**) unless resulting in profit to a director (***Daniels v Daniels* [1978] Ch 406**).

[5] Remember to make your comparison

The common law also required 'wrongdoer control'—actual voting control, not mere de facto control through dominance of shareholding and management position: ***Prudential Assurance Co Ltd v Newman Industries Ltd (No. 2)* [1982] Ch 204**. Wrongdoer control is no longer a condition for a statutory derivative claim but remains relevant, as if the company could commence proceedings itself, this is an important element in the court's decision whether to allow the claim to continue (***Bamford v Harvey* [2012] EWHC 2858 (Ch)**). Accordingly a claimant's position is only marginally improved.[6]

[6] Link your discussion to the focus of the question—improvement and value to shareholders

Procedural Hurdles

At common law, derivative claims were equitable and discretionary. The procedural hurdles could be off-putting, and claims could be rejected for many reasons. This position has been little altered by **CA 2006**, although the process and grounds for dismissal are clearer.

Members must apply to the court for permission to continue the claim (**s. 261(1)**), which will be refused if the application and evidence filed do not disclose a prima facie case: **s. 261(2)**. *Iesini v Westrip Holdings Ltd* **[2009] EWHC 2526 (*Iesini*)** held the court should take a provisional view on the strength of the claim, not hold a mini-trial of the action. The court must also refuse permission to continue if satisfied that a person acting in accordance with **CA 2006, s. 172** (duty to promote the company's success) would not seek to continue the claim: **s. 263(2)(a)**. Gibbs argues this prima facie stage is 'seemingly redundant' as weak cases pass this, but then fall at the next stage ('Has the statutory derivative claim fulfilled its objectives?' (2011) 32 Co Law 41)[7] but *Langley Ward Ltd v Trevor* **[2011] EWHC 1893** criticized attempts to omit the first stage and go straight to the permission hearing as undermining the statutory scheme. In *Iesini*, the court held that **s. 263(2)(a)** required the court to be satisfied that no director acting in accordance with **s. 172** would seek to continue the claim. If some would and others would not then it is simply a factor to be considered in the exercise of discretion under **s. 263(3)(b)**. The court must also refuse permission where the action arises from a prospective act or omission that has been authorized by the company or from an existing act or omission that was previously authorized or subsequently ratified: **s. 263(2)(b)–(c)**.

[7] Bring in some wider reading to show your appreciation of how the procedure works

If the claim is not rejected under **s. 263(2)**, the court considers whether to give permission. **Section 263(3)** gives a (non-exhaustive) list of relevant factors, many of which echo the approach of the courts at common law.[8] For example, the court must consider whether the

[8] This demonstrates concisely (when combined with the case examples) an awareness of common law cases as well as the new statutory procedure

member is acting in good faith in seeking to continue the claim—at common law in *Barrett v Duckett* [1995] 1 BCLC 243 the claimant's ulterior motive led the court to refuse permission to continue. Other factors are whether authorization or ratification is likely (reflecting the general principle of majority rule); whether the company has decided not to pursue the claim; whether the act or omission gives rise to a personal cause of action for the member; and the importance someone with the duty under s. 172 would attach to continuing the claim. The court must also have particular regard to the views of any independent members (s. 263(4)), echoing *Smith v Croft (No. 2)* [1987] 3 All ER 909 at common law.

More than one factor can be relevant. In *Mission Capital plc v Sinclair* [2008] EWHC 1339, the court refused permission as it felt the notional director would not attach great weight to continuing the claim, and was also influenced by the availability of an unfair prejudice petition (see also *Franbar Holdings Ltd v Patel* [2008] EWHC 1534 and *Stimpson v Southern Landlords Association* [2009] EWHC 2072). Although the existence of an alternative remedy is relevant it is not decisive (*Kiani v Cooper* [2010] EWHC 577): a derivative claim was allowed to proceed notwithstanding the existence of a s. 994 claim in *Phillips v Fryer* [2012] EWHC 1611. As well as the s. 263(3) factors, the courts will consider any other relevant matters, including in *Kleanthous v Paphitis* [2011] EWHC 2287 the fact that any recoveries from directors would largely be returned to them as majority shareholders.

Remedy and Costs

Under **CA 2006**, as under the common law, a successful derivative claim leads to relief for the company. It thus benefits a claimant only indirectly (as well as benefiting all other shareholders), which may discourage action being taken. Other remedies, particularly **CA 2006, s. 994**, offer greater flexibility,[9] although the tendency to favour buy-out orders under s. 996 may not suit a shareholder who does not want to leave.

A member bringing a derivative claim is potentially liable for costs, though acting on behalf of the company, which could deter claims. The courts have been willing to order the company to indemnify claimants where it was reasonable to bring an action and it was brought in good faith: *Wallersteiner v Moir (No. 2)* [1975] 1 QB 373, although not if the action is thought unreasonable: *Smith v Croft*. Since the 2006 reforms the courts have continued to grant indemnities (eg *Stainer v Lee* [2010] EWHC 1539; *Kiani v Cooper*) although Keay notes costs indemnities are relatively uncommon and often subject to limits ('Assessing and rethinking the statutory scheme for derivative actions under the Companies Act 2006' [2016] JCLS 39).

[9] Show an awareness of how derivative claims relate to other shareholder remedies

Conclusion

The statutory derivative claim has improved the law for minority shareholders by widening the cause of action, and clarifying the procedure and grounds for dismissal. Nonetheless, as it deliberately mirrors the common law, it retains many of its problems—even when a shareholder can discover sufficient information to bring a claim (**s. 261(3)** enables the court to order the production of evidence), the procedural hurdles are significant and the remedy inflexible. The fact that the statutory claim has not resulted in the flood of cases feared by some shows it has retained strict limitations.[10] Accordingly, although derivative claims are an important exception to the rule in *Foss v Harbottle*, in most cases a shareholder unhappy with a company's management will seek an alternative remedy.

[10] This point could be expanded, using some academic literature as support, to show the initial concerns and how things have worked in practice

LOOKING FOR EXTRA MARKS?

- Reflect on whether the statutory derivative claim differs significantly from the common law—here you could engage with the academic discussion surrounding the introduction of the statutory remedy

- Show your wider appreciation of the issues by considering whether the derivative claim can better operate as a tool of corporate governance now it is on a statutory footing

- Indicate an awareness of the other options available to a minority shareholder, but don't lose focus on the question itself

- Explore gaps in the reform, such as the multiple derivative claim

QUESTION | 2

Until recently Ellie was one of the five directors of Drango plc. The shares in Drango plc are owned by Lily, Millie, Nelly, Ollie, and Polly. At the end of last year Ellie's negligence caused a loss of £250,000 to Drango plc. Her actions have resulted in a drop in the value of the company's shares.

Ellie has now left the company but the remaining directors have decided that it is not in the company's interest to take any action against her. Polly is not happy with this decision and would like to bring proceedings against Ellie or otherwise recoup her losses.

Advise Polly on the options open to her as a shareholder in this position.

CAUTION!

- Look carefully at the question: the company is a public limited company, so you need to reflect on this in your response

- Make sure that you identify what a shareholder is complaining about so that you can focus your legal discussion and application appropriately

- As the instruction is broad you will need to consider all the potential shareholder remedies, but think through your answer before you start so that you can focus on those that are most relevant

DIAGRAM ANSWER PLAN

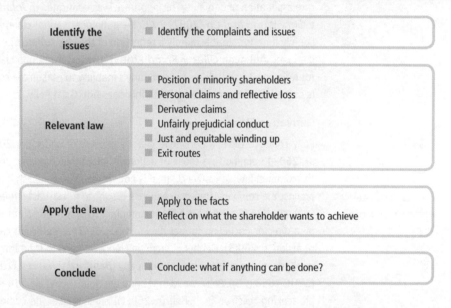

Identify the issues
- Identify the complaints and issues

Relevant law
- Position of minority shareholders
- Personal claims and reflective loss
- Derivative claims
- Unfairly prejudicial conduct
- Just and equitable winding up
- Exit routes

Apply the law
- Apply to the facts
- Reflect on what the shareholder wants to achieve

Conclude
- Conclude: what if anything can be done?

SUGGESTED ANSWER

Drango plc appears to have a prima facie case against Ellie for breach of the duty of care, skill, and diligence under **Companies Act 2006 (CA 2006), s. 174**, and possibly, but controversially, breach of **CA 2006, s. 172** if she failed to declare her wrongdoing to the company (*Item Software (UK) Ltd v Fassihi* **[2004] EWCA Civ 1244**). The company is not taking action against Ellie however, and Polly is unhappy, particularly as she has suffered loss (through the loss in value of her shares) as a consequence of the breach. As the wrong has been done to the company, members are normally prohibited from bringing action under the rule in *Foss v Harbottle* **(1843) 2 Hare 461**, but there are exceptions to this rule[1] which will be considered in order to advise Polly of her

[1] There is a lot to cover in this question, so the background has to be dealt with very concisely

options. Polly might also allege the directors' failure to pursue Ellie is a breach of **s. 172**, but in the absence of evidence of bad faith or lack of consideration, this will not be pursued.

Personal Claim

A personal claim is outside the rule in *Foss v Harbottle*, which relates to wrongs done to the company rather than wrongs done to a shareholder personally.[2] Polly has suffered financial loss through the drop in share value, which might indicate she could bring a personal claim. However, *Prudential Assurance Co Ltd v Newman Industries Ltd (No. 2)* **[1982] Ch 204** held that a shareholder could not bring a personal claim in respect of a fall in the value of his shares caused by the wrongdoing of the company controllers who had disposed of a corporate asset at an undervalue. This approach was confirmed in *Johnson v Gore Wood and Co* **[2002] 2 AC 1**—a member cannot claim personally for a loss that is merely a reflection of the loss suffered by the company. Although *Giles v Rhind* **[2003] 1 BCLC 1** permits claims for reflective losses where the company's inability to pursue the claim is caused by the wrongdoing itself, this does not assist Polly.

Derivative Claim

Polly could consider a derivative claim against Ellie under **CA 2006, ss. 260–4**, relating to a cause of action vested in the company. Unlike the common law derivative claim, it is not necessary to establish 'fraud' against the company: 'mere' negligence is sufficient (contrast *Pavlides v Jensen* **[1956] 2 All ER 518** at common law).[3] Any breach of duty by a director (including former directors: **s. 260(5)**) is sufficient cause of action: **s. 260(3)**. Neither is there any longer a need to establish the wrongdoers are in control of the company (*Bamford v Harvey* **[2012] EWHC 2858 (Ch)**). Polly would thus bring the claim on behalf of Drango plc seeking relief on its behalf (**s. 260(1)**) against Ellie. The company would be joined as a defendant to make it party to the proceedings.

[3] An essential point to make given the nature of the director's wrongdoing

However, Polly would face a number of hurdles in bringing a derivative claim. At the first stage she would have to ensure that her application and supporting evidence disclose a prima facie case; if not, the court would refuse permission to continue the claim: **s. 261(2)**. The 'prima facie' stage is intended to remove unmeritorious cases at an early stage rather than conduct a 'mini-trial' (*Iesini v Westrip Holdings Ltd* **[2009] EWHC 2526 (*Iesini*)**), and it seems likely that Polly could satisfy this stage. The court would then have to consider whether or not to grant permission to continue, having regard to the provisions of **s. 263**. If the court considers a person acting to promote the interest of the company in accordance with **CA 2006, s. 172** (duty to promote the success of the company), known as 'the hypothetical director', would not seek to continue the claim (**s. 263(2)(a)**), or that the breach was authorized or ratified by the company (**263(2)(b)–(c)**), it must refuse permission. As **(a)** requires the court to be satisfied that no such hypothetical director would seek to continue the claim, and not just that some would and some wouldn't (*Iesini*), it seems probable (depending on all the surrounding facts) that the claim would not be dismissed on this ground, neither does it appear that the breach has been authorized or ratified.[4]

On Polly passing this hurdle, the court must then exercise its discretion as to whether or not to give permission, and in so doing must in particular take into consideration the factors in **s. 263(3)**: whether Polly is acting in good faith in bringing the claim, the importance the hypothetical director would attach to continuing the claim, whether authorization or ratification is likely, whether the company has decided not to pursue the claim, and whether the act gives rise to a cause of action that Polly could pursue in her own right. The court must have particular regard to the views of members of the company who have no personal interest in the matter (**s. 263(4)**). Taking the factors into account (particularly the hypothetical director and the company's decision), the court might well refuse permission, although we need more information on the views of the other shareholders, and the reasons why the directors had chosen not to proceed against Ellie.[5]

If Polly were granted permission to bring a derivative claim, any remedy would go to the company, not to her directly, and so she would only benefit indirectly. Polly would have to weigh this benefit against the difficulties of bringing the claim; the risk of a costs order against her (although the court may order the company to indemnify her for her costs if she is acting reasonably: *Wallersteiner v Moir (No. 2)* **[1975] 1 All ER 849**); and the fact that publicity from any action might impact negatively on the share price (see Arsalidou, 'Litigation culture and the new statutory derivative claim' (2009) 30 Co Law 205).[6]

Unfair Prejudice

Another possible option for Polly would be an unfair prejudice petition under **CA 2006, s. 994**. (As Polly has no apparent wish to 'kill' the company, a petition under **Insolvency Act 1986, s. 122(1)(g)** —winding up on the just and equitable ground—will not be considered.)[7] **Section 994** requires there to have been conduct of the company's affairs that unfairly prejudices the interests of a member. This includes breaches of duty by directors: *Atlasview Ltd v Brightview Ltd* **[2004] EWHC 1056**; *Re Tobian Properties Ltd* **[2012] EWCA Civ 998**—s. 994 can be used to 'outflank' the rule in *Foss v Harbottle* (*Re Saul D Harrison & Sons plc* **[1995] 1 BCLC 14**).

There is clearly financial prejudice to her interests, but Polly also needs to show unfairness, which normally requires either a breach of the terms of association, or the use of legal rules in an inequitable

---

[4] Explicitly consider how the law applies to the facts of the problem

[5] It is fine to take a provisional view and indicate where you would need more facts to advise more confidently

[6] Bringing in a practical point shows you have really thought about the issues; in this particular instance it also allows you to show your wider reading

[7] If you don't think a particular option is relevant, it can be helpful to give a reason for your view— that way the examiner knows you haven't just forgotten it

manner (*O'Neill v Phillips* **[1999] 1 WLR 1092**). It is highly unlikely that equitable constraints would be found here: this does not appear to be a quasi-partnership company (*Ebrahimi v Westbourne Galleries Ltd* **[1973] AC 360**) and although this is not essential (*Brett v Migrations Holdings Ltd* **[2016] EWHC 523**) the courts are very reluctant to impose equitable constraints in a public company[8] (*Re Astec (BSR) plc* **[1998] 2 BCLC 556**). Is there a breach of the terms of association? Despite suggestions to the contrary in *Re Charnley Davies Ltd (No. 2)* **[1990] BCLC 760**, breach of the duty of care can give rise to a **s. 994** claim (*Re Macro (Ipswich) Ltd* **[1994] 2 BCLC 354**) and there is no requirement to remedy such breaches through a derivative claim rather than **s. 994**: *Zedra Trust Company (Jersey) Ltd v The Hut Group Ltd* **[2020] EWHC 5**.

If Polly can establish unfair prejudice, the most likely remedy under **s. 996** would be an order for the purchase of her shares (*Grace v Biagioli* **[2006] 2 BCLC 70**). This does not appear to be what Polly wants, as although recouping her investment, she will lose the potential for future dividends and capital growth. She would also bear the risk of costs if unsuccessful.[9] Accordingly, this option is not very attractive here, particularly in light of the courts' reluctance to engage **s. 994** in public companies and the risk that a timely offer to purchase her shares at a fair price could bring a swift end to any petition (*O'Neill v Phillips*).

Conclusion

Polly's case demonstrates the difficult position of a minority shareholder. A derivative claim is possible if she is determined to try to remedy the breach and stay in the company, but she will face significant hurdles in bringing the claim. Her other legal options are perhaps even less attractive. Pragmatically, Polly might be better advised to seek to persuade her fellow shareholders to put pressure on the directors to bring an action, or to seek sufficient support to remove the directors (needing a simple majority under **CA 2006, s. 168**).[10] If Polly has no support and is really unhappy with the way the company is being run, she might prefer to sell up and invest elsewhere, as legal proceedings may prove expensive and futile.

[8] Remember that the company is a public company, so you need to indicate where this is relevant to how the law applies

[9] Consider what the client wants, and think about the drawbacks as well as any benefits

[10] This shows you are not just producing a 'standard form' answer but are considering what the particular client could possibly do, as well as demonstrating wider knowledge

➕ LOOKING FOR EXTRA MARKS?

- Consider further the positions of minority shareholders in public companies compared with private companies: how far do, and should, the available remedies differ, and why?

- Explore the interaction of derivative claims and unfair prejudice where the claim is based on breach of duty, and also whether an unfair prejudice claim may effectively allow a shareholder to claim for 'reflective loss'

QUESTION | 3

Assess the significance of the House of Lords' decision in *O'Neill v Phillips* [1999] 1 WLR 1092 to the unfair prejudice remedy under Companies Act 2006, section 994.

CAUTION!

- You will need a good understanding of the unfair prejudice remedy generally in order to assess the decision in *O'Neill v Phillips* effectively

- The question is about the significance of the case, and not about the case generally, so don't waste time setting out case facts in great detail

- Don't just look at the concept of 'unfairness'; look at other important elements of the case such as the advice given on how to approach an offer to purchase the petitioner's shares

DIAGRAM ANSWER PLAN

Introduction: issues to be considered

▼

Context of *O'Neill v Phillips*

▼

Unfairness: meaning and scope

▼

Unfairness and 'legitimate expectations'

▼

Offer to purchase and effect on petition

▼

Evaluation of broader significance

▼

Conclusion: summarize points

SUGGESTED ANSWER

This essay will argue that *O'Neill v Phillips* [1999] 1 WLR 1092 (*O'Neill*) has been significant in developing the 'unfair prejudice' remedy (**Companies Act 2006 (CA 2006), s. 994**) but is significant as a strong restatement of principle rather than a fundamental change of approach. After briefly considering the context, two key elements of the case will be analysed—the concept of 'unfairness', and the effect of offers to purchase a petitioner's shares, considering cases and proposed reform before and after *O'Neill*, to evaluate its significance.[1]

¹ It can be effective to both indicate the argument and explain what will be covered in the first paragraph. But if you are not sure how your argument will go before you start writing, you can just explain your approach, linking clearly to the question

Context

CA 2006, s. 994 allows a member to petition for relief when the company's affairs have been conducted in a manner unfairly prejudicial to a member's interests. *O'Neill* was the House of Lords' first opportunity to consider the remedy (then **Companies Act 1985, s. 459**) which had proved very popular in contrast to its predecessor, **Companies Act 1948, s. 210**, which required 'oppression', restrictively interpreted by the courts. But there were concerns about the number, length, and 'appalling' cost of proceedings (*Re Unisoft Group Ltd (No. 3)* [1994] 1 BCLC 609); for example, in *Re Elgindata Ltd* [1991] BCLC 959, costs of £320,000 were incurred on shares valued at £24,600. These concerns explain the court's generally restrictive approach to the remedy.[2]

² This makes the connection between otherwise fairly general points about the remedy and the approach taken in *O'Neill* itself to avoid overly descriptive writing

Unfairness

Lord Hoffmann, giving the only speech in *O'Neill*, identified unfairness as the key element of the remedy. Although this conferred 'a wide power to do what appeared just and equitable',[3] it must be applied judicially and the content based upon rational principles. Lord Hoffmann recognized both that a company has a commercial nature—a legal association for an economic purpose—and that company law developed from the law of partnership, so incorporates equitable concepts of good faith. This, he held, gives two aspects to unfairness. First a member cannot ordinarily complain of unfairness unless there has been some breach of the terms on which they agreed the affairs of the company should be conducted. Secondly, in some cases equitable considerations make it unfair for those conducting the affairs of the company to rely upon strict legal powers. The judge drew a parallel with the approach of *Ebrahimi v Westbourne Galleries Ltd* [1973] AC 360 (*Ebrahimi*) for just and equitable winding up—legal rights may be subject to equitable considerations in certain circumstances. This is typically justified where the company is a 'quasi-partnership', ie displaying one or more of the characteristics identified in *Ebrahimi*:[4] (i) an association formed or continued on the basis of a personal relationship involving mutual confidence, (ii) an agreement or understanding that the shareholders will participate in the conduct of the business, and (iii) restrictions on the transfer of the shares.

³ If you can't remember precise phrases when in an exam, don't worry, just give the essence of what was said

⁴ You need to be familiar with *Ebrahimi* and be able to set out and apply the quasi-partnership characteristics

⁵ This paragraph gives just enough of the facts to show the examiner you know the case well, while using the facts to show a good understanding of how the law (previously explained) is applied

In *O'Neill*,[5] O's primary complaint was that P had failed to award him additional shares as expected and discussed. Lord Hoffmann's analysis of unfairness led to the conclusion that this was not unfair as the 'promise' to give O more shares was not legally binding. Furthermore, although the company was a quasi-partnership, so excluding O from management would have been unfair, the court found that O had not been forced out; he had chosen to leave.

This interpretation of unfairness was not particularly significant as it mirrored the analysis (of Hoffmann LJ) in *Re Saul D Harrison & Sons plc* [1995] 1 BCLC 14 (*Saul D Harrison*). More significantly, *O'Neill* explicitly rejected of the concept of 'legitimate expectations',[6] a notion introduced in *Saul D Harrison*. In *O'Neill*, Lord Hoffmann held that 'legitimate expectations' was just a label for the equitable restraint and 'should not be allowed to lead a life of its own': a focus on legitimate expectations had led the Court of Appeal to find in favour of O, and (wrongly) loosen the boundaries of unfair prejudice.

Accordingly, while *O'Neill* did not break new ground it made the boundaries clearer. Following the decision, the Law Commission thought the remedy would be less readily available while the Company Law Review Steering Group ('Modern Company Law for a Competitive Economy: Final Report' (2001)) believed it remained substantially unchanged but agreed with the *O'Neill* analysis.[7] There was perceived to be no need for reform, contrary to the views of the Law Commission prior to *O'Neill*, suggesting the judgment was effective in clarifying the boundaries of the remedy.

Later cases have accepted *O'Neill* as providing the necessary guidance for unfair prejudice, eg *Oak Investment Partners XII v Boughtwood* [2010] 2 BCLC 459 (*Oak Investment*). *Re Tobian Properties Ltd* [2012] EWCA Civ 998 (*Tobian*) reflects its essence in describing the remedy as 'elastic but not unbounded'. The *O'Neill* analysis means that for the majority of companies, where the relationship is purely commercial, unfairness lies only in a breach of terms of association—such as the articles, company law, or binding agreements. Only where equitable constraints can be justified, can the petitioner rely on a wider notion of 'unfairness'. This will most commonly be in quasi-partnership companies but equitable constraints may also be found elsewhere (*Brett v Migrations Holdings Ltd* [2016] EWHC 523).

Prior to *O'Neill*, the Law Commission had considered providing a more general exit route for aggrieved shareholders but *O'Neill* made clear the remedy does not provide 'no fault divorce', allowing a petitioner to be bought out wherever trust and confidence has broken down. This was followed in *Re Phoenix Office Supplies Ltd* [2003] 1 BCLC 76. Even deadlock between the shareholders is not enough in itself to trigger s. 994: *Hawkes v Cuddy* [2009] 2 BCLC 427. These limits show how important it is to place dispute resolution mechanisms and exit provisions in the articles or shareholder agreements from the start.[8]

---

[6] Pull your discussion back to the question by focusing on 'significance'

[7] Awareness of reform proposals is always valuable, but it is particularly helpful to use this knowledge to support your argument, which is what this paragraph goes on to do

[8] Bring in your wider understanding of a minority shareholder's position

Although *O'Neill* tightened the concept of 'unfairness', in other respects it took a broad approach. For example it held that 'interests of a member' for the purposes of the provision should be interpreted widely and not be 'too narrowly or technically construed'. This has been followed in later cases, eg *Gamlestaden Fastigheter AB v Baltic Partners Ltd* [2007] 4 All ER 164.

Offer to Purchase

Another significant element of *O'Neill* is the guidance given regarding offers to purchase the petitioner's shares—given expressly to encourage parties to avoid litigation. It was already established that an offer could lead to a petition being dismissed—the petitioner having received the full relief that might eventually be awarded (eg *Re A Company (No. 836 of 1995)* [1996] BCLC 192). Lord Hoffmann in *O'Neill* asserted that such an offer prevents conduct from being unfair as the minority is no longer trapped. Providing practical guidance, *O'Neill* set out the principles expected of a 'fair' offer—normally a pro-rata valuation without a minority discount to be determined by a competent expert with both parties having equal access to information and the opportunity to make submissions to the expert. An offer should usually include legal costs incurred, although a respondent should have 'a reasonable opportunity to make an offer' before any costs obligation arises. A reasonable offer does not need to be capable of becoming legally binding as soon as accepted, although the likelihood of it being followed through may influence whether it is reasonable: *Re Sprintroom Ltd* [2019] EWCA Civ 932.

[9] Think PEA: the point about offers to purchase has been made and explained in the previous paragraph, now it is time to analyse its importance (and support this with academic opinion)

Because of its value in bringing petitions to a speedy close, the guidance on offers to purchase is arguably the most significant element of *O'Neill* (Boyle, 'Unfair prejudice in the House of Lords' (2000) 21 Co Law 253)[9] and it has been followed in later cases, eg *North Holdings Ltd v Southern Tropics Ltd* [1999] 2 BCLC 625. However an offer within *O'Neill* guidance will not inevitably lead to the striking out of a petition: *Harborne Road Nominees Ltd v Karvaski* [2011] EWHC 2214.

Conclusion

O'Neill is significant because it emphasizes the boundaries to **s. 994** and increases opportunities for resolving disputes out of court. However, it does not change the law materially, nor unduly restrict this important flexible remedy. **Section 994** continues to be praised for its 'adaptability' (Arden LJ in *Tobian*, also recognizing it as a tool for encouraging good corporate behaviour) and its 'wide and flexible' nature (*Re Coroin Ltd* [2013] EWCA Civ 781). Courts have not been deterred from developing the jurisdiction in appropriate cases, within the parameters of *O'Neill*, for example considering the conduct of a holding company towards its subsidiary (*Gross v Rackind* **[2004] 4 All ER 735**) or the conduct of a senior manager (*Oak Investment*).

Unsurprisingly given the restrictions of other remedies and the limited relief they offer, **s. 994** continues to be the most favoured option in shareholder disputes. Unfortunately, although helpful in reducing the number and length of proceedings, *O'Neill* has not entirely resolved this problem. Arden LJ has commented upon 'heavy' and 'resource intensive' **s. 994** cases and the need to reduce hearing times (*Re Coroin Ltd* and similarly in *Graham v Every* **[2015] 1 BCLC 41**),[10] so the significance of *O'Neill* in this regard should not be overstated.

[10] This brings the essay full circle by returning to concerns about the number and cost of unfair prejudice cases

LOOKING FOR EXTRA MARKS

- Show your wider awareness by reflecting on views of the law reform bodies and whether the Law Commission proposals were preferable

- Incorporate further academic evaluations of the case and its importance to shareholder remedies

- You could also think about whether the case may have impacted on other shareholder remedies (but be careful not to stray too far away from the question itself)

QUESTION | 4

Between 2013 and 2018 Suzie and Tara ran a successful business in partnership. In 2018, they decided to incorporate the business, and to take this opportunity to bring in a mutual friend, Urma, who had previously been working informally with them. Esteyu Ltd was incorporated with an issued share capital of 1,000 £1 shares, Suzie and Tara each taking 450 shares, and Urma taking 100 shares. All three became directors of Esteyu Ltd on incorporation.

About a year after incorporation, Suzie and Tara voted to remove Urma from her directorship, and thereafter have not allowed Urma to be involved in management. They claim that she is difficult to get on with and doesn't work as hard as they do. The company has never paid any dividends. Suzie and Tara claim that the company is not profitable enough to pay dividends but Urma says profits are being kept to a minimum because Suzie and Tara are paying themselves substantial remuneration and perks.

Advise Urma, who is very unhappy with the current position, considering both Companies Act 2006, s. 994 and Insolvency Act 1986, s. 122(1)(g). Would your answer differ if Suzie and Tara had recently offered to buy Urma's shares, the value to be determined by the company's auditor?

CAUTION!

■ If you are asked to advise in relation to a specific remedy or remedies, keep this focus and don't waste your time discussing shareholder remedies more generally

■ Keep linking the law to the facts to avoid being too descriptive

■ Don't forget to consider any additional points raised, here the 'offer to purchase' point

◻ DIAGRAM ANSWER PLAN

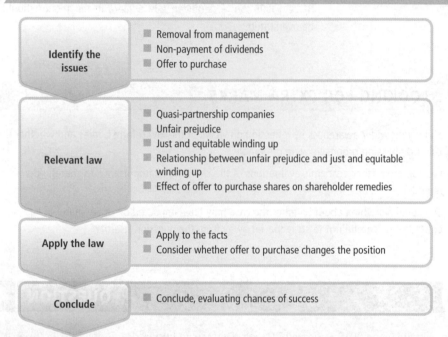

| Identify the issues | ■ Removal from management
■ Non-payment of dividends
■ Offer to purchase |

| Relevant law | ■ Quasi-partnership companies
■ Unfair prejudice
■ Just and equitable winding up
■ Relationship between unfair prejudice and just and equitable winding up
■ Effect of offer to purchase shares on shareholder remedies |

| Apply the law | ■ Apply to the facts
■ Consider whether offer to purchase changes the position |

| Conclude | ■ Conclude, evaluating chances of success |

 SUGGESTED ANSWER

[1] A short introductory paragraph is often all that is necessary in a problem question

Urma is a minority shareholder in Esteyu Ltd. Her complaint relates to her removal as a director and failure to pay dividends. This essay will advise on her prospects[1] if she were to bring a petition under **Companies Act 2006, s. 994** or **Insolvency Act 1986, s. 122(1)(g)**, also considering the effect of an offer to purchase her shares.

Unfair Prejudice

[2] A neat little device to convince the examiner you are looking at the question—saying 'a member's complaint' would be just as valid, but would give the impression of being less strong on application

Under **CA 2006, s. 994** Urma's complaint[2] must relate to the conduct of the company's affairs. This has been interpreted broadly: provided the complaint does not relate solely to the conduct of an individual's affairs (such as the sale of shares between members: *Re Leeds United Holdings plc* [1996] 2 BCLC 545) this will be satisfied. Suzie and Tara's behaviour would clearly fall within the requirement.

Urma must also establish that her interests as a member have been prejudiced. 'Interests as a member' extends beyond pure 'membership rights' and can include participation in management (*O'Neill v Phillips* **[1999] 1 WLR 1092** (*O'Neill*)) so is satisfied here. Prejudice is relatively straightforward, and need not be financial loss (*Re Coroin Ltd* **[2013] EWCA Civ 781**): here Urma's removal and lack of financial return would amount to prejudice.[3]

The aspect of **s. 994** that is potentially more difficult for Urma is unfairness. The conduct must not just be prejudicial, but unfairly so: *Re Saul D Harrison & Sons plc* **[1995] 1 BCLC 14**. 'Unfairness' is a broad concept but must be applied judicially and within established boundaries. The key case is *O'Neill*[4] where the House of Lords held that unfairness will normally, in a standard commercial association, lie only in a (non-trivial) breach of the terms on which it was agreed the company's affairs would be conducted. This would require some breach of the constitution, law, or binding agreement, for example, which does not appear to be the case here, as we will assume Urma's removal was in accordance with **CA 2006, s. 168** (requiring a simple majority and special notice) and there is nothing else prohibiting her removal. Additionally, however, unfairness may lie where equitable considerations make it unfair for those conducting the affairs of the company to rely on their strict legal powers. This is typically (but not invariably, see eg *Re Westshield Ltd* **[2019] EWHC 115**) where a company is a 'quasi-partnership company', as identified in *Ebrahimi v Westbourne Galleries Ltd* **[1973] AC 360** (*Ebrahimi*): a company formed on the basis of a personal relationship involving mutual confidence with all (or most) members involved in management, and a restriction on the transfer of shares.

Applying the *Ebrahimi* factors to Esteyu Ltd, it appears to be a quasi-partnership. Although Urma was not initially a partner, she had been working with the partners and was brought in as a member and director at incorporation with Suzie and Tara. Restrictions on share transfers are very common in private companies, and there will be practical restrictions anyway due to the lack of market for private company shares. Urma seems to have joined the company in reliance on the understanding she would be involved in management (reliance is necessary to give rise to the equitable constraint: *Re Guidezone Ltd* **[2000] 2 BCLC 321**) and accordingly, it would prima facie be unfair for Suzie and Tara to exclude her. *Re Ghyll Beck Driving Range Ltd* **[1993] BCLC 1126** held it was unfair when one of four members in a quasi-partnership was excluded[5] following arguments.

A further factor is the failure to pay dividends, as with Urma no longer a director receiving remuneration, she has no return on her investment. A failure to pay dividends can be unfair, particularly if one class

[3] Think IRAC: having established the issue, and the rule, remember to apply and conclude on each point. This paragraph uses IRAC concisely to raise and conclude on three minor issues

[4] You need to be able to set out the *O'Neill* analysis of 'unfairness' confidently (and fairly concisely) in problem questions such as this

[5] Support your conclusion with reference(s) to a case or cases that are on point

is treated differently without authority or justification (*Routledge v Skerritt* [2019] EWHC 573) or when only some members benefit from director remuneration (*Re Sam Weller & Sons Ltd* [1990] Ch 682) as here. In *Re C F Booth Ltd* [2017] EWHC 457, a no-dividend policy was unfairly prejudicial when directors received objectively excessive remuneration and other perks.

[6] Think about possible arguments that could be made for the other side

Suzie and Tara might argue Urma's removal was still not unfair,[6] because of Urma's perceived failings. Exclusion was not unfair in *Re RA Noble & Sons (Clothing) Ltd* [1983] BCLC 273 because the individual had been paying no attention to company affairs, nor in *Grace v Biagioli* [2006] 2 BCLC 70 where the individual had been purchasing a competing company. However, Urma's alleged failings— even if proven—seem hardly sufficient to make apparently unfair conduct, fair; indeed *Re Sprintroom* Ltd [2019] EWCA Civ 932 makes clear even committing a breach of duty will not necessarily render exclusion fair.

On balance, Urma seems to have a strong case under **s. 994**. The court has a wide discretion as to the remedy granted (**s. 996**). Urma must specify the remedy sought: *Hawkes v Cuddy* [2009] BCLC 427. The most common order is a share purchase order buying out the minority shareholder, as it frees the petitioner and removes the possibility of future discord (*Grace v Biagioli*). The valuation date is usually the date of the order (although it can be backdated if losses have been continuing: *Re London School of Electronics Ltd* [1986] Ch 211). In a quasi-partnership company as here, the valuation is usually pro-rata without a minority discount: *Re Bird Precision Bellows Ltd* [1984] Ch 419.

Just and Equitable Winding up

Urma's chances of succeeding on a petition under **Insolvency Act 1986 (IA 1986), s. 122(1)(g)** are lower although not because she doesn't have a good case per se. Following *Ebrahimi* (see also eg *Re A & BC Chewing Gum Ltd* [1975] 1 WLR 579), exclusion from management in a quasi-partnership company can make it just and equitable to wind up the company. *O'Neill* drew parallels between the unfair prejudice and 'just and equitable' jurisdictions (see also *Re Paramount Powders Ltd* [2019] EWCA Civ 1644) but *Hawkes v Cuddy* confirmed (rejecting *Re Guidezone Ltd* on this point) that unfair prejudice and just and equitable winding up continue to exist as separate jurisdictions.

[7] It is important to remember s. 125(2) when dealing with just and equitable winding up

However, under **IA 1986, s. 125(2)** [7] the court must not wind up a company on the just and equitable ground if it is of the opinion that the petitioner has some other remedy and she is acting unreasonably in seeking winding up instead of pursuing that remedy. As Urma has another remedy (**s. 994**) and it would be unreasonable to wind up a viable company without good reason, her petition under **s. 122(1)(g)** would almost certainly be dismissed. **Section 122(1)(g)** is potentially of most use in a deadlock situation such as *Re Yenidje Tobacco Ltd* **[1916] 2 Ch 426**—there is no deadlock in this case as Suzie and Tara have a clear majority. Urma should also note that bringing the two petitions in the alternative is strongly discouraged because of the serious effect a winding up petition has on a company.

Offer to Purchase

The offer to purchase would potentially change Urma's position. If a reasonable offer to purchase the petitioner's shares is made, an unfair prejudice petition will usually be dismissed. This is because a successful petitioner will most likely obtain a share purchase order. The offer to purchase therefore gives the petitioner all she is likely to achieve (*Re A Company (No. 836 of 1995)* **[1996] BCLC 192**). Lord Hoffmann in *O'Neill* also indicated that an offer means there is no unfairness, as the petitioner is no longer trapped.[8] The same consequence would follow for an **IA 1986, s. 122(1)(g)** petition as the offer would be an alternative remedy that would (usually) be unreasonable not to pursue.

[8] Although this doesn't make any difference to your conclusion, it is a valuable additional point as it shows you have a deeper appreciation of the issues

The critical factor is whether the offer is 'reasonable'. In *O'Neill*, guidance was given (obiter, but followed in later cases) on what constitutes a reasonable offer. This will normally be an offer to purchase shares at a 'fair value' on a pro-rata basis without minority discount, with the value (if not agreed) to be determined by a competent expert and both parties having access to information to make submissions to the expert. The offer should also normally include payment of the petitioner's costs to date. Here it is not clear that the offer is reasonable as the valuation is by the company's auditor, who will probably not be regarded as sufficiently independent[9] (*North Holdings Ltd v Southern Tropics Ltd* **[1999] 2 BCLC 625**). Furthermore, no allowance is made for costs, although this may not matter if the offer is made promptly: *O'Neill*. A court may still allow a petition to proceed notwithstanding an offer to purchase within the *O'Neill* guidelines, depending on all the facts: *Harborne Road Nominees Ltd v Karvaski* **[2011] EWHC 2214**.

[9] Even if unaware of authority on this point, you should think about the significance of the valuation being by the auditor—it must be in the case facts for a reason! The examiner wants to see you've thought about it, even if your conclusion differs from theirs

Conclusion[10]

[10] A brief conclusion is fine if you've concluded on points as you've gone along

On balance Urma has good prospects of success if she brings an unfair prejudice petition, provided Suzie and Tara do not make a reasonable offer to purchase her shares within the *O'Neill* guidelines. If successful she is likely to be bought out, rather than reinstated as a director, with the valuation not discounted for its minority status. She should not, however, bring a petition for just and equitable winding up, as this is unlikely to succeed.

LOOKING FOR EXTRA MARKS?

- Support your points with authority as much as you can, while recognizing there are lots of cases in this area so you can't use them all. Give case facts sparingly and only where pertinent to save time for analysis and application
- Explore the relationship between **section 994** and **section 122(1)(g)** in more depth, considering how far they overlap

TAKING THINGS FURTHER

- Arsalidou, D., 'Litigation culture and the new statutory derivative claim' (2009) 30 Co Law 205
  Reviews the benefits of the statutory derivative claim generally and in light of cases under the new provisions, reflecting on whether there is a risk of additional litigation against directors.

- Baxter, C., 'The true spirit of *Foss v Harbottle*' (1987) 38 NILQ 6
  An entertaining analysis of the rule in Foss v Harbottle *and its exceptions following the case of* Prudential Assurance v Newman. *There is much of value here as it ranges through a number of 'mind-bending problems', but remember that it predates the introduction of the statutory derivative claim.*

- Boyle, A. J., 'Unfair prejudice in the House of Lords' (2000) 21 Co Law 253
  A case note on O'Neill v Phillips, *highlighting the practical importance of the guidance on a 'reasonable' offer to purchase a petitioner's shares.*

- Gray, A. M., 'The statutory derivative claim: an outmoded superfluousness?' (2012) 33 Co Law 295
  Explores the distinction between derivative claims and unfair prejudice petitions, concluding the derivative claim continues to add value to company law and provides a deterrent to directors considering breaching their duties.

- Griffin, S., 'Shareholder remedies and the no reflective loss principle—problems surrounding the identification of a membership interest' [2010] JBL 461
  Suggests that the unfair prejudice jurisdiction effectively blurs the conceptual boundaries of 'membership interest', bringing together a number of issues including membership interests, personal claims, corporate claims, and reflective losses.

- Griffin, S., 'Alternative shareholder remedies following corporate mismanagement—which remedy to pursue?' (2010) 281 Co LN 1
  A useful summary of the different options open to shareholders, contrasting their nature and scope, distinguishing between them, and highlighting areas where they overlap.

- Hannigan, B., 'Drawing boundaries between derivative claims and unfairly prejudicial petitions' [2009] JBL 606
  Criticizes the failure of some courts to distinguish adequately between derivative and personal claims, in particular when ordering corporate relief in an unfair prejudice petition. See also Reisberg, A., 'Shareholders' remedies: in search of consistency of principle in English Law' (2005) 16 EBLR 1063, and Cheung, R., 'Corporate wrongs litigated in the context of unfair prejudice claims: reforming the unfair prejudice remedy for the redress of corporate wrongs' (2008) 29 Co Law 98.

- Keay, A., 'Assessing and rethinking the statutory scheme for derivative actions under the Companies Act 2006' [2016] JCLS 39

  Reviews the operation of the new statutory derivative claim, including consideration of its purpose, exploring why it has not been used more frequently. See also Keay, A. and Loughrey, J., 'Derivative proceedings in a brave new world for company management and shareholders' [2010] JBL 151, and Gibbs, D., 'Has the statutory derivative claim fulfilled its objectives? Parts 1 and 2' (2011) 32 Co Law 41 and 76.

- Mitchell, C., 'Shareholders' claims for reflective loss' (2004) 120 LQR 457

  Examines the justifications and policy reasons for the bar on claims for 'reflective loss', exploring when and why shareholders can claim for loss in share value.

- Paterson, P., 'A criticism of the contractual approach to unfair prejudice' (2006) 27 Co Law 204

  An account of the unfair prejudice remedy including a review of conduct that can be 'unfair', arguing that the modern approach is not properly explained by contractual analysis.

- Payne, J., 'Section 459 and public companies' (1999) 115 LQR 368

  Considers the reasons why unfair prejudice claims are unlikely to be successful in public companies, with particular reference to Re Astec (BSR) plc.

- Wedderburn, K. W., 'Shareholders' rights and the rule in *Foss v Harbottle*' [1957] 15 CLJ 194, [1958] 16 CLJ 93

  This classic article (in two parts) examines the rule in Foss v Harbottle *and its exceptions, linking to the enforceability of the articles of association and focusing on when a minority shareholder can take action.*

 Online Resources   www.oup.com/uk/qanda/

For extra essay and problem questions on this topic, as well as advice on revision and exam technique, please visit the online resources.

8 Corporate Liability: Contracts, Torts, and Crimes

ARE YOU READY?

In order to attempt the questions in this chapter you will need to have covered the following topics:

- Principles of corporate liability
- Pre-incorporation contracts
- Contractual capacity, the ultra vires doctrine, ss. 31 and 39
- Authority: actual, usual, and apparent
- Restrictions on authority, the *Turquand* rule and s. 40
- Contracts with connected persons and s. 41
- Tortious and criminal liability
- Corporate manslaughter
- Connections (in particular) with: corporate personality, directors' duties, company management

 KEY DEBATES

Debate: how should liability for torts and crimes be attributed to companies?

This is a problem that has long exercised the finest corporate, tort, and criminal law minds. Currently the 'directing mind and will' test appears to live on, despite widespread criticism, and some optimism at a change of focus in *Meridian*. There is something for everyone in this topic, with articles ranging from the highly theoretical to the intensely practical, all trying to cope with the application of established legal concepts to the corporate entity.

Debate: corporate manslaughter

Unsurprisingly given the huge public interest in this area, corporate manslaughter has been a particularly fruitful area for law reform and academic discussion. Views range from those advocating

⏵

◉

more specifically 'corporate' liability, to those insisting that liability should remain based on individual culpability, with many critical opinions of CMCHA 2007.

QUESTION | 1

How effective have the legislature's efforts been at removing the problems associated with pre-incorporation contracts?

CAUTION!

- The question is fairly straightforward and the topic fairly narrow, so you will need a good understanding of the wider and deeper issues to impress the examiner
- Avoid a chronological approach that sets out the pre-reform law and then the current law; instead use your structure effectively to highlight and address the problems

⬭ DIAGRAM ANSWER PLAN

> Introduction: the problem of pre-incorporation contracts

▼

> Validity of a pre-incorporation contract

▼

> Who is bound? Considering agents, companies, and novation

▼

> Avoidance of liability

▼

> Areas where statute does not apply

▼

> Conclusion: evaluate effectiveness of reform

SUGGESTED ANSWER

[1] Use your introduction to define any important terms

Pre-incorporation contracts are contracts purportedly entered into by or on behalf of a company prior to its incorporation.[1] Since a company comes into existence only on incorporation (**Companies Act 2006 (CA 2006), s. 16**), it cannot be party to a contract entered into before that point. The primary concern for the law is to determine the status of and parties to that 'pre-incorporation contract', but there are other connected issues. To evaluate the effectiveness of the legislature's attempts to remove problems in this area,[2] it is necessary to compare the position at common law with that under statute (now **CA 2006, s. 51**), looking in particular at the parties to the contract, liability, and ongoing problems in this area.

[2] Refer specifically to the question statement to show your focus, and then set out what you are going to do

At common law there was a degree of confusion surrounding the validity of a pre-incorporation contract. Because the company was non-existent at the time of the contract, there was no doubt that the company itself could not be bound by a pre-incorporation contract, nor could it adopt or ratify such a contract after incorporation (*Natal Land Co & Colonization Ltd v Pauline Colliery and Development Syndicate Ltd* [1904] AC 120). But would the contract be void, or treated as a valid contract with the person acting for the non-existent company? This apparently turned on the intentions of the parties, as revealed by the contract (*Phonogram Ltd v Lane* [1982] QB 938). In *Kelner v Baxter* (1866) LR 2CP 174, the court found the person contracting on behalf of the company personally liable on the agreement. However, *Newborne v Sensolid* (GB) *Ltd* [1954] 1 QB 45 held that a contract signed in the name of the unincorporated company (and 'authenticated' by the signature of the 'director'), was purportedly made by the company itself and so was void. The potential injustice in such a distinction was clear, and reform came via the **First Company Law Directive 68/151/EEC (9 March 1968), Article 7**, which became part of UK law in the **European Communities Act 1972, s. 9(2)** (later incorporated into the **Companies Act 1985** and now **CA 2006, s. 51**).[3]

[3] Indicate the legislative history (not least as it gives the background to the arguments in *Phonogram v Lane*), but don't spend too much time reciting the details

Under **s. 51(1)** a person purporting to act on behalf of a company or as agent for it in entering into a contract (prior to incorporation) is personally liable on that contract. The section itself is slightly ambiguous as to whether it has the effect of creating a full contract between the 'agent' and the third party, or simply imposes liability on the 'agent'. In *Braymist Ltd v Wise Finance Co Ltd* [2002] **Ch 273**, the court confirmed that **s. 51** does create a contract between the parties that can be relied on by the 'agent' as well as his being liable. The section thus ensures a valid contract between the third party and the person acting for the unincorporated company,

[4] This shows that you understand the impact s. 51 has on the particular problem highlighted earlier

and deals with the discrepancy between *Kelner v Baxter* and *Newborne v Sensolid (GB) Ltd*—all such contracts will be valid, however the contract is signed.[4] The courts have ensured that the section is construed purposively, rejecting arguments designed to narrow its scope in *Phonogram Ltd v Lane* [1982] QB 938. In that case Lane argued, referring back to the original French text of the Directive, that a company must be in the process of being formed for the section to apply. Here, not only was the company not in the process of being formed, it was never actually formed. The court held that the section applied regardless. Neither did the court accept that there must have been some belief that the company was already in existence—the section still applied even where both parties were aware that the company had yet to be created.

[5] It is important to consider the limits of s. 51 as well as its achievements

Although a binding contract is created with the 'agent', it is clear that **s. 51** does not create what the parties to such a contract probably intend, which is a contract with the company.[5] It does not make the contract automatically binding on the company when (or if) it comes into existence, nor does it provide for a company to adopt or ratify a pre-incorporation contract. This is contrary to the recommendations of the Report of the Jenkins Committee (Cmnd 1749, 1962) which recommended a right for companies unilaterally to adopt pre-incorporation contracts. This approach has been taken in many Commonwealth countries and was included in the abortive Companies Bill 1973, but has not been adopted in the UK.

[6] A quick way of saying that the law hasn't changed in this regard

Accordingly, just as under the common law,[6] a company wishing to take up a pre-incorporation contract must go through the process of novation, entering into a new contract with the original contractor on the same terms. This requires the agreement of both parties (so may not be possible), and novation cannot simply be assumed from the fact that both parties acted as if they were bound: *Re Northumberland Avenue Hotel Co* (1886) 33 Ch D 16. The **Contracts (Rights of Third Parties) Act 1999** could possibly come to the aid of the company, as it can apply to individuals not in existence at the time of contracting (**s. 1(3)**), but the Act is aimed at contracts where there is an intention to benefit the third party, rather than where the 'third

[7] You could go into more detail if you had good recollection of Savirimuthu's arguments

party' is intended to be a party to the contract. Savirimuthu has raised the issue of whether the 'agent' could assign the contract to the company[7] ('Pre-incorporation contracts and the problem of corporate fundamentalism: are promoters proverbially profuse?' (2003) 24 Co Law 196) but this would clearly be less straightforward than ratification.

Although from the third party's perspective the situation is better than the common law, the fairness of binding the 'agent' without providing for the company to take on the contract following incorporation can be questioned. It could be a matter of chance which one of several founding members put their name to a contract, and yet **s. 51** makes that individual personally liable, when he might not be in a position to ensure subsequent novation. It might be argued in response that the person acting for the company was free to exclude liability,[8] as **s. 51** applies 'subject to any agreement to the contrary'. This requires clear and express exclusion of liability, the way in which the contract is entered into (for example) is not sufficient: *Phonogram Ltd v Lane*. Few individuals acting for a company pre-incorporation will have sufficient legal awareness to protect themselves in this way.

[8] Think PEA: make the point (exclusion of liability), evidence and explain it (s. 51 and *Phonogram*), and then assess it by considering whether it is of any use in practice

   Section 51 has further limitations.[9] Clearly it only applies to pre-incorporation contracts and not more generally to the problem of non-existent or misnamed companies. This limitation has led to some criticism (eg Griffiths, 'Agents without principals: pre-incorporation contracts and section 36C of the Companies Act 1985' (1993) 13 LS 241). The section has been held not to apply where a company trades under a new name before the change is operative: *Oshkosh B'Gosh Inc v Dan Marbel Inc & Craze* **[1989] BCLC 507**—once a company is in existence (even if not using its intended name) **s. 51** cannot operate, which is obviously an issue where companies are purchased 'off the shelf'. Similarly it does not apply where a company had been described by an incorrect name: *Badgerhill Properties Ltd v Cottrell* **[1991] BCLC 805**. It was also held not to apply where a person contracted in the name of a company that had been struck off the register and a new company of the same name was subsequently incorporated to continue the business as there had been no intention to create the new company at the time of the contract: *Cotronic (UK) Ltd v Dezonie* **[1991] BCLC 721**. Furthermore, the common law position still applies to companies registering outside the UK: *Rover International Ltd v Cannon Films Ltd* **[1989] 1 WLR 912**.

[9] This paragraph is important as it deals with several areas where s. 51 does not apply. This helps you to consider how far s. 51 can help with associated problems

   To conclude, it has been seen that **s. 51** deals with the primary problem of whether a pre-incorporation contract is binding, protecting the person dealing with the non-existent company, and so the legislature's efforts have been effective to that extent. But it is not a panacea for all problems concerning wrongly named or non-existent companies, and gaps remain where individuals deserve protection. Although creating a binding contract, the section does not provide parties with what they expect, nor does it provide a simple route for companies to adopt a pre-incorporation contract (as in many other countries), leaving companies reliant on the common law process of novation. As Milman has observed ('Company contracts: a review of the current and restated law' (2008) 240 Co LN 1) it is 'inexplicable' that the **CA 2006** reforms did not provide a ratification facility to bring the UK in line with other developed systems of corporate law. Furthermore, although it is understandable that the primary concern of the legislature is the third party (unsurprising as the origins of the section lie in the European provisions designed to protect persons dealing with companies),[10] it does not appear fair to leave an unsuspecting 'agent' facing significant personal liabilities. Given the remaining gaps and deficiencies, further legislative reform would be beneficial.

[10] Bring in your understanding of the origins of the provision and thus its focus

LOOKING FOR EXTRA MARKS?

- Use your further reading to develop your ideas and raise issues and problems
- Show an awareness of reform proposals and the origins of the provision, particularly where this supports or informs the points you are making
- Incorporate your basic knowledge concisely and within your discussion. This shows you are using your knowledge (rather than simply presenting it) and also leaves you maximum space for deeper analysis

QUESTION | 2

Extreem Ltd was incorporated in January by ten friends, to sell party decorations and related items. The ten friends took equal shareholdings in the company. Three of the friends were appointed to be the officers of the company—Caspar as Managing Director, Feliz as Operations Director, and Rudy as company secretary.

Shortly after incorporation, Caspar ordered a large consignment of party balloons, streamers, and table decorations (for £15,000) from Soiree Ltd on behalf of the company. The following week Feliz ordered two small delivery vans (for £40,000) from a local dealer, Noelle, who is Feliz's mother. (Feliz had told the other directors of Noelle's relationship to him.) In the same week Rudy ordered 200 boxes of drinking glasses (for £6,000). Rudy assured the seller, Kriss, that as company secretary he had the authority to make the purchase, and with this assurance, Kriss went ahead with the contract.

The other shareholders are now getting nervous about the rate of spending in this new company and would like to get out of these contracts.

Advise the shareholders, considering how, if at all, your advice would differ if Extreem Ltd's articles of association contained a clause stating, 'All contracts for a value in excess of £3,000 must be approved in advance by the general meeting'.

CAUTION!

- Separate the different contracts and deal with them one at a time, and one stage at a time, to avoid muddling issues
- Contracts questions almost inevitably involve some overlap with directors' duties so keep an eye out for these, while keeping your focus on the validity of the contracts
- There is a lot to cover in this question, so refer back to earlier discussion if the same point arises again rather than repeat yourself

DIAGRAM ANSWER PLAN

Identify the issues
- Are the contracts valid?
- What is the effect of any limitations on capacity and/or authority?

Relevant law
- Corporate capacity and the ultra vires doctrine
- Unrestricted objects: s. 31
- Restricted objects: operation of s. 39
- Types of authority: actual, usual, apparent
- Restrictions on authority: *Turquand's* rule
- Restrictions on authority: s. 40
- Connected persons and s. 41
- Directors exceeding authority: s. 171(a) and substantial property transactions

Apply the law
- Apply the relevant law to the facts

Conclude
- Conclude on each contract

SUGGESTED ANSWER

This question concerns the validity of several contracts—with Soiree, Noelle, and Kriss—entered into on Extreem Ltd's behalf. It raises various issues concerned with corporate capacity and directors' authority, and connected breaches of directors' duties.[1]

[1] Just set out the main areas in your introduction; otherwise you'll cover too much material before you get the chance to apply it to the facts

Soiree Contract

Historically, capacity was a major issue in contractual validity as the ultra vires doctrine made void any contract outside a company's capacity (as determined by the company's objects): ***Ashbury Railway Carriage & Iron Co v Riche* (1875) LR 7 HL 653**. But under **Companies Act (CA 2006), s. 31**, provided Extreem Ltd's articles do not specifically restrict its objects, its capacity will be unlimited. This is the most likely position.[2] If Extreem Ltd did have restricted objects, the contract appears to be within the scope of a 'party decoration' business in any event. Even if it wasn't, Soiree would be protected by **CA 2006, s. 39**, which prevents anyone challenging a contract on the ground of lack of capacity arising from anything in its constitution. Clearly capacity is not a problem for this contract.

[2] As you are not told whether the company has restricted objects or not, you can say what position is most likely, but you need to cover other possibilities as well, albeit concisely

The validity of the contract depends also on the authority of the person acting for the company. There is no evidence that Caspar has actual authority to enter into this contract (and he could not have actual authority if the restriction were in place) but usual or apparent authority is also sufficient to bind the company. Usual authority is the authority that is usual for someone in the position of that individual to have. This has been analysed as a form of implied actual authority (eg Hannigan, *Company Law*, 5th edn, Oxford, 2018), or a form of apparent/ostensible authority (eg *Mayson, French & Ryan on Company Law*, 36th edn, Oxford, 2019), but the difference doesn't matter here.[3] A managing director's usual authority is extensive (eg **Hely-Hutchinson v Brayhead Ltd [1967] 3 All ER 98**) and so this contract appears to be within the scope of Caspar's usual authority. Extreem Ltd will be bound by the contract.

[3] A quick nod to the examiner that you have looked into this point

If the restriction was there,[4] the contract should have been approved by the general meeting. But even if approval were not obtained, the contract will be binding on the company. In balancing the interests of shareholders (seeing the restriction upheld) and the third party (ensuring the contract is binding), both courts and statute have leant firmly in favour of the third party.

[4] Make clear when you are discussing the alternative scenario—you could even use a further sub heading if you wanted

At common law the **Turquand** rule (**Royal British Bank v Turquand (1856) 6 El & Bl 327**) permits the third party to assume all matters of internal management and procedure have been complied with, provided there was no knowledge/suspicion of the irregularity. So provided Soiree was unaware of the irregularity it would be protected. **CA 2006, s. 40** goes even further. Where a person deals with a company in good faith, the power of the directors to bind the company or authorize others to do so, is deemed free of any limitation under the company's constitution: **s. 40(1)**. Soiree is dealing with the company as a party to the transaction (**s. 40(2)(a)**), and under **s. 40(2)(b)** is presumed to be acting in good faith, is not bound to enquire as to any limitations on the powers of directors, and will not be regarded as in bad faith even if it knew the act was outside the limitation. Soiree will therefore be protected by **s. 40**, and the contract will be binding notwithstanding the restriction in the articles. The shareholders have the right to bring proceedings to restrain acts outside the powers of directors (**s. 40(4)**), but this will not help them as the act is completed.[5]

[5] Shows that you know the point of law, and also recognize why it won't help here

By acting without approval Caspar would breach **CA 2006, s. 171(a)**. This requires him to act in accordance with the company's constitution and is not affected by validation of the contract under **s. 40** (**s. 40(5)**). The company could therefore claim against Caspar if his breach caused loss. The shareholders could not make the directors bring proceedings as they would need a special resolution to direct the directors (**Article 4, Model Articles for Private Companies**:

Companies (Model Articles) Regulations 2008, Sch 1) and they only have 70 per cent of the shares. Neither would they be likely to get permission for a derivative claim as they are majority shareholders. However they could dismiss the directors by ordinary resolution under **CA 2006, s. 168** and appoint new directors. Whether this is advisable would depend on how concerned the shareholders are about the direction of the company, and would not change the fact that the Soiree contract is binding on Extreem Ltd.[6]

[6] This paragraph covers a lot of ground—duties, management, and remedies—but crucially links it all back to the validity of the contract

Noelle Contract

[7] If the same points arise, it is fine to refer back to previous discussion. But do remember to check that there aren't any different facts to take into account

There is no problem with the company's capacity, for the reasons given in relation to Soiree.[7] But there are problems with Feliz's authority, and his relationship to Noelle.

Feliz seems to have usual authority to enter into this contract. Although the usual authority of an individual director is fairly limited, it expands within the ambit of an executive role. The purchase of vans would arguably come within the remit of an Operations Director, and so within the scope of Feliz's usual authority and therefore, prima facie, be binding on Extreem Ltd. However, this could be a substantial property transaction[8] within **CA 2006, ss. 190–6**. Noelle is a connected person as Feliz's mother (**CA 2006, ss. 252(2)(a) and 253(2) (e)**) and the transaction is over £5,000, and probably over 10 per cent of the company's asset value. If so, it needed prior approval of the shareholders (**s. 190**), and without this the contract is voidable unless certain exceptions apply (**s. 195(2)**). Feliz's disclosure of Noelle's involvement to the other directors, would prevent a possible breach of **CA 2006, s. 177** but not **s. 190**.

[8] Remember that breach of some obligations can impact on the validity of a transaction

[9] Don't forget to cover the alternative scenario

If the restriction in the articles were in place,[9] the contract would be voidable regardless of whether the contract is a substantial property transaction. Although **s. 40** would appear to apply, where a contract's validity depends on **s. 40** but the contract is between the company and a director or connected person, the contract is voidable at the instance of the company (**s. 41(2)**) unless affirmed by the company or another exception in **s. 41(3)** applies. The shareholders should therefore be advised that in these circumstances the company could avoid this contract. Feliz would also be in breach of **s. 171(a)** for acting outside the company's constitution, as for Caspar.

Kriss Contract

Although the purchase of glasses may be outside the business of party decorations, capacity is not a problem, because of **CA 2006, s. 31** (and **s. 39** if necessary), as discussed for Soiree. Here the primary problem is one of Rudy's authority. Rudy does not appear to have actual authority, and as company secretary his usual authority is quite limited. *Panorama Developments (Guildford) Ltd v Fidelis Furnishing Fabrics Ltd* [1971] 2 QB 711 accepted a company secretary was not a 'mere clerk' and had authority to deal with the administrative side of the company's affairs, but as the contract with Kriss does not fall within 'administrative' matters, it would not be within the scope of Rudy's usual authority. However, the company will still be bound if Rudy was acting within his apparent (or ostensible) authority.

Apparent authority is authority as it appears to others, and requires a representation that the agent had authority, made by someone with actual authority to manage the business, and inducing the third party to enter into the contract (*Freeman & Lockyer v Buckhurst Park Properties (Mangal) Ltd* [1964] 2 QB 480). As a form of estoppel, apparent authority cannot be relied on if the other party knows (or should have known) of the individual's lack of actual authority, although **s. 40** offers a great deal of protection in this regard. The problem for Kriss is that the representation was by Rudy himself, so apparent authority does not arise and the contract does not bind the company. If there was apparent authority, **s. 40** would allow Kriss to rely on this notwithstanding any restriction in the articles (even if he knew of it) but it cannot operate so as to 'create' authority in these circumstances. Similarly, the rule in *Turquand's Case* cannot create authority here, as Rudy's lack of authority is not due to some internal irregularity. Accordingly, the company is not bound by this contract (although could ratify it if it chose), and Rudy may face a claim by Kriss for breach of warranty of authority.

[10] The conclusion gives you the last chance to check that you have advised explicitly on the validity of each of the contracts

Conclusion[10]

The shareholders should be aware that the Soiree contract is binding on Extreem Ltd, even if the restriction is in place. For the Noelle contract, if the restriction is in place, the contract will be voidable: **s. 41**, and may be voidable even without the restriction if this contract is a substantial property transaction (**ss. 190–6**). Both Caspar and Feliz will have breached their duty to the company under **CA 2006, s. 171(a)**. As Rudy does not have authority at all, the contract with Kriss is not binding on the company, although the shareholders can ratify it if they choose to do so.

LOOKING FOR EXTRA MARKS?

■ Recognizing links between topics shows your deeper understanding of the subject: here you can bring in relevant points from directors' duties (and even shareholder remedies and company management) at appropriate points, while keeping the focus on the validity of the contracts

■ Delve more deeply into the complexities surrounding establishing authority, for example in relation to who can make representations for the company, and the extent to which a third party can rely on apparent authority when the director is clearly acting contrary to the company's interests

QUESTION | 3

'The **Companies Act 2006** has finally removed all issues of capacity and authority for anyone entering into a contract with a company.'

Discuss.

CAUTION!

- Remember to consider both capacity and authority issues

- The statement refers to 'all issues' so you need to think about things where the Act has no effect, as well as the more obvious things that the Act addresses explicitly

- It is easy to slip into an overly descriptive approach, so make sure you comment and relate your discussion back to the question regularly. Remember markers still expect you to explain, analyse, and criticize in 'discuss' questions

DIAGRAM ANSWER PLAN

Introduction: issues in corporate contracts

▼

Capacity and ultra vires

▼

Dealing with ultra vires: s. 31 and s. 39

▼

Authority: types of authority and restrictions

▼

Dealing with authority problems: s. 40 and *Turquand's* rule

▼

Limitations: charitable companies and connected persons

▼

Conclusion: review the question

SUGGESTED ANSWER

A company as a separate legal person can enter contracts in its own right, but does so through the agency of its representatives, particularly the directors. Corporate contracts can cause problems because limitations can be imposed on the company or its agents' ability to enter into contracts, of which the third party may not be aware. Although historically the law appeared keener to protect a company's shareholders by upholding internal limitations, the need to protect third parties dealing with a company has now long been favoured. It will be seen that **Companies Act 2006 (CA 2006)** has gone a very long way in dealing with issues arising in both capacity and authority for someone dealing with a company, but has not removed absolutely all issues.[1]

[1] Linking to the question and indicating your line of argument helps both to reassure and interest the examiner

Capacity Issues

CA 2006 has almost entirely removed issues of capacity within corporate contracting, with more success than previous reforms, although not quite laying 'to rest the corpse of the ultra vires doctrine'[2] (Milman, 'Company contracts: a review of the current and restated law' (2008) 240 Co LN 1). The ultra vires doctrine held that contracts outside a company's objects were void: *Ashbury Railway Carriage & Iron Co v Riche* (1875) LR 7 HL 653. Although designed to uphold the constitution and protect shareholders, the doctrine could cause hardship to the company as well as to the third party. Its effect was mitigated by company draftsmen creating long, essentially meaningless, objects clauses and including 'independent objects' clauses (*Cotman v Brougham* [1918] AC 514) and subjective objects clauses (*Bell Houses Ltd v City Wall Properties Ltd* [1966] 1 QB 207). Even so, contracts could occasionally fall foul of the doctrine (eg *Re Introductions Ltd* [1970] Ch 199). In *Rolled Steel Products (Holdings) Ltd v British Steel Corpn* [1986] Ch 246, the courts took a more pragmatic approach to such issues than in *Re Introductions Ltd*, but this could not entirely remove capacity as a potential threat to a corporate contract.[3]

[2] Making use of a memorable phrase can add a spark to your work, as well as gaining credit for using your wider reading

[3] This paragraph packs in a lot of information as a compromise between getting straight to CA 2006 (which would be focused but miss the context) and telling the examiner everything about ultra vires (which would show lots of knowledge but not be sufficiently focused)

Statutory attempts at reform prior to **CA 2006** (particularly **Companies Act 1989**, amending **Companies Act 1985 (CA 1985)**), went some way towards removing issues related to capacity, but the provisions were not entirely clear, nor fully effective. For example[4] **CA 1985, s. 3A**, designed to stop long objects clauses, simply had the effect of adding an additional clause (as predicted by Ferran, 'The reform of the law on corporate capacity and directors' and officers' authority Part 2' (1992) 13 Co Law 177).

[4] Rather than spend a lot of time detailing the problems with the earlier provisions, an example suffices

The position is significantly clearer after **CA 2006**, which takes a different approach. Following a recommendation of the Company

Law Review (Final Report), companies now have unrestricted capacity unless they specifically restrict their objects (**CA 2006, s. 31**). So most new companies (and existing companies which alter their articles) will have no restriction on capacity. Where a company does have objects and acts outside them, the contract is saved by **CA 2006, s. 39** (a modified version of **CA 1985, s. 35**), which prevents any person calling the validity of the company's act into question on the ground of lack of capacity by reason of anything in the company's constitution. Accordingly all issues in this area have been removed as far as third parties are concerned (a couple of exceptions will be considered later).[5] Internally a director acting outside restricted objects will remain liable to the company for breach of **CA 2006, s. 171(a)** but this does not affect the contract.

[5] You could instead deal with the exceptions at this point, and then again (referring back) when looking at authority

Authority Issues

A crucial issue for the validity of corporate contracts is the authority of the person acting for the company. The board of directors is given all the powers of the company (Article 3, Model Articles for Private Companies: **Companies (Model Articles) Regulations 2008, Sch 1**), but companies often act through individual directors or other agents, rather than through the board. A contract only binds a principal if the agent is acting within the scope of his authority, so whether an individual has authority is very important.

As observed in *First Energy (UK) Ltd v Hungarian International Bank Ltd* **[1993] BCLC 1409**, the court has to strike a balance between two conflicting commercial considerations: (i) a contracting party cannot be expected to know all internal procedures to be sure they are dealing with a fully authorized agent, and (ii) a contracting party cannot simply rely on any person purporting to represent the company.

[6] Recognizes that statute is not concerned with all issues of authority

At the basic level of determining authority, statute has had little impact,[6] and normal agency rules governing authority (as applied in company law cases such as *Freeman & Lockyer v Buckhurst Park Properties (Mangal) Ltd* **[1964] 2 QB 480**) remain relevant. Accordingly not everyone purporting to act for a company will be found to have authority, although in many cases apparent authority will be found either through a direct or indirect representation of authority. Where the nature of the transaction is itself suspicious though, a court is unlikely to find apparent authority (*Re Capitol Films Ltd* **[2010] EWHC 2240**) with cases moving towards considering the third party's 'honest belief' (*Quinn v CC Automotive Group Ltd* **[2010] EWCA Civ 1412**, endorsing *Thanakharn v Akai Holdings Ltd* **[2011] HKLC 357**). Statute's main involvement is to protect a third party where authority appears to be present, but in fact was restricted by some constitutional limitation. This is dealt with by **CA 2006, s. 40**.

Section 40 is a modified version of CA 1985, s. 35A, clarifying some aspects of the former provision. This provides that in favour of a person dealing with a company in good faith, the powers of the directors to bind the company or authorize others to do so are deemed free of any constitutional limitation.[7] Dealing with a company is widely defined (s. 40(2)(a)), although it won't include 'inside' transactions such as a bonus issue of shares: *EIC Services Ltd v Phipps* [2004] 2 BCLC 589. 'Good faith' is also generously defined: it is presumed, it is not lost simply through knowledge of the limitation, and the third party is under no obligation to make enquiries of any limitations (s. 40(2)(b)).

[7] There isn't much choice here but to pretty much repeat the words of the section

Before statutory reform, those dealing with a company could rely on the rule in *Royal British Bank v Turquand* (1856) 6 El & Bl 327, but this is limited to matters of internal procedure, and cannot be relied on where an individual has notice of an irregularity: *B. Liggett (Liverpool) Ltd v Barclays Bank Ltd* [1928] 1 KB 48. Section 40 is obviously wider as knowledge of an irregularity does not prevent a person being in good faith. Furthermore, the minor redrafting in CA 2006 is believed to have dealt with the few remaining interpretational concerns about CA 1985, s. 35A relating to restrictions on individuals, and inquorate boards, which had caused problems in *Smith v Henniker-Major & Co* [2002] 2 BCLC 655.[8] Accordingly, while CA 2006 hasn't dealt with all authority issues, those dealing with the company in good faith (which will be most people) will be protected from constitutional limitations on that authority. Shareholders could seek to restrain an act outside directors' powers (s. 40(4)) but this right is rarely, if ever, exercised as shareholders are usually unaware of the issue until after the company is bound. Directors remain liable for breach of duty for exceeding their powers under s. 171(a) (s. 40(5)).

[8] You could expand on this if you have time and have covered it on your course

Limitations on Operation of ss. 39–40

Sections 41–42 cover some specific exceptions to ss. 39–40. Section 42 limits the operation of ss. 39–40 for charitable companies so they apply only in favour of a person who does not know they are dealing with a charity, or who gives full consideration and doesn't know the act is outside the objects or directors' powers.

Section 41 restricts the protection of s. 40 when the party to the contract is a director or connected person under ss. 252–6. In such cases the contract is voidable (s. 41(2)) unless restitution is no longer possible, the company has been indemnified for any losses, rights acquired by a non-party would be affected, or the company affirms the transaction (s. 41(4)). The loss of protection under ss. 39–40 is justified because directors and connected persons will, or should, be aware of any internal restrictions.[9]

[9] This provides a bit of comment to an otherwise rather descriptive part of the essay

Conclusion

For a person entering into a contract with a company (other than charitable companies), **CA 2006** has finally, after decades of reform attempts, removed all issues of capacity. While the director will have breached their duty to the company, this need not concern the other party. **CA 2006** has not removed all issues of authority, but the combination of agency principles and **s. 40** work together to protect most contracting parties. Those who are not protected will be those who should not have assumed the authority of the person acting, and/or who are acting in bad faith, and/or are a director or connected person. It can be argued that in these cases the company is more deserving of protection than they are.

LOOKING FOR EXTRA MARKS

- Explore the overlap between the *Turquand* rule and apparent authority and the changing focus of the courts in this area

- The developing jurisprudence on when a third party is entitled to rely on apparent authority is an interesting point that could be examined further

QUESTION | 4

'The attribution of liability for torts or crimes to a company has caused great difficulties for the courts and Parliament but the position is gradually becoming a little clearer.'

Discuss.

CAUTION!

- Read the question carefully to pick up on all the points—both torts and crimes, both the courts and Parliament

- Be prepared to comment on the legal position and approaches as well as describing and explaining them

- You need to assess whether, and how, the legal position is getting clearer in order to address the question fully

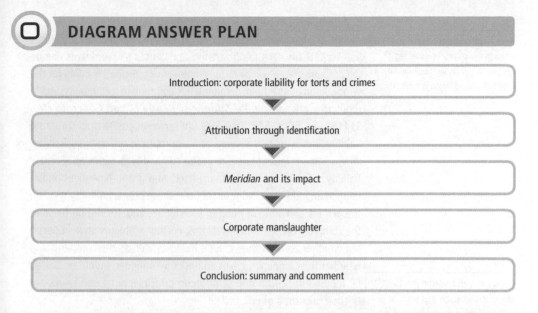

DIAGRAM ANSWER PLAN

Introduction: corporate liability for torts and crimes

▼

Attribution through identification

▼

Meridian and its impact

▼

Corporate manslaughter

▼

Conclusion: summary and comment

 SUGGESTED ANSWER

As a legal person a company can be liable for torts and crimes in its own right. However, a company is not a natural person so must act through others—its directors and agents. It is the acts of these individuals that are examined to determine what a company did, knew, etc and so attribute liability to a company.

[1] The introduction follows the classic approach of briefly setting the scene for the topic, and then explaining what will be considered

In addressing the statement, this essay will[1] examine how liability attaches to a company, considering the difficult issue of whose acts and states of mind can be attributed to the company and in what circumstances. This will involve consideration of different approaches, particularly the identification doctrine, the *Meridian* principles (*Meridian Global Funds Management Asia Ltd v Securities Commission* [1995] 2 AC 500), and statutory developments particularly the **Corporate Manslaughter and Corporate Homicide Act 2007 (CMCHA 2007)**.

Liability in Tort and Crime

Campbell v Paddington Corporation **[1911] 1 KB 869** established that a company could be liable for its own wrongs, rejecting the argument that tortious acts were ultra vires the company. Companies could even be liable for crimes requiring mens rea: *R v ICR Haulage Ltd* **[1944] KB 551**; *DPP v Kent & Sussex Contractors Co Ltd* **[1944] KB 146**. Accordingly, a company can in principle be liable for any tort or crime, except where it cannot commit the wrong (eg bigamy), or cannot be subject to the penalty (murder).[2]

[2] This makes the point implicitly that a company cannot be treated in all respects as the same as a natural person

A company can be made liable primarily (liable for its own wrongdoing) or vicariously (liable 'as if' it were a wrongdoer). Vicarious liability is relatively straightforward and causes few problems unique to companies[3]—a company (as employer or principal) is liable for the wrongdoing of its employee/agent. It is common in tort liability, and in regulatory offences, eg *Re Supply of Ready Mixed Concrete (No. 2)* [1995] 1 BCLC 613. This does not however create truly corporate liability, and is usually viewed as inappropriate for criminal liability, where some level of blame, or moral culpability, is expected. Primary liability is liability of the company itself, and is not dependent on liability of an individual. Nonetheless corporate primary liability rests on the actions and state of mind of individuals, and attributing these to the company causes some problems. Further problems arise in deciding whether an individual can be liable as well as the company, and whether the company's claim against a wrongdoer should be barred by the *ex turpi causa non oritur actio* principle, but these issues are outside the scope of this essay.[4]

[3] For a company law course you wouldn't normally be expected to go into detail on vicarious liability; a very brief explanation is sufficient

[4] You can use this technique to let the examiner know that you are aware of other related issues, even though the question doesn't explicitly direct you into them

Identification

The identification doctrine or 'alter ego' approach attributes liability through the company's 'directing mind and will': *Lennard's Carrying Co Ltd v Asiatic Petroleum Co Ltd* [1915] AC 705 (*Lennard's*). The court finds someone, sufficiently high up the corporate hierarchy, who can be identified with the company, in whom the various elements of the wrong can be found. In *R v Andrews-Weatherfall Ltd* [1972] 1 WLR 118 Eveleigh J said that the person (or persons) must have 'the status and authority' which makes their acts the acts of the company. In *HL Bolton (Engineering) Ltd v TJ Graham & Sons Ltd* [1957] 1 QB 159, Lord Denning likened a company to a 'human body', with a controlling 'brain and nerve centre', and 'hands which hold the tools' and follow instructions—only the former (the directors and managers) could be viewed as the 'directing mind and will' of a company. This 'anthropomorphic' attitude was explicitly criticized in *Meridian* as well as by many writers[5] (eg Ferran, 'Corporate attribution and the directing mind and will' (2011) 127 LQR 239).

[5] You need to be aware of Denning's memorable analogy in *HL Bolton*, but it is only right to recognize that it has not been met with universal enthusiasm

The identification approach has limitations. One obvious problem lies in identifying someone who is the directing mind and will of a company. This may depend on the wrong in question (*R v ICR Haulage Ltd; HL Bolton (Engineering) Ltd v TJ Graham & Sons Ltd*, although this was doubted in *Tesco Supermarkets Ltd v Nattrass* [1971] 2 All ER 127). Unless a 'directing mind and will' can be identified, a company will avoid liability under this doctrine. In *Tesco Supermarkets Ltd v Nattrass*, a branch manager was not identified with the company and so was 'another person', which allowed the company to avoid liability for misleading pricing.

A connected problem is what to do when individual elements of the wrong are made out, but are not located within a single individual. This caused particular problems in the area of manslaughter. The courts accepted that a company could in principle be liable for manslaughter (*R v HM Coroners for East Kent, ex p Spooner* **(1987) 3 BCC 636**) but this depended on identifying the company with an individual guilty of the crime. The courts rejected the option of aggregating the acts and states of mind of various individuals to found liability. Consequently no corporate liability resulted from the ferry disaster in Zeebrugge (*R v P&O Ferries (Dover) Ltd* **(1991) 93 Cr App Rep 72** (*P&O Ferries*)) despite the company being 'infected with the disease of sloppiness'[6] from top to bottom (Department of Transport, *MV Herald of Free Enterprise: Report No. 8074* (1987)).

[6] A particularly telling finding that highlights the corporate (and not just individual) failings

Under the identification doctrine, liability becomes harder to establish the larger and more complex a company becomes. As in *P&O Ferries*, liability could not be established in the Southall rail crash (*A-G's Reference (No. 2 of 1999)* [2000] QB 796). In contrast, corporate liability was established in relation to the Lyme Bay canoeing accident in *R v Kite and OLL Ltd*, Independent, 9 December 1994, where the company was small.

The Meridian Approach

In *Meridian*, the Privy Council appeared to signal a move away from the identification doctrine. In what the Supreme Court in *Singularis Holdings Ltd v Daiwa Capital Markets Europe Ltd* [2019] UKSC 50 described as the 'classic exposition' of when acts and intentions will be treated as those of the company, Lord Hoffmann identified three types of attribution rules:[7] (i) primary rules of attribution (generally found in the company's constitution); (ii) general rules of attribution that are also applicable outside companies (such as agency and vicarious liability); and (iii) special rules of attribution, which are (exceptionally) fashioned by the courts to deal with laws that exclude attribution through the primary or general rules of attribution. The starting point is therefore an examination of the purpose or policy of the rule in question, using this to determine whose acts or state of mind should be relevant. Lord Hoffmann explained the *Lennard's* approach as based on the language and purpose of the provision in question, indicating the 'directing mind and will' test should be viewed as a special rule of attribution based on the particular rule, rather than an all-encompassing approach to liability.

[7] You should be able to explain the three types of attribution rules from *Meridian*

At first sight *Meridian* seemed to make significant inroads into the identification doctrine, and knowledge lower down the corporate hierarchy has been held sufficient for particular charges: *Morris v Bank of India* [2005] EWCA Civ 693; *Meridian*. Nonetheless, the 'directing mind and will' rule still applies in most cases, at least for criminal offences involving mens rea as seen in *A-G's Reference*

(No. 2 of 1999) [2000] QB 796, and *R v St Regis Paper Company Ltd* [2012] 1 Cr App R 14, where the Court of Appeal applied the principle and rejected any alternative special rule of attribution.

Attribution and Corporate Manslaughter

[8] There is a lot of academic writing surrounding CMCHA 2007. Try to bring a little of this in, even in a general essay like this one where you have to be brief. If the question was just on corporate manslaughter you should engage more deeply with a selection of materials

Parliament took a different approach to attribution in **CMCHA 2007**,[8] following disquiet over failures to secure manslaughter convictions against large companies. **CMCHA 2007** moves away from identification. Instead it looks at the way in which the company's activities are managed or organized (**s. 1(1)**), allowing the courts to consider multiple individuals and the corporate culture. The involvement of 'senior management' must still be a substantial element (**s. 1(3)**) which has been criticized for retaining significant focus on people rather than truly 'corporate' liability (Price, 'Finding fault in organisations—reconceptualising the role of senior managers in corporate manslaughter' (2015) 35 LS 385). **CMCHA 2007** was used in *R v Cotswold Geotechnical Holdings Ltd* [2011] EWCA Crim 1337, finding the company guilty where there was a gross breach of duty through a demonstrably unsafe system of work, but liability would probably have resulted under the 'directing mind and will' test in any event.

Conclusion

Attributing criminal and tortious liability to a company causes difficulties because of complex interactions of human actors and the company as a separate entity. The courts tend to require an embodiment of the company, and although *Meridian* offers some flexibility, the directing mind and will test still dominates. While Parliament has finally created a uniquely corporate form of liability in **CMCHA 2007**, this is limited to corporate manslaughter, and its impact is questionable. Elsewhere Parliament has sought to deal specifically with corporate liability in other ways, for example the 'failure to prevent' model under **Bribery Act 2010** gives 'grounds for cautious optimism': Copp & Cronin, 'New models of corporate criminality' (2018) 39 Co Law

[9] Links back to the words of the question

104. While the courts and Parliament have gradually made some areas of the law clearer,[9] much remains to be done.

LOOKING FOR EXTRA MARKS?

■ There is a lot of academic work in this area, from a variety of perspectives: engage further with this to add depth and strengthen your analysis

■ You could raise connected issues such as individual liability and operation of the *ex turpi causa non oritur actio* principle (see *Jetivia SA v Bilta (UK) Ltd* [2015] UKSC 23 and *Singularis Holdings Ltd v Daiwa Capital Markets Europe Ltd* [2019] UKSC 50) in this question (if covered by your course) to show your grasp of the bigger picture

TAKING THINGS FURTHER

■ Copp, S. and Cronin, A., 'New models of corporate criminality: the development and relative effectiveness of "failure to prevent" offences' (2018) 39 Co Law 104

Explores the introduction and growth of new legislative approaches to corporate criminal liability, particularly the 'failure to prevent' model used in the Bribery Act 2010 which 'blurs the line with regulatory offences'. Focuses on 'economic crime' rather than criminal liability more generally.

■ Ferran, E., 'The reform of the law on corporate capacity and directors' and officers' authority: Parts 1 and 2' (1992) 13 Co Law 124 and 177

Critique of the 'technically defective' statutory reform brought in by Companies Act 1989 (in particular CA 1985, ss. 35–35A) aimed at problems of capacity and authority. Useful to compare with the approach of CA 2006 and to understand some of the reasons behind further reform.

■ Ferran, E., 'Corporate attribution and the directing mind and will' (2011) 127 LQR 239

Revisits Meridian, *questioning its long-term impact on attribution in UK law. Also helpful in highlighting the views of other leading writers. (Note: discussion of* Stone & Rolls Ltd v Moore Stephens *[2009] UKHL 39 should be read in the light of the recent critical view of the case in* Jetivia SA v Bilta (UK) Ltd *[2015] UKSC 23.)*

■ Field, S. and Jones, L., 'Death in the workplace: who pays the price?' (2011) 32 Co Law 166

Provides a summary of the pre- and post-CMCHA 2007 position and looks at sentencing for corporate manslaughter and health and safety offences causing death. See also Field, S. and Jones, L., 'The Corporate Manslaughter and Corporate Homicide Act 2007 and the sentencing guidelines for corporate manslaughter: more bark than bite?'(2015) 36 Co Law 327 that challenges a 'somewhat timid prosecutorial policy' and penalties which 'lack bite'.

■ Gobert, J., 'The Corporate Manslaughter and Corporate Homicide Act 2007—thirteen years in the making but was it worth the wait?' (2008) 71 MLR 413

An in-depth critical view of CMCHA 2007. Describes the Act as 'limited in its vision and lacking in imagination', not least for its failure to deal with corporate criminality more generally.

■ Griffiths, A., 'Agents without principals: pre-incorporation contracts and section 36C of the Companies Act 1985' (1993) 13 LS 241

A helpful consideration of pre-incorporation contracts, explaining the background and issues and identifying ongoing problems. Appeals for a more purposive interpretation and for inclusion of a ratification procedure. See also Savirimuthu, J., 'Pre-incorporation contracts and the problem of corporate fundamentalism: are promoters proverbially profuse?' (2003) 24 Co Law 196 for a re-evaluation of earlier cases.

■ Law Commission, 'Legislating the Criminal Code: Involuntary Manslaughter' (1996) Law Com No. 237. See also Law Commission, 'Criminal liability in regulatory contexts' (2010) Consultation Paper No. 195

■ Milman, D., 'Company contracts: a review of the current and restated law' (2008) 240 Co LN 1

A brief review of the law on corporate contracts and pre-incorporation contracts at the time CA 2006 came into force, summarizing the issues and highlighting the problems.

■ Ormerod, D. and Taylor, R., 'The Corporate Manslaughter and Corporate Homicide Act 2007' (2008) 8 Crim LR 589

A helpful critique of CMCHA 2007, explaining its origins and approach. While welcoming the Act, it raises the question of whether it might prove in practice to be 'little more than a symbolic statement about corporate responsibility'.

■ Price, L., 'Finding fault in organisations—reconceptualising the role of senior managers in corporate manslaughter' (2015) 35 LS 385

An interesting exploration of whether corporate manslaughter is a truly corporate or organizational crime, assessing in particular the emphasis on involvement of senior management in the offence under CMCHA 2007. Advocates an approach based on senior managers' role in corporate systems of work.

■ Sullivan, G. R., 'The attribution of culpability to limited companies' [1996] 55 CLJ 515

A classic article examining the principles of corporate criminal liability in depth. Considers Meridian, and the Law Commission proposals for a 'corporate killing' offence (pre-dating CMCHA 2007) arguing that corporate liability cannot be dissociated from culpability of individuals. See also Wickins, R. and Ong, C. A., 'Confusion worse confounded: the end of the directing mind theory?' [1997] JBL 524.

■ Worthington, S., 'Corporate attribution and agency: back to basics' (2017) 133 LQR 118

Offers thoughtful consideration of many issues relating to corporate attribution, actual authority, and ostensible authority, reflecting on the importance of paying careful attention to separate corporate personality.

Online Resources　　　　　　　　　www.oup.com/uk/qanda/

For extra essay and problem questions on this topic, as well as advice on revision and exam technique, please visit the online resources.

Share Capital

9

ARE YOU READY?

In order to attempt the questions in this chapter you will need to have covered the following topics:

- Share capital
- Capital maintenance: principle and purpose
- Issue of shares at a discount
- Issue of shares at a premium
- Reduction of capital
- Purchase of company's own shares
- Redemption of shares
- Distributions/dividends
- Financial assistance
- Connections (in particular) with: shares and shareholders, directors' duties, loan capital

 KEY DEBATES

Debate: the continuing relevance of the capital maintenance doctrine

Although the capital maintenance doctrine is well established, it has many critics, both of the doctrine itself, and of the way in which the current law upholds the doctrine. The legislative framework is complex and, for many, overly restrictive, but to a great extent driven by European requirements in relation to public companies. For a deeper consideration of the law in this area than offered by most textbooks, see Ferran, E. and Ho, L. C., *Company Law and Corporate Finance* (2nd edn, Oxford, 2014).

Q **QUESTION** | **1**

In May, Kapital plc issued 10,000 £1 shares to Athena in consideration for the transfer of a piece of land to the company. Prior to this the company had instructed the local estate agent to value the land for them (he placed a value of £15,000 on the land) and they notified Athena of this valuation. In a separate arrangement, Kapital plc issued 2,000 £1 shares to Cayenne for £1,000. Cayenne has since given the shares to her daughter, Suva.

In June, Kapital plc was contacted by Dublin, an elderly shareholder who wanted to give his 500 £1 shares back to the company rather than leave them to his children. The directors felt it was unfair to take the shares without payment so the company paid Dublin £500 for the shares.

In July, the directors of Kapital plc learned that a debt of £20,000 owed by Hamilton to the company is unlikely to be paid. They wish to cancel £20,000 of the company's capital to take account of this bad debt.

Advise Kapital plc in respect of all of these matters. How, if at all, would your advice differ if it was a private limited company?

! **CAUTION!**

- This question covers aspects of both raising and maintaining capital
- Here the company is a public limited company so advise accordingly. However you are also specifically told to consider if the advice would change if it was a private company so don't forget to do this
- Deal with each scenario separately, rather than discussing capital maintenance in general terms
- There is lots of statutory material to deal with; remember to apply it, don't just copy it out

▢ **DIAGRAM ANSWER PLAN**

Identify the issues	■ Identify the issues arising in each scenario
Relevant law	■ Capital maintenance: raising and maintaining capital ■ Issue for non-cash consideration: ss. 593–09 ■ Issue at a discount: ss. 580, 588, 590 ■ Purchase of a company's own shares: ss. 658–69 ■ Reduction of capital: ss. 641–53 ■ Minimum capital requirements ■ Differences between public and private companies
Apply the law	■ Apply the relevant law to the different scenarios ■ Consider different application according to whether company private or public
Conclude	■ Conclude on each point

This question raises issues of law that have their origins in the capital maintenance doctrine. The capital maintenance doctrine requires a company to raise and maintain its share capital (ie not return it to shareholders), on the basis that creditors must rely on the company's assets as the liability of members is limited (*Trevor v Whitworth* **(1887) 12 App Cas 409**). Although common law in origin, the current law is mostly statutory and found in the **Companies Act 2006 (CA 2006)** which regulates public companies (such as Kapital plc) much more stringently than private companies.[1] Each scenario will be examined in turn to advise Kapital plc, before considering whether the position would be different if the company was a private company.

[1] Show briefly that you understand the origins of the law, and that you've recognized what law applies to Kapital

Athena

[2] The requirement for subscribers to the memorandum of a public company to pay in cash (s. 584) is omitted as not relevant on the facts; the examiner won't expect comment on it

Companies can issue shares for money or money's worth (**CA 2006, s. 582**).[2] Public companies are not however entirely free to issue shares other than for cash, and face various restrictions. The applicable provisions here are **ss. 593–7** which establish detailed rules for valuing non-cash consideration, and it appears that Kapital plc has breached these.

Under **CA 2006, s. 593** a public company can only issue shares other than for cash if an independent valuation report is made in compliance with the statute. The report must be made to the company in the six months immediately preceding the allotment of the shares and a copy of the report sent to the allottee, ie Athena[3] (**s. 593**). A copy must also be sent to the registrar (**s. 597**). The report must be by an independent valuer (**s. 596(1); ss. 1150–3**) and the report must contain the details set out in **s. 596(2)**, including the value of the shares, a description of the consideration, and the method and date of valuation. Although here a valuation has been obtained (and it will be assumed is within the six-month timeframe), there is no suggestion that a full report has been completed, nor does a 'local estate agent' appear to be an independent valuer within **s. 1150**.[4] Neither is there any evidence the valuation report (if there was one) has been sent to Athena—merely informing her of the valuation would not comply with **s. 593**.

[3] Adding in Athena's name indicates you know what the provision actually means and aren't just reciting the section

[4] Don't assume an 'expert' would fall within the definition of an independent valuer

If, as seems to be the case, **s. 593(1)** has been breached, the company, and any officers in default, will commit an offence and be liable for a fine (**s. 607**). Athena will be liable to pay the company the aggregate amount of the nominal value of the shares, the whole of the premium, and interest at the appropriate rate: **s. 593(3)**; even if she didn't know the payment was in contravention of the rules (*System Controls plc v Munro Corporate plc* **[1990] BCLC 659**). Athena could apply to the court for relief from liability under **s. 606** which gives the court discretion to exempt her from liability in whole or in part if it is 'just and equitable' to do so. The court will take into account whether the company has actually received value for the shares (**s. 606(4)**; *Re Bradford Investments plc (No. 2)* **[1991] BCLC 688**).

[5] You can't do more than speculate on the value of the shares, but as you are given some figures, you can at least indicate a possible outcome

If the valuation of £15,000 is correct, and Athena's shares are not carrying a significant premium,[5] then it appears the company has received full value and she may well be granted relief (as in *Re Ossory Estates plc* **[1988] BCLC 213**, where the consideration had already been sold by the company for more than the value of the shares).

Cayenne

In issuing 2,000 shares to Cayenne for only £1,000, Kapital plc has issued the shares at a discount to their nominal value, which is prohibited. The prohibition was established in *Ooregum Gold Mining Co of India v Roper* **[1892] AC 125**, which held that a company could not issue shares at a discount, even though the market price had dropped below the nominal value. The prohibition is now in **CA 2006, s. 580(1)**. As Kapital plc has breached **s. 580(1)**, Cayenne is liable to pay the company the amount of the discount (ie £1,000) with interest (**s. 580(2)**).

[6] Don't forget the subsequent holder of the shares is also potentially liable

Furthermore, under **s. 588**, Suva will be jointly and severally liable with Cayenne, as Suva is a subsequent holder of the shares who is not a purchaser for value without notice.[6] Kapital plc and its officers in default have also committed an offence and are liable to a fine (**s. 590**).

Dublin

Trevor v Whitworth established that a company must not purchase its own shares. **CA 2006, s. 658** now prohibits a company from acquiring its own shares other than in accordance with the statute. Had Kapital plc simply accepted the shares as a gift, this would have been lawful, as acquisition other than for valuable consideration is permitted (**s. 659(1)**). **CA 2006, s. 690(1)** does give companies the power to purchase their own shares, but only by following the

[7] It can be helpful to find ways of summarizing these points, as you don't have space to set them out in detail

complex statutory procedure in **ss. 690–708**.[7] This permits either a market purchase (on a recognized investment exchange) or an off-market purchase (**s. 693**). The former requires an ordinary resolution setting boundaries for the proposed purchase (number of shares, price, time, etc), while the latter requires a special resolution approving the terms of the purchase contract. As a public company the purchase can only be funded out of distributable profits or the proceeds of a fresh issue of shares (**s. 692(2)**). As it appears Kapital plc has not complied with **ss. 690–708**, the purchase is in breach of **s. 658** and so void (**s. 658(2)(b)**). Furthermore the company and any officer in default commit an offence, and are liable to a fine/imprisonment (**s. 658(2)–(3)**).

Hamilton

The capital maintenance doctrine prohibits the reduction of capital by a company, other than in accordance with the statutory framework (*Trevor v Whitworth*). Under **s. 641(1)(b)** a public company may reduce its capital by special resolution confirmed by the court. A company can reduce its capital in any way, and **s. 641(4)(b)(i)** states a company can cancel any paid-up share capital that is lost or unrepresented by available assets. To obtain the court's confirmation Kapital plc may need to settle a list of creditors (**ss. 645–7**), and the court may also consider whether the reduction is fair as between the members, applying 'broad standards of fairness, reasonableness and equity' (*Scottish Insurance Corp v Wilsons & Clyde Coal Co Ltd* **[1949] AC 462**). Assuming the court confirms the reduction, it takes effect only when the order is registered. If the reduction takes Kapital plc's capital below the authorized minimum of £50,000 (**s. 763**), the company would normally need to be re-registered as a private company[8] using an expedited procedure under **s. 651** before the registrar can register the order.

[8] A minor issue but it does show appreciation of a point that only applies because Kapital is a public company

[9] You could just as effectively deal with the 'what if' points as you go along (ie after each scenario)

Differences for Private Limited Company[9]

If Kapital was a private company, the issue to Athena would be lawful. Despite the opportunity it provides for avoiding the prohibition on issue at a discount, the courts have declined to question the value placed by a company on non-cash consideration provided it is not dishonest or 'colourable' (*Re Wragg Ltd* **[1897] 1 Ch 796**). So provided there is no evidence of fraud and the consideration is not illusory (*Hong Kong and China Gas Co Ltd v Glen* **[1914] 1 Ch 527**)—and neither appears to be the case here—the issue will be lawful and there will be no legal consequences for Athena, Kapital Ltd, or the directors.

The position with regard to the issue at a discount to Cayenne would be unchanged: the prohibition and consequences apply equally to public and private companies.

The purchase of Dublin's shares would still only be lawful if in accordance with the statute (as the general prohibition on the acquisition of a company's own shares in **s. 658** applies to both public and private companies). As a private company, the purchase would have to be an off-market purchase, but the company would have more freedom in funding the purchase as **s. 692(1ZA)** allows private companies to make payment out of capital up to (the lower of) £15,000 or 5 per cent of the paid-up share capital.

As a private company Kapital Ltd need not go to the time and expense of court confirmation in order to reduce its capital (to reflect the Hamilton bad debt). Under **s. 641(1)(a)** a private company can reduce its capital by special resolution supported by a solvency statement. This must be in accordance with **s. 643** and made no more than 15 days before the resolution (**s. 642**). The resolution, a copy of the solvency statement, and a statement of capital must be sent to the Registrar within 15 days of the resolution.

[10] As the essay concludes on each point as it comes, there isn't much to finish off the essay with—a final comment can help to complete the picture though

Overall, it can be seen[10] that the statutory requirements would be significantly less onerous if Kapital was a private company, but most of the scenarios would still be subject to some regulation.

LOOKING FOR EXTRA MARKS?

■ Even if you want to be really thorough, avoid working through provisions subsection by subsection, as this can look as if you are reading through your statute book rather than applying law you already know. Instead, select particularly pertinent aspects of the provisions to slot in at appropriate points

■ You could add some brief comment and critique about the justifications behind various provisions, or explore further the reasons for difference in approach between public and private companies

QUESTION | 2

'Paid-up capital may be diminished or lost in the course of a company's trading; that is a result which no legislation can prevent; but persons who deal with, and give credit to, a limited company, naturally rely upon the fact that the company is trading with a certain amount of capital already paid, as well as upon the responsibility of its members for the capital remaining at call; and they are entitled to assume that no part of the capital which has been paid into the coffers of the company has been subsequently paid out, except in the legitimate course of its business.'

(Lord Watson, ***Trevor v Whitworth*** (1887) 12 App Cas 409 at 423)

Critically discuss the extent to which this statement accurately reflects the present law.

CAUTION!

■ The statement isn't just about the requirements of the capital maintenance doctrine, but about the justifications behind it. So to discuss this 'critically', you need to assess the value of the capital maintenance principle more generally as well as reviewing the present law relating to capital maintenance

■ Best to avoid discussion of the rules of raising capital—it isn't directly covered by the question and you would rapidly run out of time

DIAGRAM ANSWER PLAN

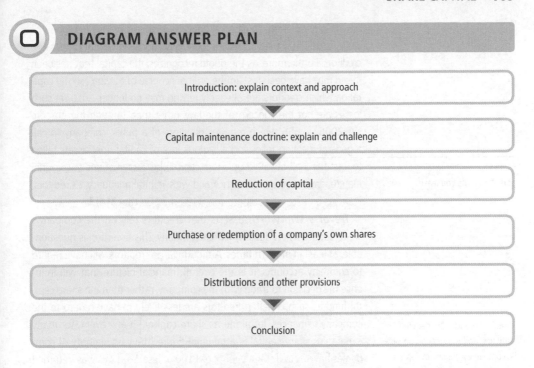

Introduction: explain context and approach

Capital maintenance doctrine: explain and challenge

Reduction of capital

Purchase or redemption of a company's own shares

Distributions and other provisions

Conclusion

A SUGGESTED ANSWER

The capital maintenance doctrine requires share capital raised by the company to be 'maintained', meaning it must not be returned to shareholders, rather than kept intact. In order to address the question, the doctrine and its justifications will be examined. Then the circumstances in which the law (currently in **Companies Act 2006 (CA 2006)**) allows capital to be returned to shareholders will be considered to evaluate how far the statement reflects the present law.[1]

[1] Use the introduction to explain what you are going to do, and why it relates to the question

Capital Maintenance

The quote justifies the capital maintenance doctrine by saying that creditors dealing with the company rely on the company's capital. A similar point was made in *Re Exchange Banking Co, Flitcroft's Case* (1882) **21 Ch D 519**: a creditor can only rely on the assets of the business, and gives credit in faith that the capital will be applied only for the purposes of the business and not returned to shareholders. But the justification in the quote can be questioned on several grounds.

At the time of *Trevor v Whitworth* (1887) **12 App Cas 409** it was common for companies to have shares of high nominal value, issued partly paid. The quote reflects this in referring to members' responsibility for capital remaining at call.[2] Accordingly, there would commonly be a fund (the amount remaining unpaid on the shares) that could be called on from shareholders on the company's insolvency. But the position

[2] This shows you have thought about the content of the quote

now is very different. Most companies have shares of very low nominal value, issued fully paid, meaning there is no uncalled capital to reassure creditors. Furthermore, as the quote recognizes, the capital that has been raised may have been lost 'in the ordinary course of trading', so the capital on which creditors are allegedly relying may no longer exist. Yet such losses are not the concern of the law, other than through the obscure **CA 2006, s. 656** which requires directors of a public company to call a general meeting following a 'serious loss of capital' (net assets fallen to less than half of called-up share capital). As Ferran points out, capital maintenance rules are not concerned with 'capital adequacy' ('Creditors' interests and "core" company law' (1999) 20 Co Law 314).[3]

[3] Use your further reading to support the points you make

Trevor v Whitworth asserts that creditors rely on the company's share capital when dealing with a company. This assertion is questionable, at least in modern times. Although large creditors will have regard to company accounts, it is the overall financial picture that will influence the decision to trade with the company, rather than the share capital fund as such. Smaller creditors are less likely to have regard to the company's finances, let alone its share capital. In any event, for many companies share capital is a minimal figure (the vast majority of companies have issued share capital of £100 or less)[4]—if this was 'returned to shareholders' it would make very little difference to creditors.

[4] You could add more detailed statistics, and information on public companies' minimum capital requirements here if you wanted

The assumptions in *Trevor v Whitworth* underlying capital maintenance are thus questionable. Despite this, a great deal of law puts a great deal of effort into upholding the principle. While the present law makes some inroads into the doctrine, companies still usually need to jump through hoops before doing anything that might return capital to shareholders. These circumstances will now be examined.

Reduction of Capital

The capital maintenance doctrine only prohibits reduction of capital other than as permitted by statute. Statute makes provision (**CA 2006, s. 641–9**) for a company lawfully to reduce its capital. This can be done in any way (**s. 641(3)**) but in particular a company can (a) extinguish or reduce liability on shares in respect of unpaid capital, (b) cancel paid-up capital that is lost or unrepresented by assets, or (c) repay paid-up capital in excess of the company's wants (**s. 641(4)**). It can be seen that (b) simply restores reality to the share capital figure and causes no (further) damage to creditors' interests, and (c) will not harm creditors as the company has more money than it needs. While (a) potentially removes a valuable fund for creditors, the statutory procedure ensures this will not be done when creditors might be at risk.[5] This procedure allows private companies to reduce capital through a special resolution supported by a solvency statement, indicating the company can pay all its debts (**s. 641(1)(a)**, **ss. 642–4**). The procedure for public companies requires a special resolution and then court confirmation (**s. 641(1)(b)**, **ss. 645–51**), which usually

[5] You need to link your discussion of capital reduction to the principle and justifications of capital maintenance to ensure your essay is not too descriptive

requires the company to settle a list of creditors and ensure fairness between members (*Scottish Insurance Corp v Wilsons & Clyde Coal Co Ltd* [1949] AC 462). Accordingly, while capital can be reduced, statute ensures creditors are protected.

Purchase and Redemption of a Company's own Shares

Trevor v Whitworth established that a company could not purchase its own shares. This prohibition is now in **CA 2006, s. 658**: breach is an offence by the company and officers in default. However, the statute does provide a lawful route for a company to purchase its own shares.

To be lawful, a purchase must be in accordance with **ss. 690–708**: either an off-market purchase (requiring a special resolution), or a market purchase (requiring an ordinary resolution establishing various limits for the purchase) and, usually, cancelling the shares after purchase. However, public companies cannot use capital to purchase their shares (they must use distributable profits or the proceeds of a fresh issue of shares made for the purpose (s. 692)), so upholding the capital maintenance principle.[6] While private companies may use capital, the risk to creditors is small: private companies can use a small amount of capital (£15,000 maximum, or 5 per cent of the share capital if lower, **s. 692(1ZA)**) but thereafter must use the same funding sources as public companies, or use the complex process (which includes a solvency statement and auditor's report) in order to use a 'permissible capital payment' under **ss. 709–23**. In essence a lawful share repurchase either doesn't use capital, or does so only where risk to creditors is minimized.

Companies can also issue redeemable shares[7] under **CA 2006, s. 684**, which would seem to be contrary to the *Trevor v Whitworth* statement. However, even here, the basis of the principle is observed, as the funding of the redemption (**s. 687**) echoes that for a purchase of a company's own shares, thus protecting capital and creditors.

Distributions and other Provisions

To ensure companies do not return capital to shareholders through dividends, there are restrictions on when distributions (including dividends) can be made. These can only be out of 'profits available for the purpose', ie 'accumulated realised profits less accumulated realised losses' (**s. 830**). Further restrictions apply to public companies (**s. 831(1)**). Directors authorizing an unlawful dividend are liable to repay the distribution to the company if aware of the facts that render it unlawful (*Burnden Holdings (UK) Ltd v Fielding* [2019] **EWHC 1566**; *Bairstow v Queens Moat Houses plc* [2001] **2 BCLC 531**). Members are liable to repay an unlawful distribution if they knew or had reasonable grounds to believe it was paid contrary to the statute.

[6] Again, indicate the significance of the point you make to the theme of the essay

[7] You could add more detail on redeemable shares, but the simple point relating to capital maintenance can be dealt with concisely by referring to previous discussion

The courts have also been alert to transactions with shareholders that may be a disguised return of capital.[8] In **Re Halt Garage (1964) Ltd** [1982] 3 All ER 1016, the court overturned payments to shareholders labelled as director remuneration. In **Progress Property Co Ltd v Moorgarth Group Ltd** [2010] UKSC 55, the court highlighted the need to examine the substance of a transaction rather than merely the name given it by directors to ensure capital was not being returned other than through the statutory framework. In a further nod to creditor interests, even otherwise lawfully paid dividends may breach **Insolvency Act 1986, s. 423** (transactions defrauding creditors): **BTI 2014 LLC v Sequana SA** [2019] EWCA Civ 112.

Another area of law with its origins in the capital maintenance doctrine (although now with stronger links to preventing market abuse) is financial assistance. **CA 2006, s. 678** prevents a public company from assisting a purchaser of its shares, by eg paying for the shares, or providing or guaranteeing a loan. While many examples of financial assistance do not diminish the company's capital, there is obviously potential to do so, and the courts have interpreted exceptions very strictly (**Brady v Brady** [1989] AC 755). However, since **CA 2006** these rules only apply to public companies, showing the legislature's preference to minimize the impact of the capital maintenance doctrine on private companies at least.

[8] It is easy to concentrate on the statutory provisions and forget about this line of cases

Conclusion

[9] A very concise summary of the second part of the essay

There have been inroads into the capital maintenance principle: companies can reduce their capital, purchase and redeem their own shares, and, if a private company, fund share purchases out of capital and give financial assistance for the purchase of its own shares.[9] But there are still very few opportunities for companies to return capital to shareholders and where it is permissible, statute seeks to ensure there is no sensible risk to creditors. **Trevor v Whitworth** is thus still very much part of our law. The bigger issue is arguably whether the statement is correct in the assumptions and justifications it relies on.[10] As this is questionable, the law may be misplacing its energy in continuing to support the capital maintenance doctrine, and might be better directed at improving protection for creditors on insolvency.

[10] This reminds the examiner that you have questioned the principle, as well as discussing the provisions themselves

LOOKING FOR EXTRA MARKS?

- Develop the point about 'disguised return of capital' and develop the link between capital maintenance and creditor protection

- Show you understand why the law has departed from the strict principle on occasion, for example why the law does sometimes allow capital to be reduced, shares purchased, etc

- Explore the various rules and procedures in further depth to evaluate how well they fit either with the capital maintenance principle in an absolute sense, or with the wider justifications behind the principle

Gary is the managing director and major shareholder (holding 5 million shares) of Takeout plc, a property development company. In negotiations to bring Howard, a wealthy businessman, into the company, Gary agreed on behalf of Takeout plc to acquire a property with planning permission for commercial development from Howard for £3m. (The property was recently valued at £1.5m.) Howard then obtained an unsecured loan of £2m from Eastern Bank and purchased 50 per cent of Gary's shareholding in Takeout plc for £5m. Howard joined the board of Takeout plc, and shortly after, Takeout plc created a floating charge over its property portfolio to secure Howard's loan from Eastern Bank.

Advise on the legality of the transactions entered into by Takeout plc and the rights and liabilities of Gary, Howard, and the Bank.

! CAUTION!

■ Work through the financial assistance provisions step by step in order to cover all the points and draw clear conclusions

■ Remember that although CA 2006 changed the law by removing private companies from the ambit of the financial assistance provisions, pre-2006 case law is still relevant on many points

■ Follow the instructions: advise on the consequences for the transaction and the various parties involved in it

☐ DIAGRAM ANSWER PLAN

Identify the issues	■ Is the transaction legal: has there been unlawful financial assistance? ■ If so, what effect does this have on the transaction and the parties?
Relevant law	■ Prohibition on financial assistance ■ Exemptions/defences ■ Consequences of breach: effect on transaction ■ Consequences of breach: liability of company and individuals
Apply the law	■ Apply the law to the transactions
Conclude	■ Conclude, considering the effect on the transactions and liability of the parties

SUGGESTED ANSWER

This problem raises the question of whether Takeout plc has been guilty of the offence of providing financial assistance for the acquisition of its own shares under **Companies Act 2006 (CA 2006), ss. 677–83**. Although **CA 2006** abolished financial assistance for private companies, it remains applicable to public companies (and private companies in a group with public companies), meaning Takeout plc is subject to the prohibition. As well as potentially offending the capital maintenance doctrine, financial assistance is prohibited because it gives companies scope to manipulate their share price and/or allow new controllers to engage in asset-stripping to the detriment of existing shareholders and creditors.[1]

There are two situations here which could constitute financial assistance: the purchase of the commercial property from Howard for £3m and the creation of a floating charge to secure Howard's loan of £2m. The transactions will be considered to see if they amount to financial assistance, together with any potential exceptions to the offence, and the liability of the parties discussed.[2]

CA 2006, s. 678 prohibits a public company (or its subsidiary, other than a foreign subsidiary: *Arab Bank plc v Mercantile Holdings Ltd* [1994] 2 All ER 74) from giving financial assistance to any person for the purpose of the acquisition of its shares. This is prohibited whether given directly or indirectly, and whether given before or at the same time as the share acquisition (contemporaneous financial assistance), or after the acquisition takes place (subsequent financial assistance): **s. 678**.

According to *British and Commonwealth Holdings plc v Barclays Bank plc* [1996] 1 WLR 1 the provision 'requires that there should be assistance or help for the purpose of acquiring shares and that that assistance should be financial' (Aldous J). Financial assistance is not defined as such in **CA 2006** but **s. 677** states[3] that it includes financial assistance given by way of a guarantee, security, or indemnity: **s. 677(1)(b)(i)**. This would cover the creation of the floating charge, which is indirect subsequent financial assistance, enabling Eastern Bank to enforce the charge against Takeout plc's assets in the event of Howard defaulting on the loan.

Under **s. 677(1)(d)(i)** financial assistance also includes any other financial assistance given by the company where the net assets of the company are reduced to a material extent by the giving of the assistance (or where the company has no net assets). This would cover the purchase of Howard's property as[4] the purchase price significantly exceeds the value of the property acquired. For example, in *Belmont Finance Corpn Ltd v Williams Furniture Ltd* [1979]

[1] While in a problem question you should focus on application of the law to the facts, there is usually the opportunity to show a little bit more of your knowledge and understanding

[2] Even in a problem question it can be helpful to set out your approach in your introduction, but it is less important than in an essay

[3] It is tempting to view s. 677 as a definition provision, but it isn't and the examiner will be pleased to see you recognize this

[4] Remember to apply the law explicitly to the facts—just setting out the relevant law isn't enough in itself

Ch 250 directors of the defendant company, with the connivance of some of the directors of the claimant, sold its property at a substantial overvalue. The four directors then used the money to purchase all the issued shares in the plaintiff company. The Court of Appeal held that the transaction was illegal financial assistance and a breach of what is now **CA 2006, s. 678(1)**. While the courts have indicated that they will view potential financial assistance pragmatically and look at the overall commercial realities of a situation (*Charterhouse Investment Trust Ltd v Tempest Diesels Ltd* [1986] BCLC 1; *Anglo Petroleum Ltd v TFB Mortgages* [2008] 1 BCLC 185), the timing and detail of this purchase suggest it is very much part of a deliberate scheme to assist financially in the purchase of Takeout plc's shares, rather than a genuine commercial arrangement. It therefore seems likely that the purchase of the commercial property from Howard was contemporaneous financial assistance.

Prima facie, then, Takeout plc has been involved in two examples of unlawful financial assistance. However both offences are subject to the purpose exceptions under **CA 2006, s. 678(2) and (4)**.[5] The first of these (**ss. 678(2)(a) and 678(4)(a)**) permits a company to give financial assistance if its principal purpose in giving the assistance is not to give it for the purpose of any such acquisition (in the case of contemporaneous financial assistance) or to reduce or discharge any liability incurred (in the case of subsequent financial assistance) and the assistance is given in good faith in the interests of the company. The second purpose exception (**ss. 678(2)(b) and 678(4)(b)**) permits a company to give financial assistance if the giving of the assistance (or the reduction or discharge of liability) is only an incidental part of some larger purpose of the company and the assistance is given in good faith in the interests of the company.

Although clearly designed to ensure genuine commercial transactions were outside the ambit of the prohibition, the scope of the purpose exceptions was severely restricted by *Brady v Brady* [1989] AC 755. In this case the House of Lords rejected[6] the decision of the lower courts that the financial assistance fell within the purpose exceptions, despite being given as part of a major company reorganization to resolve intractable conflict between the two controlling parties and so avoid the company's likely liquidation. The House of Lords distinguished between a purpose and the reason why a purpose is formed and held that a 'larger purpose' must be something more than the reason why the transaction was entered into. This decision has rendered the purpose exceptions of 'little, if any, practical value' (Mercouris, 'The prohibition on financial assistance: the case for a commercially pragmatic interpretation' (2014) 35 Co Law 321),[7] although the exception was held to have been satisfied in *Re Uniq plc* [2011] EWHC 749 (on very different facts to the present case).

[5] The two purpose exceptions are both contained within subsections (2) and (4), rather than one in each, so make sure you know where to find them before you are in the exam

[6] As it is such a significant case it is helpful to give some case facts, but you should still be concise and focus on the points that relate to the issue at hand

[7] You could make the point about the problem with *Brady* without specific support, but it is good to show your further reading if you can

Applying the cases and the reasoning in *Brady v Brady* it is highly unlikely that Takeout plc could argue that the financial assistance is to achieve the larger purpose of bringing Howard and his expertise into the company, even if this were in the interests of the company. Neither is the financial assistance incidental to some larger purpose of the company, which requires there to be some 'larger overall corporate purpose' in which the assistance is merely incidental (*Brady v Brady*).

There are other exceptions to the prohibition on financial assistance, for example when in relation to a reduction of capital or purchase of shares undertaken in accordance with the statutory schemes (**s. 681**) but these do not apply to Takeout plc's case. Neither do the exemptions for money-lending companies or employee share schemes apply (**s. 682**). Accordingly, it seems highly probable that Takeout plc will be found to have breached the prohibition on financial assistance.

Breach of the financial assistance provisions is a criminal offence by the company and every officer of the company who is in default: **CA 2006, s. 680(1)**. The company would be liable to a fine and any officer liable to a fine and/or imprisonment: **s. 680(2)**. Although the statute does not make provision for the civil consequences of the breach, the courts have held that any unlawful financial assistance is unenforceable by either party,[8] meaning that the floating charge granted to Eastern Bank will be illegal and unenforceable against the company by the bank: *Heald v O'Connor* [1971] 1 WLR 497. However, the courts are willing to sever any illegal element from the rest of a transaction where possible (*Carney v Herbert* [1985] 1 All ER 438), so the rest of the arrangement should remain valid.

Gary, as a director of Takeout plc, will be in breach of his duty to the company[9] by authorizing the giving of financial assistance (*Re In a Flap Envelope Co Ltd* [2004] 1 BCLC 64) and liable to account to the company for any losses caused. He may have breached multiple duties in causing the company to purchase Howard's property and giving security for Howard's loan (for example using his powers for an improper purpose under **CA 2006, s. 171(b)**, or not acting in good faith to promote the success of the company under **s. 172**). Howard too, in authorizing the giving of security after being appointed a director, will be in breach of his duties as a director, including a potential conflict of interest. In addition, if Howard received payment for his property knowing that the transaction was improper and an abuse of Gary's fiduciary duties, he could also be liable as a constructive trustee to account to Takeout plc: *Belmont Finance Corpn Ltd v Williams Furniture Ltd (No. 2)* [1980] 1 All ER 393; *Royal Brunei Airlines Sdn Bhd v Tan Kok Ming* [1995] 2 AC 378. It is also possible for the company to sue Gary and Howard for damages for conspiracy, despite the company being a party to the transaction:

[8] Remember to think about the civil consequences of breach, as well as criminal liability

[9] Directors' duties will inevitably be relevant, but don't get too distracted and provide too much detail—the focus of the question is financial assistance rather than duties per se

Belmont Finance Corpn Ltd v Williams Furniture Ltd [1979] Ch 250. Should Takeout plc get into financial difficulties there is also the possibility that the purchase of Howard's property could be challengeable under **Insolvency Act 1986** (as a transaction at an undervalue: **s. 238**), while causing a company to give financial assistance is evidence of unfitness under **Company Directors Disqualification Act 1986, s. 6:** *Re Continental Assurance Co of London plc* [1997] 1 BCLC 48.

 ## LOOKING FOR EXTRA MARKS?

- Explore the purpose exception in more depth and examine some of the criticism surrounding *Brady v Brady*

- Examine the reasons behind the financial assistance prohibition and assess whether those justifications are present in the case at hand

- Show your awareness of how directors' duties are relevant to financial assistance, but be careful not to spend too much time on this element of the question

 ## TAKING THINGS FURTHER

- Armour, J., 'Share capital and creditor protection: efficient rules for a modern company law' (2000) 63 MLR 355

  Questions whether the rules on capital raising and maintenance fulfil the stated aim of creditor protection, through the prism of economic analysis. Concludes that while such rules could enhance efficiency, the form of existing regulation is not justified by such principles.

- Clementelli, F., '(Under)valuing the rules on capital maintenance' [2012] ICCLR 191

  Explores the capital maintenance rules and argues that legislation has not kept up with changes to the economic climate with the result that companies have attempted to find other ways of returning capital to shareholders.

- Daehnert, A., 'The minimum capital requirement—an anachronism under conservation: Parts 1 and 2' (2009) 30 Co Law 3 and 34

  Discusses the value of a minimum capital requirement and its link to limited liability and creditor protection, with particular reference to the position in Germany.

- Ferran, E., 'Creditors' interests and "core" company law' (1999) 20 Co Law 314

  An exploration of the role of debt finance in the corporate capital structure, and the impact and value of the capital maintenance rules to creditors and more generally.

- Ferran, E., 'Corporate transactions and financial assistance: shifting policy perceptions but static law' (2004) 63 CLJ 225

  A critical account of the financial assistance provisions pre-CA 2006. Many of the comments and criticisms are still relevant to the current law.

■ Hudson, A., 'BHS and the reform of company law' (2016) 37 Co Law 364

A critical look at how company law enables the extraction of value from companies through the lens of the collapse of BHS, with suggestions for reform in a number of areas including the capital maintenance rules.

■ Mercouris, S., 'The prohibition on financial assistance: the case for a commercially pragmatic interpretation' (2014) 35 Co Law 321

Considers the policy arguments behind financial assistance and examines recent case authorities. Argues that the financial assistance prohibition fails to offer adequate protection while also putting legitimate commercial transactions at risk.

■ Micheler, E., 'Disguised returns of capital—an arm's length approach' (2010) 69 CLJ 151

An interesting article considering when payments to shareholders may be viewed as a disguised return of capital, and examining the relationship with the doctrines of capital maintenance, ultra vires, and abuse of corporate power.

Online Resources   www.oup.com/uk/qanda/

For extra essay and problem questions on this topic, as well as advice on revision and exam technique, please visit the online resources.

Loan Capital 10

ARE YOU READY?

In order to attempt the questions in this chapter you will need to have covered the following topics:

- Corporate borrowing
- Fixed charges
- Floating charges
- Registration of charges
- Priority of charges on insolvency
- Vulnerability of floating charge on insolvency
- Connections (in particular) with: share capital, directors' duties, corporate insolvency

 KEY DEBATES

Debate: distinguishing between fixed and floating charges

The efforts of creditors to gain the advantages of fixed charges in situations where floating charges might be thought more appropriate (in particular in relation to charges over book debts) led to some much criticized cases and academic dispute. The distinction between fixed and floating charges is now tolerably clear, but grey areas remain. Keep in mind when reading academic commentary whether it pre- or post-dates the decisions in *Re Brumark* (Privy Council), and *Re Spectrum* (House of Lords). See also more generally Ferran, E. and Ho, L. C., *Principles of Corporate Finance Law* (2nd edn, Oxford, 2014).

Debate: reforming the company charge registration system

Reform of the registration system had been long anticipated, but the eventual changes (in 2013) were not particularly extensive. In this area the Law Commission papers are helpful in explaining problems and alternative solutions, but you should weigh up the much more ambitious proposals against the final cautious reform.

QUESTION | 1

'A specific charge, I think, is one that without more fastens on ascertained and definite property or property capable of being ascertained and defined; a floating charge, on the other hand, is ambulatory and shifting in its nature, hovering over and so to speak floating with the property which it is intended to affect until some event occurs or some act is done which causes it to settle and fasten on the subject of the charge …'

Lord Macnaghten, *Illingworth v Houldsworth* [1904] AC 355

Critically assess the characteristics of fixed and floating charges, and how the law distinguishes between them.

CAUTION!

- Remember to address both parts of the instruction—it is easy to forget to deal with 'how' the law distinguishes them, ie the process, not just the distinguishing features

- As part of your critical assessment, make sure you identify why it has become so important to distinguish between fixed and floating charges—in particular the attempts to create fixed charges over fluctuating assets

DIAGRAM ANSWER PLAN

Introduction: companies, security, and fixed and floating charges

Fixed charges: features and benefits

Floating charges: features, benefits, and drawbacks

Distinguishing between fixed and floating charges: the courts' approach

Charges over book debts/receivables

Conclusion: review of distinguishing features and approach

A company may grant security to a creditor by creating fixed (or specific) or floating charges over its assets, whereas sole traders and partnerships (other than LLPs) cannot create floating charges. The two types of charge do not offer equal security to creditors in the event of a company's insolvent liquidation and this makes it particularly important to be able to distinguish between the two types of charge.[1] This essay will explore the characteristics of both forms of charge, highlighting their distinguishing features, and will explain the approach adopted by the courts in distinguishing between them.

[1] This shows you know why the distinction matters

Fixed Charges

Fixed charges are legal or equitable charges created by the company over specific, identified assets. However, the quote's focus on the nature of the charged asset[2] is slightly misplaced, as the critical feature of a fixed charge (and the element distinguishing it from a floating charge) is that the company cannot deal with or dispose of the charged asset without the chargeholder's consent, rather than the type of asset as such. Accordingly, while a fixed charge is generally created over property such as land, fixed plant, and machinery, with care fixed charges can also be created over less permanent assets.

[2] Although the question itself doesn't ask specifically about the quote, your answer should still reflect on the issues raised by the quote

A fixed charge gives the holder priority over other creditors[3] on the company's insolvency—a creditor with a fixed charge can realize their debt from the charged asset. Unlike floating charges, assets subject to a fixed charge are not vulnerable to meeting the costs of the liquidation or paying preferential creditors, and no part of such assets is taken for the benefit of unsecured creditors. Furthermore, a fixed charge does not risk invalidation under **Insolvency Act 1986 (IA 1986), s. 245** if created in the period prior to the commencement of winding up. Other provisions such as **IA 1986, s. 239** (preferences) may operate to remove the benefit of the security for the creditor but these are harder to establish than **s. 245**. Unsurprisingly, creditors will seek to create a fixed charge rather than a floating charge where possible, in order to achieve these advantages.

[3] This paragraph is important as it sets out why fixed charges tend to be preferred to floating charges and so backs up the brief comment in the introduction

Floating Charges

The floating charge is 'an equitable charge on the assets for the time being of a going concern' (*Governments Stock and Other Securities Investment Co Ltd v Manila Railway Co Ltd* [1897] AC 81; see also *Re Panama, New Zealand and Australian Royal Mail Co* (1870) 5 Ch App 318). Three characteristics were identified by Romer LJ in *Re Yorkshire Woolcombers Association Ltd* [1903] 2 Ch 284 (*Yorkshire Woolcombers*):[4] (i) it is a charge on a class of assets of a company present and future; (ii) the class is one which,

[4] You don't need to remember the precise words, but you should be able to summarize these three characteristics

in the ordinary course of business of the company, changes from time to time; and (iii) until some future step is taken (and the charge 'crystallizes'), the company can carry on its business using the assets as if uncharged. It is the final characteristic, the company's ability to use the assets in the ordinary course of business, rather than the class of assets, that is the essential characteristic distinguishing a floating charge from a fixed charge.

Crystallization is when the charge ceases to float over the body of assets covered by the charge and attach to those assets comprising that class at that time. The crystallizing event will usually be a formal act of the chargeholder (such as appointing an administrator or giving notice) but it need not be directly triggered by the chargeholder (eg the commencement of winding up, or the company ceasing to be a 'going concern' (*Re Woodroffes (Musical Instruments) Ltd* [1985] 3 WLR 543)). Charges may even use an automatic crystallization clause (*Re Brightlife Ltd* [1987] Ch 200). However, floating charge-holders cannot claim that by crystallization they gain the benefit of being a fixed chargeholder on winding up. IA 1986, s. 251 provides that charges created as floating charges rank as such and so do not change position in the priority order of creditors even if crystallizing before commencement of winding up or administration.

⁵ This paragraph sets out some of the benefits of a floating charge, but then goes on to give some more detail on its drawbacks, filling out the detail of the points raised earlier

A floating charge is a flexible device[5] that enables creditors to take security over the entire undertaking of a company, but leaves the company free to deal with its assets in the ordinary course of business (*Agnew v IRC; Re Brumark Investments Ltd* [2001] 2 AC 710 (*Brumark*)). It is valid even if when created the company does not have assets that could be subject to it: *SAW (SW) 2010 Ltd v Wilson* [2017] EWCA Civ 1001. The holder of a 'qualifying' floating charge also has the right to appoint an administrator over the company (IA 1986, Sch B1). However, it has drawbacks compared with a fixed charge. Assets subject to a floating charge may be used to pay the expenses of the liquidation and to pay preferential debts where the company's free assets (those not subject to any charge) are insufficient to meet those claims (IA 1986, s. 176ZA and s. 175(2)) and part of the recoveries will usually be available to unsecured creditors as the 'prescribed part' under IA 1986, s. 176A. Furthermore, floating charges created other than for new consideration will be invalid if created during a relevant time (one or two years prior to the commencement of the winding up) (IA 1986, s. 245).

Distinguishing between Fixed and Floating Charges

⁶ It is important to deal with the process for determination as well as the distinguishing features

It is for the court to determine whether a charge is a fixed or a floating charge, irrespective of how the parties have described the charge: *Re Armagh Shoes Ltd* [1984] BCLC 405. In *Brumark*, the Privy Council held that determination is a two-stage process.[6]

The court must first identify the rights the parties intended to create (looking at the rights rather than the label attached to the charge by the parties) and then decide, as a matter of law, whether those rights create a fixed or floating charge. The *Brumark* approach was accepted by the House of Lords in *Re Cosslett Contractors Ltd* [2002] 1 BCLC 77.

In deciding whether a charge is fixed or floating, the third *Yorkshire Woolcombers* characteristic—the ability to deal with the assets charged in the ordinary course of trading—is clearly more important than the others. In *Re Spectrum Plus Ltd* [2005] 2 AC 680 (*Spectrum*), Lord Scott said this was 'the essential feature of the floating charge, the characteristic that distinguishes it from a fixed charge'. Other characteristics are thus not determinative. However, the nature of the asset charged may well be indicative, with Lord Scott in *Spectrum* connecting the company's ability to remove assets from the security, with the circulating character of assets typically subject to a floating charge.

The *Brumark* approach, focusing on the rights and obligations actually given, guards against the mislabelling of charges, but does not necessarily mean attempts to create fixed charges in novel situations are bound to fail. A particular area of difficulty for the courts was whether fixed charges could be created over book debts (or receivables)[7]—a valuable asset that by its nature is constantly changing and over which a company usually needs to retain some control.

In *Siebe Gorman & Co Ltd v Barclays Bank Ltd* [1979] 2 Lloyd's Rep 142 (*Siebe Gorman*), the court upheld a fixed charge over book debts: the terms of the charge required debts to be credited to a specific bank account and restricted the company's rights to dispose of those monies. As it was not always possible for a chargeholder to restrict a company's rights in this way, a 'hybrid' charge (a fixed charge over book debts while outstanding and a floating charge over the proceeds) was created in *Re New Bullas Trading Ltd* [1993] BCC 251 (*New Bullas*). However, this was heavily criticized[8] and held in *Brumark* to have been wrongly decided. In *Spectrum*, the House of Lords unanimously overruled both *Siebe Gorman* and *New Bullas*.

Post-*Brumark* and *Spectrum*, it is not impossible to create a fixed charge over book debts, but only if the assets are permanently appropriated to the payment of the debt—the chargeholder must have control of the proceeds. Although some dealings in the charged property are not necessarily fatal to the existence of a fixed charge (eg *Arthur D Little Ltd v Ableco Finance LLC* [2003] Ch 217), in practice it is now very difficult to create a fixed charge over book debts as the chargeholder will need to require and control an account into which proceeds are paid.

[7] You will need to consider the book debts saga, but concentrate on the current law

[8] If you had time you could consider some of the criticisms here

Conclusion

Fixed and floating charges have different characteristics but the key distinguishing feature is the extent to which the company retains the ability to deal with the charged asset. The nature of the asset charged is not determinative but it is significant (as the quote indicates)[9] and may strongly influence the level of control retained by the company. The courts' approach to distinguishing between fixed and floating charges looks at the true picture of what has been created, rather than that presented by the draftsman. This ensures that creditors do not gain the benefit of a fixed charge in situations when in truth they have created a floating charge.

[9] Linking back to the quote at the end shows that you have understood the significance of the point it raises

LOOKING FOR EXTRA MARKS?

■ Engage with some of the (many) critical pieces relating to fixed charges over book debts and academic views of the various cases in this saga

■ Consider some of the practical elements of corporate lending, and whether changes (such as *Brumark*, and the 'prescribed part') have impacted on lending practices

■ Develop the examination of floating charges by exploring differing academic views about the nature of the charge and its proprietary status prior to crystallization

QUESTION | 2

Two years ago Haggis Ltd granted a charge over its book debts to its bank, Leeward Bank plc. Leeward registered the charge the following week. The charge instrument states that it is a fixed charge. It gives Leeward the right to require Haggis Ltd to pay all proceeds of its book debts into its principal account with the bank and to seek the bank's permission before utilizing those monies.

Last year Haggis Ltd borrowed £10,000 from Aviemore Loans Ltd, granting Aviemore a charge over its investments (shareholdings in two public companies) and proceeds of those investments. This charge was stated to be a fixed charge. The charge instrument requires Haggis to pay any proceeds of those investments into a specific bank account, and prohibits Haggis from disposing of or otherwise dealing with the investments or their proceeds without the permission of Aviemore.

Haggis Ltd is now in some financial difficulty which has caused Leeward and Aviemore to review their respective securities. Leeward has not exercised its right to insist that Haggis pays proceeds of its book debts into its account, and even when they have been, Leeward has allowed Haggis to make use of them without restriction. In contrast, the terms of Aviemore's charge have been fully complied with, but Aviemore has just noticed that due to an administrative oversight, its charge was not registered.

Advise Leeward and Aviemore.

CAUTION!

- You will need to have a good understanding of the test for distinguishing between fixed and floating charges, but don't waste time repeating the same principles for both parts of the question

- To avoid an answer that is too descriptive, just summarize why a fixed charge would be better than a floating charge. Your focus should be on applying the law—both distinguishing between fixed and floating charges and the failure to register

DIAGRAM ANSWER PLAN

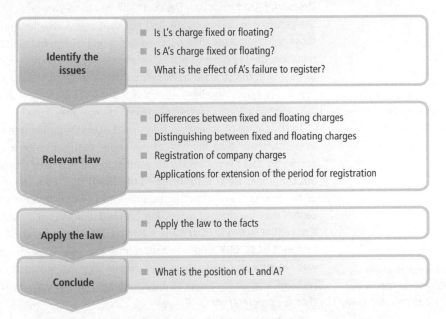

Identify the issues
- Is L's charge fixed or floating?
- Is A's charge fixed or floating?
- What is the effect of A's failure to register?

Relevant law
- Differences between fixed and floating charges
- Distinguishing between fixed and floating charges
- Registration of company charges
- Applications for extension of the period for registration

Apply the law
- Apply the law to the facts

Conclude
- What is the position of L and A?

SUGGESTED ANSWER

Although the charges granted by Haggis are stated to be fixed charges, the label attached to a charge by the parties is not conclusive: *Re Armagh Shoes Ltd* **[1984] BCLC 405**. It will therefore be necessary to determine whether each charge is fixed or floating as this will be particularly important should Haggis' financial difficulties result in liquidation. Creditors prefer fixed charges because they are not subordinated to the liquidator's costs and preferential creditors, and are not subject to the percentage share taken for unsecured creditors. For Aviemore a further issue arises, the effect of the non-registration of their charge, and whether this can be remedied.

[1] This line isn't essential but it can be helpful to show you have thought about potential issues and ruled out what doesn't arise on the facts

[2] In a problem question with lots of points to cover you are unlikely to have time to deal in depth with the older 'book debts' cases but should show you are aware of them

[3] You could look at the characteristics of fixed and floating charges in more depth if you had time

[4] This paragraph applies the test concisely by linking the law very closely to the facts at each point

[5] The introduction set out the main reasons why fixed charges are preferred to floating charges so there is no need to recite them again

[6] There is no need to set out the test again, and the facts are fairly straightforward here, so make sure you apply the law to the facts but then move on

As the charges are over different assets no issue of priority as between Leeward and Aviemore arises.[1]

Leeward

Although Leeward has attempted to create a fixed charge, it is for the courts not the parties to determine the nature of the charge (*Agnew v IRC; Re Brumark Investments Ltd* [2001] 2 AC 710 (*Brumark*)). While it is possible to create a fixed charge over book debts, it is much harder to do so following the rejection of *Siebe Gorman & Co Ltd v Barclays Bank Ltd* [1979] 2 Lloyd's Rep 142 and *Re New Bullas Trading Ltd* [1993] BCC 251[2] in *Re Spectrum Plus Ltd* [2005] 2 AC 680 (*Spectrum*).

To determine the nature of Leeward's charge, the two-stage test of *Brumark* must be applied. The court will first determine what rights the parties intended to create, and will then assess whether, in law, those rights make the charge a fixed or floating charge. In that determination, the key point of distinction is whether the company is free to deal with the charged asset without the chargeholder's consent. It is the company's ability to use the assets as if uncharged that is indicative of a floating, rather than fixed, charge: *Spectrum*.[3]

The first stage of the test considers what rights the parties intended to create, rather than the type of charge the parties wanted to create. So the fact the parties clearly wanted to create a fixed charge is not conclusive: *Re G E Tunbridge Ltd* [1994] BCC 563. The terms of the charge indicate the parties intended Leeward to have some control over the charged assets. But Leeward didn't actually exercise that control. In *Royal Trust Bank v National Westminster Bank plc* [1996] 2 BCLC 699 a right to gain control that was never exercised was not sufficient to create a fixed charge. In practice Haggis (and Leeward) treated the assets as unencumbered, the mark of a floating charge, per *Spectrum*.[4]

It is therefore probable that Leeward's charge is floating, not fixed. Fortunately there is no risk of potential challenge by the liquidator under **Insolvency Act 1986, s. 245** in the event of Haggis Ltd's liquidation. This is because even if granted to secure existing debt, it was created in favour of an unconnected person more than 12 months before any possible commencement of winding up. Nonetheless it is less desirable for Leeward than a fixed charge for the reasons summarized previously.[5] Leeward still has power to appoint an administrator over the assets but this might well precipitate the failure of Haggis so should not be done lightly.

Aviemore

Applying the *Brumark* test,[6] it is probable that Aviemore has a fixed charge, as labelled. Here the parties intended to impose, and in fact operated, tight restrictions on Haggis Ltd's ability to deal with the investments and their proceeds. Accordingly, following *Spectrum*, the charge should be recognized as a fixed charge.

The problem for Aviemore is that charges on company property must be registered at Companies House. As the charge was created on or after 6 April 2013 the relevant provisions are **Companies Act 2006 (CA 2006), Part 25 Chapter A1**. The registration system enables those dealing with a company to check for charges; it warns 'unsuspecting creditors' that the company has charged its assets: *Re Welsh Irish Ferries Ltd* [1985] BCLC 327. More pertinently for Aviemore,[7] failure to register a 'registrable charge' renders the security void when it matters.

Pre-2013 the law provided a list of registrable charges under which all floating charges but not all fixed charges were registrable. A fixed charge on shares was not registrable (*Arthur D Little Ltd v Ableco Finance LLC* [2003] Ch 217) which could have protected Aviemore from the consequences of non-registration. Unfortunately for Aviemore, under Chapter A1 all charges are registrable unless specifically excluded in **s. 859A(6)**. The excluded charges, relating to landlord deposits, Lloyd's members and charges excluded by other Acts, clearly do not include Aviemore's charge. Accordingly it was registrable and should have been registered by Aviemore or Haggis within 21 days of its creation (**s 859A**). While the 2013 reforms[8] mean that Haggis Ltd's failure to register is no longer a criminal offence, the impact on Aviemore is potentially serious.

Failure to register means the charge will be void against any liquidator, administrator, or creditor of Haggis Ltd (**s. 859H**). The charge is not void against the company while not in administration or winding up (*Re Cosslett (Contractors) Ltd* [2002] 1 BCLC 77) and non-registration does not affect the validity of the debt itself which remains payable (*Re Monolithic Building Company* [1915] 1 Ch 643). But if Haggis were to go into liquidation, the liquidator would be able to take and sell the charged assets without regard to Aviemore's charge, and Aviemore will rank as an unsecured creditor. And if another creditor has subsequently registered a charge over the investments they are free to ignore Aviemore's charge.

However Aviemore may, and should as a matter of urgency, apply for an extension to the time for delivery under **s. 859F(3)**. This gives the court discretion (on application of Haggis or Aviemore) to extend the period for delivery if satisfied the failure to deliver the documents in time was 'accidental or due to inadvertence or to some other sufficient cause', or is 'not of a nature to prejudice the position of creditors or shareholders of the company', or that it is just and equitable to grant relief. Aviemore clearly falls within the first category as an administrative oversight is clearly accidental/inadvertent, but they

[7] Make sure you focus on the points that are particularly relevant to the parties you are advising

[8] This paragraph brings in some of the reform changes to show deeper knowledge, but carefully keeps the focus on the current law and the facts of the problem

must support their application with evidence to this effect: *Re Telomatic Ltd* **[1994] 1 BCLC 90** (*Telomatic*).

[9] Knowing a few of the facts from the relevant cases will help you in applying the law convincingly to the facts of the problem

The courts are generally willing to extend the period,[9] provided that rights acquired in the meantime are not prejudiced. In *Re Braemar Investments Ltd* **[1989] Ch 54** (*Braemar*) Hoffmann J said that the 'underlying guide' should be whether it would be just and equitable to grant relief. Accordingly, while delay in making an application and Haggis Ltd's financial position will both be relevant, neither will necessarily be fatal.

Aviemore should make the application as soon as possible, not least as Haggis' financial position could worsen. If Haggis is in danger of imminent liquidation an application may well be refused: *Re Resinoid and Mica Products Ltd* **[1983] Ch 132**, where there was also substantial delay. *Barclays Bank plc v Stuart Landon Ltd* **[2001] 2 BCLC 316** (*Stuart Landon*) explained the reason for this is because once winding up commences, unsecured creditors obtain vested interests under the insolvency code and so making a previously unregistered charge enforceable would infringe those rights. But financial difficulties will not inevitably lead to rejection (*Re Ashpurton Estates Ltd* **[1983] Ch 110**; *Braemar*) as until winding up unsecured creditors have no vested rights (*Stuart Landon*).

If Aviemore succeeds in its application, as seems likely unless Haggis is on the brink of liquidation, the order will probably contain the standard proviso (*Re Joplin Brewery Co Ltd* **[1902] 1 Ch 79**) that registration is without prejudice to rights acquired prior to actual registration. And if Haggis Ltd seems likely to go into liquidation or administration, the order will probably give a liquidator/administrator the right to challenge the order (a '*Charles* order': *Re L H Charles and Co Ltd* **[1935] WN 15**).

[10] Show you have thought about alternatives, and potential problems in pursuing them

Another possibility for Aviemore would be to seek a new charge contract[10] with Haggis, and this time ensure the charge is registered correctly within 21 days by sending a certified copy of the charge instrument to the registrar, together with a 'statement of particulars' (**s. 859D**). However, if agreement is unlikely Aviemore should not waste time trying. Repeated failures to create a new charge led to significant delays in *Telomatic*, and then rejection of the application to extend the period for registration.

Conclusion

The problem shows how the nature of a charge is determined by the rights given to the parties: although both labelled fixed charges, Leeward will have the lesser rights of a floating chargeholder. While Aviemore does have a fixed charge, the benefit of the security is currently negated by the failure to register the charge. Aviemore needs to apply to extend the registration period as a matter of urgency and is likely to be successful, provided Haggis does not decline into insolvent liquidation in the meantime.

LOOKING FOR EXTRA MARKS?

- Show an appreciation of how the law was changed in 2013 and why, engaging with some academic discussion where relevant
- Explore the consequences for the parties of your conclusions and consider practical steps they might wish to take

QUESTION | 3

Francis is the controlling shareholder and managing director of two companies, Gato Ltd and Canis Ltd.

Gato Ltd suffered a financial crisis in 2017 and it was agreed in January 2018 that Canis Ltd would pay off its outstanding debts and advance a further £50,000 on the security of a floating charge on Gato Ltd's assets. Canis Ltd settled the debts and advanced the money to Gato Ltd in March 2018, although the debenture containing the charge was not actually executed until July 2018. The charge was registered within 21 days of its creation.

Gato Ltd had a major supplier, Lapin plc, which in September 2018 refused to make further deliveries to Gato Ltd on credit since it was already owed £40,000 for previous deliveries. Following talks between the directors of Gato Ltd and Lapin plc, Lapin plc agreed to continue to supply Gato Ltd on condition that Gato Ltd created in its favour a fixed charge over its freehold premises to cover the existing debt of £40,000. The charge was created in October 2018 and registered within 21 days.

Gato Ltd went into creditors' voluntary liquidation in March 2019.

Advise the liquidator of Gato Ltd on the validity of the charges created in favour of Canis Ltd and Lapin plc.

CAUTION!

- Although at first sight this looks like a question on corporate insolvency, it expressly asks you to advise on the validity of the charges, rather than more generally on insolvency or liability matters. Make sure you focus your answer accordingly
- Nonetheless, there is a lot of overlap between company charges and corporate insolvency. Here you need to be aware in particular of the possibility of a liquidator invalidating a charge under IA 1986, either using s. 245 (floating charges only) or s. 239
- Don't forget to draw conclusions after explaining the relevant law

DIAGRAM ANSWER PLAN

Identify the issues	■ Validity of Canis charge ■ Validity of Lapin charge
Relevant law	■ Fixed charges ■ Floating charges ■ Invalidation of certain floating charges: IA 1986, s. 245 ■ Preferences: IA 1986, s. 239
Apply the law	■ Apply the law to the facts
Conclude	■ Are the charges valid?

SUGGESTED ANSWER

[1] Indicate that you know why the issue matters

It is important for the liquidator of Gato Ltd to consider the validity of the charges, as this will determine whether Canis Ltd and Lapin Ltd are secured creditors (benefiting from priority over unsecured creditors in winding up) or unsecured creditors.[1] A charge may be invalidated on liquidation either because it has not been registered, or because a liquidator successfully challenges it under provisions of the **Insolvency Act 1986 (IA 1986)**. In this case both charges (in favour of Canis Ltd and Lapin plc) have been registered within 21 days of creation, so will not be void for non-registration by virtue of **Companies Act 2006, s. 859H**.[2] The validity of the charges therefore turns on the application of **IA 1986, s. 245** (which relates to floating charges only) and **IA 1986, s. 239** (which relates to preferences, which can include the creation of a charge, whether fixed or floating).

[2] This confirms to the examiner that you realize why the mention of 21 days in the question is significant

Charge in Favour of Canis Ltd

The charge created in favour of Canis Ltd is a floating charge and therefore vulnerable to challenge by the liquidator under **IA 1986, s. 245**. This provides that floating charges created at a 'relevant time' are invalid, except to the extent that they are created for new consideration.

The relevant time is 12 months ending with the onset of insolvency (**s. 245(3)(b)**), provided that the company was unable to pay its debts within **IA 1986, s. 123** (or became unable to pay its debts as a consequence of the transaction) (**s. 245(4)**). However, if the floating charge is given to a connected person this period is extended to two years (**s. 245(3)(a)**) and there is no need to show the company was unable to pay its debts at the time the charge was created.

IA 1986, s. 249 provides that a connected person is a director (or shadow director) of the company or an associate of the director or the company, with associate defined in **IA 1986, s. 435**. Canis Ltd will be a connected person as the same person has control of both Canis Ltd and Gato Ltd (**s. 435(6)**). Accordingly, the relevant time will be two years ending with the 'onset of insolvency', which is the commencement of the winding up (**s. 245(5)**). It is clear therefore that the creation of the charge was at a relevant time,[3] as the company entered winding up (March 2019) less than two years after the charge was created (July 2018), and the liquidator does not have to show that Gato Ltd was unable to pay its debts at the time the charge was created.

[3] Think IRAC within each individual point: the issue (relevant time) has been identified, and the rule/law explained. The various elements of this have been applied to the facts, allowing the conclusion to be reached here

The floating charge in favour of Canis Ltd will therefore be invalid, except to the extent of the value of any (i) money paid or goods or services supplied to the company, (ii) discharge or reduction of any debt of the company, and (iii) interest payable, provided as consideration for and at the same time as, or after, the creation of the charge (**s. 245(2)**). Clearly in this case the money paid and the discharge of the debts by Canis Ltd were consideration for the charge, but were they paid 'at the same time or after the charge was created'?[4] They were paid after the agreement to give the charge, but before the charge was actually executed.

[4] It can sometimes be helpful to set out the issue as a question; not least as it reminds you that you've got to answer it

In *Re F & E Stanton Ltd* **[1929] 1 Ch 180**, applying an earlier equivalent section, a floating charge was held to be valid when the company had resolved to create the charge prior to the loan being advanced, even though the charge was not actually created until after all the money had been received. However, a much stricter approach was taken in relation to **IA 1986, s. 245** in *Re Shoe Lace Ltd; Power v Sharp Investments Ltd* **[1994] 1 BCLC 111** (*Shoe Lace*) where the Court of Appeal declined to follow the earlier authority.

In *Shoe Lace*, the court considered the ordinary words used in **s. 245** and concluded that no monies paid prior to the creation of the charge could be taken into account, unless the interval between payment and creation of the charge was minimal (the example of a 'coffee break' was given by Sir Christopher Slade). Accordingly, although in *Shoe Lace* loans had been made between April and early July in consideration of the proposed creation of a debenture, they could not be said to have been made at the same time as the creation of the charge, which was finally executed in late July. The reason for any delay was immaterial and the floating charge was invalid.

[5] Connecting discussion of the authority with your conclusion in this way makes it abundantly clear that you are actively applying the authority

Applying *Shoe Lace*,[5] it is clear that the liquidator can avoid Canis Ltd's floating charge under **s. 245(2)** as the charge was created only after the payment had been received by Gato Ltd. This means that Canis Ltd is no longer a secured creditor of Gato Ltd and the charged property is released for the benefit of unsecured creditors. Canis Ltd will be an unsecured creditor[6] and will have to claim alongside the other unsecured creditors.

[6] Show that you've thought about the consequence of invalidating the charge

Charge in Favour of Lapin plc

IA 1986, s. 245 will not apply in relation to the charge in favour of Lapin plc, even though the charge was created to secure an existing debt, as it is a fixed rather than a floating charge. However, the charge is potentially vulnerable as a preference under **IA 1986, s. 239**, which would open up a range of possible orders under **s. 241**, including the release of security.

A preference is where the company (at a relevant time) does something that puts a creditor (or guarantor or surety) in a better position that he would have been in in the event of the company's insolvent liquidation. Giving Lapin plc a fixed charge makes it a secured rather than unsecured creditor and so puts it in a much better position as it would be significantly higher up the creditor priority order on liquidation.[7]

[7] Don't forget to identify explicitly what the 'preference' consists of on the facts of the problem

The relevant time for preferences is two years (for connected persons) and six months (for non-connected persons) ending with the onset of insolvency: **s. 240(1)(a)–(b)**, provided that the company was unable to pay its debts (within **IA 1986, s. 123**) at the time of the preference (whether or not the person is connected). Here Lapin plc does not seem to be a connected person,[8] so the relevant time is six months, ending with start of winding up. The charge will therefore fall within the relevant time, provided that the liquidator can show Gato Ltd was unable to pay its debts when the charge was created in October 2018.

[8] As there is nothing in the facts to suggest a connected person, you can assume there is no connection; there is no need to cover both possibilities in your answer

However, the problem for the liquidator is that he must show that Gato Ltd in deciding to give the charge was influenced by a desire to prefer Lapin plc: **IA 1986, s. 239(5)**. This is presumed for connected persons (**s. 239(6)**) but as Lapin plc is not a connected person, the onus remains on the liquidator to prove the requisite 'desire'. In *Re MC Bacon Ltd* [1990] BCLC 324 (*MC Bacon*), the desire to prefer was interpreted as being a subjective concept requiring that the company 'positively wished' to improve the creditor's position. Accordingly, in *MC Bacon* the court held there was no desire to prefer, because the company granted charges to its bank only because it was concerned that the bank would otherwise call in its debts and stop the company trading. Similarly in *Re Fairway Magazines Ltd* [1992] BCC 924 the court held that the company's payment to

[9] You could explore issues such as this a little further if you have the time

its bank was motivated by commercial considerations and not by a desire to improve the bank's position. Accordingly, creditor pressure can operate as an effective defence to a preference, a position which could be criticized as encouraging undesirable behaviour in creditors but remains the law.[9]

For Gato Ltd, the decision to give Lapin plc the fixed charge is clearly motivated by the desire to ensure further deliveries from their major supplier, rather than to improve Lapin plc's position. Even if Gato Ltd was fully aware that Lapin plc's position would be improved as a consequence of the action, this is not sufficient: *MC Bacon* makes clear that desire is distinct from intention, and a company is not to be taken as desiring all the consequences of its actions. The liquidator would thus have great difficulty in establishing the requisite desire to improve Lapin plc's position.

[10] As the individual issues have been concluded on fully within the answer, all that is needed in the conclusion is a final brief summary

Conclusion[10]

The floating charge in favour of Canis Ltd will be invalid under **IA 1986, s. 245** as created at a relevant time and after the payments made by Canis Ltd. The fixed charge in favour of Lapin plc is not worth challenging however. Although it was created at a relevant time and puts Lapin plc in a better position than it would have been in, it was created as a result of pressure from the chargeholder, which negatives the desire to prefer required by **IA 1986, s. 239(5)**. Lapin plc's fixed charge will thus remain valid.

LOOKING FOR EXTRA MARKS?

- Make sure you deal with all elements of the relevant provisions: remember the relevant time and defences, as well as the key concepts
- Recognize and explore criticisms of the provisions, particularly where these are relevant to the issues arising in the question
- Examine the key cases on both provisions and don't forget to then apply them to the facts of the problem

TAKING THINGS FURTHER

- Atherton, S. and Mokal, R., 'Charges over chattels: issues in the fixed/floating jurisprudence' (2005) 26 Co Law 10
  Examines the features of fixed and floating charges, including the nature of the asset charged, and the degree of control over the charged asset. Also considers the process for distinguishing between types of charge and the relevance of post-contract conduct in this regard.

■ Capper, D., 'Fixed charges over book debts—the future after *Brumark*' (2003) 24 Co Law 325

Provides a brief examination of the floating charge's place in secured lending, including a review of various academic articles, before critiquing Brumark *itself and identifying particular areas of interest or concern.*

■ Graham, P., 'Registration of company charges' [2014] JBL 175

A useful article considering the 2013 reforms to the company charge registration system. Explores the historical background, the problems in the previous system, the changes made, and areas where reform has not been followed through. See also Castellano, G., 'Reforming non-possessory secured transactions laws: a new strategy?' (2015) 78 MLR 611 for a broader consideration of the role of registration and disclosure.

■ Law Commission, 'Company security interests' (2005) Law Com No. 296, Cm 6654

■ McCormack, G., 'Extension of time for registration of company charges' [1986] JBL 282

Discusses the significance of the company's financial position in applications to extend time for registration/delivery and the provisos commonly applied.

■ McCormack, G., 'The Law Commission Consultative Report on company security interests: an irreverent riposte' (2005) 68 MLR 286

Considers and critically discusses the Law Commission report in depth, including exploring doubts about whether wholesale change in this area is desirable.

■ Pennington, R., 'Recent developments in the law and practice relating to the creation of security for companies' indebtedness' (2009) 30 Co Law 163

A thoughtful consideration of a range of issues relating to fixed and floating charges.

■ Smart, P., 'Fixed or floating? *Siebe Gorman post-Brumark*' (2004) 25 Co Law 331

Some useful consideration of the Brumark *approach, but bear in mind that the article was written before the House of Lords decision in* Spectrum.

 Online Resources www.oup.com/uk/qanda/

For extra essay and problem questions on this topic, as well as advice on revision and exam technique, please visit the online resources.

Corporate Insolvency

11

ARE YOU READY?

In order to attempt the questions in this chapter you will need to have covered the following topics:

- Corporate rescue, particularly administration and CVAs
- Winding up—petitions and 'inability to pay debts'
- Assets available for distribution to creditors
- The distribution hierarchy and *pari passu*
- Dispositions of property after the commencement of winding up
- Transactions at an undervalue
- Preferences
- Vulnerable floating charges
- Wrongful and fraudulent trading
- Disqualification of directors
- Connections with (in particular): corporate personality, directors, directors' duties, loan capital

KEY DEBATES

Debate: Corporate rescue, administration, and 'pre-packs'

In recent years much of the focus in corporate insolvency law has been on developments in corporate rescue, and in particular the role of administration, rather than insolvent liquidation. The rise of pre-packaged administrations ('pre-packs'), which make up a large proportion of administrations, has led to much discussion and criticism, with modifications such as those recommended by the Graham Report in 2014 (including the 'pre-pack pool') having had little obvious impact.

(▶)

Debate: Liability of directors on insolvent liquidation

How far should those who managed a company in insolvent liquidation bear personal responsibility for creditor losses? This obviously overlaps with fundamental concepts of separate corporate personality and limited liability. The law must tread a fine line between protecting creditors from irresponsible management and discouraging entrepreneurship and responsible risk-taking. Some argue the risk of wrongful trading and disqualification can have a stifling effect, encouraging premature liquidation, while others see the statutory framework as an inadequate and ineffective response to directorial inadequacies.

QUESTION | 1

Midas plc is a successful publisher with several bestselling authors. Unfortunately problems (not of Midas plc's making) with printing facilities overseas, where their books are produced, meant that the full autumn production was lost. The company was unable to find alternative printers and so lost significant sales over the lucrative Christmas period. The company has found it difficult to continue to meet its salary bills and rental for its UK warehouse.

Midas plc granted a floating charge over its undertaking to Gold Bank several years ago. At present it is unable to meet the interest payments on the bank loan. Once the immediate production problems are over, there is every expectation that the business should return to its normal profitable state.

Advise Midas plc and Gold Bank of the legal options available to resolve the problems.

CAUTION!

■ As the question states that a return to profitability is likely, you should be considering alternative solutions to liquidation, focusing on CVAs and administration, rather than winding up itself

■ Tailor your response according to the emphasis of your own course: it is more likely that you will be expected to show an outline knowledge of the rescue procedures and an appreciation of their different merits, rather than detailed knowledge of the legal processes and procedures relating to CVAs and administrations

DIAGRAM ANSWER PLAN

Identify the issues	■ Identify the problem ■ Identify the options available

Relevant law	■ Insolvency and the role of corporate rescue ■ Company Voluntary Arrangements ■ Administration ■ Pre-packaged administrations

Apply the law	■ Apply the law to the facts ■ Consider advantages and disadvantages of different options in the circumstances

Conclude	■ Conclude, advising on the best option in the circumstances

A   SUGGESTED ANSWER

Midas' financial difficulties appear too serious for informal agreements with creditors or management changes to make a difference. With Midas unable to pay its creditors, it risks winding up under **Insolvency Act 1986 (IA 1986), s. 122(1)(f)** if a creditor brings a petition, despite the underlying strength of its business.

¹This links an appreciation of the problems of insolvent liquidations with the purpose of corporate rescue

The impact of a corporate collapse can cause a 'ripple effect' of insolvencies among suppliers and customers, and wider financial and social harm. Accordingly the framework of 'corporate rescue' aims to maintain viable businesses[1] through offering alternatives to liquidation with 'a discernible move from pathology to preventative medicine' (Finch, 'Corporate rescue: who is interested?' [2012] JBL 190).

There are two main legal options here: a company voluntary arrangement (CVA) or administration. Both were introduced in **IA 1986** following the Cork Report (Insolvency Law Review Committee, 'Insolvency Law and Practice' (Cmnd 8558, 1982)) and were significantly reformed by **Enterprise Act 2002 (EA 2002)**. It

²Although you are not given the date of the floating charge, it is safe to make this assumption as no examiner will expect you to interpret 'several years ago' as stretching back to 2003

will be assumed that administrative receivership is not an option as Gold Bank's floating charge was almost certainly created after 15 September 2003[2] **(EA 2002)**. Other legal options, such as a Scheme of Arrangement **(Companies Act 2006, ss. 895–901)**, are possible, but would be more complex and do not offer any obvious advantages here.

CVA

A CVA (under **IA 1986, Part 1**) is, at first sight, a good option for a company such as Midas plc with a strong business but (hopefully) temporary financial difficulties. It is a 'particularly flexible option' (*IRC v Wimbledon FC Ltd* **[2004] EWCA Civ 655**), that would allow Midas to enter into a binding agreement with its creditors where they agree to delay or otherwise change the terms of payment (a scheme of arrangement), or to receive a smaller sum in full satisfaction of their debt (a composition of debt).[3]

To pursue a CVA the directors of Midas would make a proposal providing for a nominee (who will become the CVA supervisor, and must be a qualified insolvency practitioner) and explaining why a CVA is desirable. The nominee makes a report to the court and, if the report indicates that the CVA is desirable, will call meetings of the members and the creditors. The CVA will be effective (and binds all creditors with notice of and entitled to vote at the meeting) if approved by a 75 per cent majority of creditors (by value) and a simple majority of members (**IA 1986, s. 4**). There is no need for court approval, although the CVA can be challenged under **IA 1986, s. 6** if it unfairly prejudices the interests of a creditor, member, or contributory (eg *Mourant Trustees v Sixty UK Ltd* [2011] BCLC 383) or there is some material irregularity in relation to the meeting (eg *HMRC v Portsmouth FC* [2010] EWHC 2013 (Ch)). A successful CVA would mean Midas plc could continue to exist in its current form with its directors remaining in post.[4]

A major drawback to a CVA under **IA 1986, Part 1** is that it does not provide a moratorium during the pre-agreement period meaning a creditor could take action against Midas before a CVA is approved. A new-style CVA with a moratorium under **IA 1986, Sch A1** is restricted to small private companies so is not available to Midas, and has not proved popular in any event. Its proposed replacement with a 'pre-insolvency moratorium' (BEIS, 'Insolvency and Corporate Governance: Government Response', 2018) could help Midas either as a stand-alone measure or as a 'gateway to a CVA' (Umfreville, 'Pre-packaged administrations and company voluntary arrangements' (2019) 30 ICCLR 581), or Midas could pursue a CVA with the benefit of a moratorium under the 'wrapper' of an administration.[5]

Administration

Administrations (under **IA 1986, Sch B1**) were intended to reflect the best elements of administrative receivership (an outside expert maximizing value) but acting for creditors collectively rather than for the charge holder alone. Their use was further encouraged by reforms in **EA 2002**.

[3] This concisely establishes the essence of a CVA

[4] You could comment on the attraction of such an outcome for the directors, particularly when compared with other insolvency procedures

[5] Structurally this leads in nicely to the next point

An administrator must be a qualified insolvency practitioner. They can be appointed by the court (under an administration order), or (following **EA 2002**) out of court by the holder of a qualifying floating charge or by the company or its directors. As a qualifying floating charge holder (ie with a charge over the whole, or substantially the whole, of a company's undertaking, **IA 1986, Sch B1, para 14**) Gold Bank could appoint an administrator out of court, or Midas' directors could do so, by filing notice of intention to appoint an administrator with the court, followed by notice of appointment. An interim moratorium takes effect when notice of intention is filed but notice must not be filed to gain 'breathing space' without a settled intention to appoint an administrator: *JCAM Commercial Real Estate Property XV Ltd v Davis Haulage Ltd* **[2017] EWCA Civ 267**. The moratorium becomes permanent (for the duration of the administration) on the administrator's appointment.

The administrator sets out proposals for achieving the purpose of the administration—one of the three objectives of administration (**IA 1986, Sch B1, para 3**), namely (a) rescuing the company as a going concern, (b) achieving a better result for the company's creditors than on a winding up, or (c) realizing property to make a distribution to one or more secured or preferential creditors. Objective (a) should be pursued unless the administrator thinks it is not reasonably practicable to achieve that aim, or objective (b) would achieve a better result for the company's creditors as a whole. Objective (c) can only be pursued if neither of the first two objectives is reasonably practicable and it would not unnecessarily harm the interests of creditors as a whole.

[6] Having established the aims of administration, this paragraph now applies those aims to the case at hand

The administrator would therefore have to consider whether Midas itself can be rescued[6] (which may involve seeking a CVA within the administration), or whether there are other options, including selling off Midas' business (rescuing the business, but not the company itself) to maximize returns for creditors. The proposals should be sent to the registrar, creditors, and members and the administrator should call a creditors' meeting to consider whether to accept or reject the proposal (or accept a modified version, if the administrator approves)—a simple majority by value is sufficient. The administrator takes over the management of the company, carrying out their functions with a view to achieving the administration objectives, applying to terminate the administration if they believe the purpose cannot be achieved.

[7] Pre-packs are a very topical issue in corporate insolvency so it is sensible to consider them explicitly, as well as administration more generally

Pre-pack Administration

If the business of Midas is going to have to be sold, the directors and Gold Bank may wish to pursue a pre-packaged administration (a 'pre-pack'), which make up about 30 per cent of administrations.[7] The sale of the business is arranged prior to the administration following discussion between the directors, the proposed administrator, and the proposed purchaser (often a vehicle controlled by the directors),

[8] A quick reference to the characters in the question reassures the examiner that you are still focusing on the facts

and usually the main creditor, here Gold Bank.[8] The sale is completed immediately after the company enters administration.

Pre-packs have been criticized for avoiding the statutory process (as there is no proposal and no creditors' meeting) and for lack of scrutiny and independence. The courts have recognized the criticisms (*Re Kayley Vending* [2011] 1 BCLC 114; *Re Hellas Telecommunications* [2010] BCC 295), but accepted the validity of pre-packs (*Re Transbus International* [2004] 1 WLR 2654; *DKLL Solicitors v HMRC* [2008] 1 BCLC 112). Pre-packs can maximize creditor value by allowing a quick sale avoiding negative publicity to the most likely buyer, but creditors can feel overlooked. Statement of Insolvency Practice 16 (SIP 16) provides some protection by requiring administrators to, inter alia, provide information to creditors and comply with marketing guidelines. Directors must also be careful when purchasing a business or assets, as *Re System Building Services Group Ltd* [2020] EWHC 54, somewhat controversially, held directors' duties continue during administration. If a pre-pack was proposed for Midas, the purchaser could refer it to the 'pre-pack pool', introduced following the Graham Report, to offer an independent opinion and reassure creditors. Referral to the pool is voluntary and uncommon, although mandatory referral is under consideration.[9] If the requirements of SIP 16 are substantially complied with, a pre-pack sale is unlikely to be successfully challenged in the courts (*Re Halliwells LLP* [2011] 1 BCLC 345), but Midas should be aware that the courts will require evidence of compliance (*Re Moss Groundworks Ltd* [2019] EWHC 2825).

[9] Show your awareness of recent developments in the area

Conclusion

Midas or Gold Bank should appoint an administrator over the company.[10] While a CVA is more likely to result in the rescue of Midas itself, if a CVA is desirable, pursuing this within administration should increase the prospects of success. Alternatively the administrator could sell off the viable business, distributing the purchase money within the administration (dissolution following under **IA 1986, Sch B1, para 84** without need for intervening liquidation). This would provide a swift resolution to the financial difficulty while ensuring the business can continue free of its current financial burden. A pre-pack administration should be considered but the insolvency practitioner will need to balance the benefits and drawbacks of a quick sale.

[10] Giving clear advice is always welcomed, so don't hold back even if you are worried the examiner might come to a different conclusion

LOOKING FOR EXTRA MARKS?

- Use some of the many critical academic articles and empirical research papers (particularly relating to pre-packs) to enhance and support the points you make
- You could make reference to real life examples of corporate collapses or rescues, or insolvency statistics, to highlight the use of particular provisions
- Show an awareness of ongoing debates and reforms in this area

QUESTION | 2

Critically assess the circumstances in which a creditor can bring a petition to wind up a company and the possible reasons why such a petition might be rejected.

CAUTION!

- Balance your essay carefully: if you spend too long looking at the grounds for a petition you may run out of time before adequately dealing with rejection/dismissal of a petition
- Focus on the main issues (cash flow test, balance sheet test, disputed debts, cross-claims) but don't forget to at least mention other points such as statutory demands and improper purpose

DIAGRAM ANSWER PLAN

> Introduction: creditor petitions and deemed inability to pay debts
>
> ▼
>
> Statutory demands and failed execution of judgment: s. 123(1)(a)–(b)
>
> ▼
>
> Cash flow test: s. 123(1)(e)
>
> ▼
>
> Balance sheet test: s. 123(2)
>
> ▼
>
> Disputed debts and cross-claims
>
> ▼
>
> Other grounds for rejection: settlement, improper purpose, creditor wishes
>
> ▼
>
> Conclusion: linking the two elements of the question

SUGGESTED ANSWER

[1] This introduction briefly establishes the groundwork for the discussion, so that the bulk of the essay can get straight into the detail

Creditors may petition for the compulsory winding up of a company[1] under the **Insolvency Act 1986 (IA 1986), s. 122(1)(f)** on the ground that it is unable to pay its debts. **IA 1986, s. 123** deems a company to be unable to pay its debts in four circumstances: (i) failure to pay a statutory demand for £750 or more (**s. 123(1)(a)**); (ii) failed execution of judgment (**s. 123(1)(b)**); (iii) inability to pay debts as they fall due (**s. 123(1)(e)**), and (iv) assets less than liabilities (**s. 123(2)**). This essay will examine those tests to assess the circumstances in which a creditor may bring a winding up petition, and then consider the various reasons why a creditor petition may be rejected.

Statutory Demand and Failed Execution of Judgment

The tests in **IA 1986, s. 123(1)(a)–(b)** are very specific. The statutory demand under **s. 123(1)(a)** requires a creditor to serve a written demand for payment (for a due debt that is currently payable: *JSF Finance v Akma Solutions* **[2001] 2 BCLC 307**) at the company's registered office. If after three weeks the company has failed to pay the debt (which must be at least the statutory minimum of £750) or to secure or compound for it to the creditor's satisfaction, it is presumed unable to pay its debts. For a creditor the downside to this test is the element of delay.[2]

² Even a brief comment indicates that you are not simply setting out the law, but thinking about its significance

The second option, under **IA 1986, s. 123(1)(b)** is where a creditor has a judgment or court order against the company, has tried to enforce this through the court, but has not been paid. This requires the petitioner to have gone through the process of obtaining judgment and attempting execution and so is unattractive to most creditors. This means many creditors rely on the general tests under **IA 1986, s. 123(1)(e) and (2)** which stand side by side 'as part of a single exercise' (*Re Casa Estates (UK) Ltd* **[2014] EWCA Civ 383**).

Cash Flow Test

The test under **s. 123(1)(e)**—that a company is unable to pay its debts as they fall due—is known as the cash flow test.[3] A company's failure to pay an undisputed debt is in itself evidence that a company cannot pay its debts as they fall due and so can found a creditor's petition. This was seen in *Taylor's Industrial Flooring Ltd v M & H Plant Hire (Manchester) Ltd* **[1990] BCLC 216** where the Court of Appeal rejected a claim that such a process was abusive. A company can be wound up on this basis even if it has a surplus of assets over liabilities, as made clear in *Cornhill Insurance v Improvement Services* **[1986] BCLC 26**. Crucially, the petition must relate to an undisputed debt: disputed debts will be considered later.[4]

³ The cash flow test is all about whether a company can actually pay its debts as demanded, regardless of whether it has an excess of assets over liabilities

⁴ You could happily deal with disputed debts at this point, but as the essay splits quite neatly into 'grounds for petition' and 'reasons for rejection', it makes a bit more sense to leave this until later

Under this head the court is entitled to consider debts that will fall due in the 'reasonably near' future. That will depend on all the circumstances, particularly the nature of the business: *BNY Corporate Trustee Services Ltd v Eurosail-UK plc* **[2013] UKSC 28** (*Eurosail*) and not by a 'slavish focus' only on debts due at the relevant date: *Re Cheyne Finance Ltd* **[2008] 1 BCLC 741**.[5]

⁵ If you had time you could add some more detail about these cases and judgments

Balance Sheet Test

Section 123(2) looks at whether the value of the company's assets is less than the amount of its liabilities, including contingent and prospective liabilities (but not contingent or prospective assets: *Evans v Jones* [2016] EWCA Civ 660)—the balance sheet test.[6] The test should not be applied mechanistically but with common sense and regard to 'commercial reality' (*Evans v Jones*).

In *Eurosail*, the Supreme Court stated the court must make a judgment as to whether the company cannot reasonably be expected to meet its liabilities, bearing in mind that the more distant those liabilities, the harder it will be to establish this. It is not necessary to show that a company has reached 'the end of the road' as the Court of Appeal had indicated.

Disputed Debts

In order for a creditor to petition, the debt relied on under **IA 1986, s. 123(1)(e)** must be undisputed. Someone whose debt is disputed is not in a position to present a petition as they are not established as a creditor (*Mann v Goldstein* [1968] 1 WLR 1091; *Coilcolor Ltd v Camtrex Ltd* [2015] EWHC 3202 (*Coilcolor*)).[7] The winding up jurisdiction is not intended for the resolution of disputes between parties (*Re Selectmove Ltd* [1995] 1 WLR 474; *Coilcolor*) and it is an abuse of process to bring a petition to pressure a company to pay a disputed debt (*Sell Your Car With Us Ltd v Sareen* [2019] EWHC 2332).

For the petition to be rejected, the company must establish there is a genuine and bona fide dispute, that the company honestly believes this to be the case, and that there are reasonable or substantial grounds for this belief. The court should not conduct a lengthy or elaborate hearing on this matter: *Tallington Lakes Ltd v Ancasta International Boat Sales Ltd* [2012] EWCA Civ 1712. If established it has been stated that the dismissal of the petition is not discretionary but compulsory: *Re Bayoil SA* [1999] 1 WLR 147 (*Bayoil*). Nonetheless the court has allowed a petition to proceed even with a bona fide dispute as to the amount of the debt if the company clearly owes money to the petitioner in excess of the statutory minimum: *Re Tweeds Garages Ltd* [1962] 1 Ch 406. *Re GBI Investments* [2010] 2 BCLC 624 indicated a petition might also, exceptionally, be allowed to proceed notwithstanding a dispute as to the debt if injustice would otherwise result. This might contradict the first reason given for rejecting disputed debts (unless the petitioner is a creditor, they have no standing to petition),[8] but is perhaps justified as winding up is a discretionary and collective creditor remedy.

Cross-claims

Even where a debt is due and not disputed, a petition may be dismissed where the company has a 'genuine and serious' (*Bayoil*) cross-claim

---

[6] The balance sheet test means that a company can be deemed 'unable to pay its debts' even if it is paying its debts as they fall due, provided its liabilities exceed its assets

[7] It is helpful to explain why disputed debts do not found a petition: it shows you understand the justification for the courts' approach and gives you a focus for later comment

[8] Think PEA: having made the point (about petitions based on disputed debts occasionally being allowed to proceed) and evidenced it, it can be assessed by commenting on whether the reasoning is valid or not

against the petitioner that exceeds the company's debt to the petitioner. This is so even if the company had been in a position to litigate their claim but had chosen not to (*Montgomery v Wanda Modes Ltd* [2002] 1 BCLC 289, doubting *Bayoil* on this point). The reason given is that if the cross-claim amounts to a set off, the petitioner would not have standing, while even if not a set off, the cross-claim would mean the petitioner had no sufficient interest in the winding up being ordered (*Coilcolor*).[9]

Other Grounds for Rejecting a Petition

If the debt that is the subject of the petition has been paid by the time of the hearing then the petition will be rejected—the petitioner is no longer a creditor. However, the court has the ability to substitute another creditor to the petition in certain circumstances (**Insolvency Rules 2016, r. 7.17**), and so the petition may continue regardless of payment of the initial petition debt.

Another important reason for rejecting a petition is where it is brought for an improper purpose. The courts have held that a petitioner must not act in order to obtain some private advantage or for some ulterior motive. For example in *Re Leigh Estates Ltd* [1994] BCC 292 the court rejected a petition that sought to put the petitioner in a stronger position in the company's administration—winding up is a collective remedy and petitions should be brought for the benefit of creditors generally. However, *Mann v Goldstein* made clear that the mere fact that a petitioner has acted with 'personal hostility' or hope of some indirect advantage is not in itself an abuse of process.

Finally, the court may reject a petition where the creditors disagree as to whether the company should be wound up. For example in *Re ABC Coupler & Engineering Ltd* [1961] 1 WLR 243 a petition was rejected where other creditors opposed the making of a winding up order and the court found they were reasonable in wanting the company to continue as there were good prospects of payment in due course. While the views of the majority of creditors will be highly influential, the court may still choose to make a winding up order (*Re P & J MacRae Ltd* [1961] 1 WLR 229); it remains a matter for the court's discretion.

[10]As the essay question itself did not provide much of a 'handle' for a thesis, the conclusion creates a link between the two halves of the question to show further understanding of the points raised throughout the essay

Conclusion[10]

The circumstances in which a creditor may bring a petition and the grounds for rejecting a petition are connected in several ways, particularly through the notion of disputed debts. While statute gives creditors the ability to petition to wind up a company, a creditor must also be careful not to abuse the process, and ultimately winding up remains in the court's discretion. A creditor's ability to petition must be balanced against the need to act fairly to the company and respect the collective nature of the winding up jurisdiction.

LOOKING FOR EXTRA MARKS?

- Comment on the significance of the points you make, and link between them, to avoid the answer being too descriptive

- Explore the cases on the test for 'inability to pay debts' in more depth to consider the merits (or otherwise) of different approaches

- Consider how far the winding up jurisdiction is and should be used as a 'debt-collecting' process

QUESTION | 3

A winding up order was made on 30 April 2018 against Hebejebe Ltd, following a creditor's petition which was presented to the court on 8 April 2018. Lara has been appointed liquidator. The creditors of Hebejebe Ltd include:

i. Wizzerd Bank, which is owed £250,000 and has a fixed charge (duly registered) over Hebejebe Ltd's freehold premises. Hebejebe Ltd's premises have been valued at £200,000

ii. Pocus Finance plc which provided an initial £10,000 loan to Hebejebe Ltd on 2 April 2017, and then a further loan of £5,000 on 20 April 2017. Hebejebe Ltd granted Pocus Finance plc a floating charge (which was duly registered) to secure the full £15,000 on 20 April 2017

iii. Hebejebe Ltd's senior employees who received no pay during the company's last three months of trading

iv. HM Revenue and Customs which is owed £30,000 in respect of unpaid PAYE and national insurance payments

v. Abracadabra, a trade creditor, who is owed £2,000. Abracadabra had been owed £3,000 but Hebejebe Ltd paid off £1,000 of this debt on 12 April 2018 as Abracadabra refused to continue to supply essential raw materials until the debt was reduced. Hebejebe Ltd would have had to cease trading immediately had these materials not been supplied.

Advise Lara on how the company's assets should be distributed to the creditors in light of the information above. Lara has incurred costs and expenses of £10,000.

CAUTION!

- Make sure you understand the creditor priority list and where different claimants fit within this. You need to be able to identify all the claimants and the nature of their claim and slot them into place

- Keep an eye on any dates in insolvency questions—they can be crucial to whether some provisions apply or not

- Watch out for any surrounding issues as it is easy for questions like this to add in any number of other insolvency topics

DIAGRAM ANSWER PLAN

Identify the issues	▪ In what order should the company's assets be distributed?
Relevant law	▪ Function of liquidator ▪ Creditor hierarchy and pari passu ▪ Secured creditors—fixed and floating charges ▪ Vulnerability of floating charges: IA 1996, s. 245 ▪ The 'prescribed part' ▪ Dealing with costs and expenses of liquidation ▪ Preferential creditors ▪ Position of unsecured creditors ▪ Dispositions after the commencement of the winding up: IA 1986, s. 127
Apply the law	▪ Validity of specific transactions ▪ Order of payment
Conclude	▪ Who gets what, when, and why?

SUGGESTED ANSWER

As liquidator, Lara's function is 'to secure that the assets are got in, realised and distributed to the company's creditors and, if there is a surplus, to the persons entitled to it' (**Insolvency Act 1986 (IA 1986), s. 143(1)**). Accordingly, having gathered in all the assets belonging to the company (which may be swelled by claims for, eg preferences (**IA 1986, s. 239**), transactions at an undervalue (**IA 1986, s. 239**), or wrongful trading (**IA 1986, s. 214**)), she must distribute the assets according to a strict order of priority. Creditors must submit a proof of debt in order to claim in the liquidation; it will be assumed that all have done so.[1]

The basic order for priority of payment is as follows,[2] although it will be seen that the situation is more complex than at first appears:

● Secured creditors with a fixed charge
● Expenses of liquidation
● Preferential creditors
● Secured creditors with a floating charge
● Unsecured/ordinary creditors
● Deferred creditors
● Members

[1] Most courses would not expect you to know the rules of proof of debt, so it is fine to make this assumption

[2] It isn't usually good practice to set out a list or bullet points in an essay, but this helps to establish both the basic principles and the framework of your essay

The various claims in the question will be considered in the order they might be expected to appear in this list.

Fixed Charge Holders

Secured creditors with the benefit of a fixed charge, such as Wizzerd Bank, are in a strong position, and if their security is sufficient to satisfy their debt in full they need not prove in the liquidation at all. Wizzerd Bank could choose to surrender the security to the liquidator and prove as an unsecured creditor,[3] but as an unsecured creditor Wizzerd Bank would rank rateably (*pari passu*) with other unsecured creditors and would probably only recover a small part of the debt. Wizzerd Bank should realize the security, which in this case will cover £200,000 of the debt and then prove in the liquidation for the remaining £50,000, in respect of which it will be an unsecured creditor.

[3] In more unusual cases a secured creditor might choose to give up the security, for example if there were prior secured creditors then they might be better off claiming as an unsecured creditor. That is not the case here

Lara's Expenses

The expenses of the liquidation (including Lara's costs and remuneration) are paid in priority to all other payments. If the company's free assets are insufficient to meet the liquidation expenses then assets subject to a floating charge can be used by virtue of **IA 1986, s. 176ZA** (reversing *Re Leyland Daf Ltd* [2004] UKHL 9). If there are insufficient assets to meet all liquidation expenses they are paid according to the order set out in **Insolvency (England and Wales) Rules 2016, r. 7.108** (see *Re Toshoku Finance UK plc* [2002] UKHL 6).[4]

[4] Don't waste your time setting this priority order out unless you have covered it on your course and there is something in the question to indicate that all the costs/expenses might not be met

Preferential Creditors

Preferential debts are those debts that statute provides are paid in priority to other debts, other than the expenses of winding up (**IA 1986, s. 175**) and are found in **IA 1986, Sch 6**. The main preferential debts are unpaid employee remuneration from the four months prior to liquidation (to a maximum of £800 per employee), accrued holiday pay, and loans used specifically for paying employee remuneration. Accordingly the unpaid senior employees will be preferential creditors for their unpaid salaries up to £800 plus holiday pay.[5] The category of preferential debts was reduced by **Enterprise Act 2002** in order to benefit unsecured creditors meaning HM Revenue and Customs will not be a preferential creditor for outstanding PAYE and national insurance. Although the government proposes partially to reverse these changes, making HMRC a 'secondary preferential creditor' ranking before floating charge holders for debts including PAYE and employee national insurance contributions, this will only be for liquidations from April 2020.

[5] Employees can also claim against the National Insurance Fund for arrears of wages and holiday pay, with limits, but this is unlikely to be within the scope of a company law course

If the company's free assets are insufficient to pay the preferential debts, then property subject to a floating charge can be used (**s. 175(2)**). Should there be insufficient assets to meet all the preferential debts in full, then preferential creditors are paid *pari passu*.

Floating Charge Holders

Pocus Finance claims to have a floating charge securing £15,000. However, a floating charge created at a relevant time is only valid to the extent it is created in consideration for money paid or goods or services supplied 'at the same time as, or after, the creation of the charge' (**IA 1986, s. 245**). Here the first £10,000 of the debt was provided before the creation of the charge and so would be invalid (*Re Shoe Lace Ltd; Power v Sharp* **[1994] 1 BCLC 111**).

The relevant time for a person who is not connected with the company (**IA 1986, s. 249** and **s. 435**) is 12 months ending with the onset of insolvency (**s. 245(3)**), provided the company is unable to pay its debts within the meaning of **IA 1986, s. 123**. In a compulsory liquidation the 'onset of insolvency' is the date of presentation of the petition, so this charge has been created just within the 12-month period, but Lara would need to check whether the company was unable to pay its debts at that time. If so then the floating charge is likely to be valid only in relation to the £5,000, leaving Pocus Finance to claim as an unsecured creditor for the remaining £10,000. If Hebejebe was able to pay its debts as at 20 April 2017 then it would not be a relevant time and the floating charge will be valid for the full £15,000.[6] Although providing security for an existing debt (as here) can also amount to a preference under **IA 1986, s. 239**, Lara cannot use **s. 239** as the charge was created outside the relevant time of six months.

As has been seen, even where Pocus Finance has the benefit of a floating charge, it may lose some of the benefit of that security if the company's free assets are insufficient to meet the liquidation expenses and preferential debts. In addition, following **Enterprise Act 2002**, a 'prescribed part' of the realizations of assets subject to a floating charge is reserved for unsecured creditors unless disapplied (in exceptional circumstances) by the liquidator or the court (**IA 1986, s. 176A**). The prescribed part is 50 per cent of net property under £10,000 and 20 per cent over this, to a maximum of £600,000 (likely to be increased to £800,000 in 2020).

Unsecured Creditors

Unsecured creditors share *pari passu* in the remaining assets of the company[7] and the prescribed part, although secured creditors with a shortfall (here Wizzerd Bank and Pocus Finance) cannot share in the prescribed part (*Re Airbase Ltd* **[2008] EWHC 124**).

Abracadabra is also an unsecured creditor, but her position is complicated by the company's payment of £1,000 after presentation of the petition.[8] Dispositions of the company's property after commencement of the winding up (ie the presentation of the petition: **IA 1986, s. 129**) are void under **IA 1986, s. 127** unless validated by the court. Disposition is defined widely (*Re J Leslie Engineering* **[1976]**

[6] As sufficient facts aren't given in the question, the two alternative outcomes are given. You could assume that the company could (or couldn't) pay its debts at that time, and conclude accordingly—but you need to state expressly that you've made that assumption

[7] Always try to get a reference to *pari passu* into an insolvency distribution question. In an essay you could be asked to consider the notion in more depth

[8] It is essential to keep an eye on the dates (and remember how the commencement of the winding up is backdated), or you'll miss this point

1 WLR 292) and so prima facie Lara can recover the £1,000 from Abracadabra, and Abracadabra would have to prove as an unsecured creditor for the full £3,000.

However, the court is likely to be willing to validate the payment retrospectively. In *Re Gray's Inn Construction* [1980] 1 WLR 711 the court indicated that a payment made in good faith in the ordinary course of business, where the parties were unaware of the petition and there was no intention to prefer the creditor, is likely to be validated. These factors seem to apply to Abracadabra and this conclusion is supported by *Denney v John Hudson* [1992] BCLC 901[9] where a good faith payment of a debt to a fuel supplier in order to ensure continued trading was validated.

[9] Remember to apply the law to the case at hand, and support your conclusion with case authority where you can

Conclusion

It appears that Wizzerd Bank can realize its security to recover £20,000 but will need to claim the outstanding £50,000 as an unsecured creditor. Lara's costs and expenses including her remuneration will be paid first out of the free assets of the company, and out of floating charge realizations if necessary. Next come the preferential creditors, including the senior employees to the prescribed limit, but not including HMRC. Pocus Finance's floating charge could be entirely valid (if the company was able to pay its debts as at the date of the charge) or may be valid only for the 'new debt' of £5,000. To the extent that the debt is not secured by the charge, Pocus Finance will have to claim as an unsecured creditor. So far as the charge is valid, property subject to it will have the prescribed part set aside for distribution among the unsecured creditors (other than Wizzerd Bank and Pocus Finance). Abracadabra faces having to return the £1,000 to Lara as a void disposition, but could apply to the court for validation and has quite a strong case. Depending on the outcome of that validation application, Abracadabra will claim either £2,000 or £3,000 as an unsecured creditor.

Having paid the expenses of the liquidation, the preferential debts, and the claim of any valid floating charge holder, Lara must distribute the remaining assets of the company *pari passu* among the unsecured creditors. If there were any assets remaining (which is improbable in an insolvent liquidation), she should then pay any deferred debts (which include interest on proved debts: **IA 1986, s. 189**) and pay any surplus to members. Once the winding up is complete Lara should apply to have Hebejebe dissolved (**IA 1986, s. 205**).[10]

[10] Having summarized the main points from the essay (slotting everything into the payment hierarchy) it is time to finish off the question (and the company)

LOOKING FOR EXTRA MARKS?

- Explain and explore key principles such as *pari passu* in more depth, engaging with some academic discussion
- Reflect on more practical matters, such as employee claims under the Redundancy Payments Scheme, or when the prescribed part might be disapplied, or the role of the liquidator
- Consider the justification for (and criticism of) changes to preferential creditor status for HM Revenue and Customs

 QUESTION | 4

'On the liquidation of a company, all of the assets belonging to the company at the commencement of the liquidation are available for the creditors.'

Discuss.

 CAUTION!

- At first sight this appears an innocuous question, but working out what assets belong to the company and what assets are available to creditors (and what is the 'commencement of the liquidation') requires you to cover a lot of ground
- Matters included in this question, such as transaction avoidance, disclaimer, and disposition of property, more commonly appear in problem questions, but you should be able to deal with them in essays too

DIAGRAM ANSWER PLAN

Introduction: context of question and commencement of winding up

Assets unavailable for distribution: including trusts, retention of title, security, set off, disclaimer

Swelling the assets: including post-petition dispositions of property, transactions at undervalue, preferences

Conclusion: summary and comment

SUGGESTED ANSWER

The liquidator's function includes distributing the company's assets to its creditors (**Insolvency Act 1986 (IA 1986), s. 143(1)**) but identifying what assets are available for distribution is sometimes difficult.

¹Identify the two halves of the essay—reduction of available assets, and swelling of available assets

Some assets that at first sight appear to belong to the company are not in fact available to the general creditors. Conversely, the asset pool may be swollen by the liquidator recovering assets previously disposed of.¹

The commencement of the liquidation may be backdated by statute, which can be important in identifying what assets are available. The commencement of a voluntary winding up is the date of the passing of the resolution to wind up (**IA 1986, s. 86**), while the commencement of a compulsory winding up is the date of the presentation of the petition (**IA 1986, s. 129(2)**) except where the company is already in voluntary winding up: **s. 129(1)**.

Assets Unavailable for Distribution

Assets that do not pass to the liquidator include property held as trustee for another. In *Re Kayford Ltd* **[1975] 1 All ER 604**, customer deposits paid into a special account pending delivery of goods were

²You could explore how the *Quistclose* trust enables a lender to reclaim a loan given for a frustrated purpose in full, rather than claiming *pari passu* with other unsecured creditors

held on trust and so had to be returned to the customers (see also *Barclays Bank v Quistclose Investments Ltd* **[1970] AC 567**).²

In addition, property in the company's possession under a contract containing a valid reservation of title or '*Romalpa*' clause (*Aluminium Industrie Vaassen v Romalpa Aluminium* **[1976] 1 WLR 676**) does not pass if the goods remain identifiable and removable (*Hendy Lennox v Grahame Puttick* **[1984] 1 WLR 485**). The contract may also validly include an 'all-monies' clause, reserving title until all outstanding debts between the parties have been met (*Clough Mill v Martin* **[1985] BCLC 64**).

Often many of a company's valuable assets are subject to a fixed charge. These can be realized by the charge holder to meet their own

³Security is the prime reason why so few of the company's assets are available for the general body of creditors

debt without involvement of the liquidator, so will not be available for distribution to other creditors.³ While assets subject to a floating charge also offer the benefit of security to the charge holder, not only are these charges vulnerable to challenge by the liquidator under **IA 1986, s. 245** unless given for fresh consideration, but a significant part of the realizations of these assets will usually be available for distribution to unsecured creditors through the prescribed part (**IA 1986, s. 176A**). Accordingly, while assets subject to a fixed charge will not be available to general creditors (unless the charge can be challenged as a preference under **IA 1986, s. 239**, for example), assets subject to a floating charge may be at least partially available to the company's general creditors.

A company's assets include debts owing to it, and a liquidator will normally seek to recover any money owing to the company. But not all sums due are recoverable by the liquidator. If an individual both owes money to the company and is owed money by the company, these sums must be set off (**Insolvency (England and Wales) Rules 2016, r. 14.25**) and only the balance can be claimed by the liquidator (or proved in the liquidation).

More positively for general creditors, liquidators may wish to reject onerous property belonging to the company. Liquidators have a right of disclaimer in respect of unprofitable contracts, property that is unsaleable or not readily saleable, or property giving rise to liability to pay money or perform any other onerous act: **IA 1986, s. 178**. Disclaimer terminates the rights, interests, and liabilities of the company and victims of disclaimer must prove as creditors.

Swelling the Assets

[4] This sentence provides a structural link between the two parts of the essay

While not all assets apparently belonging to the company are available to the liquidator, several statutory provisions allow the liquidator to recover previously disposed of property.[4]

Under **IA 1986, s. 127** dispositions of the company's property after commencement of the winding up are void unless validated by the court. This allows the liquidator to recover property disposed of after

[5] This is the main reason why the backdating of the commencement of the winding up can be so important (it also pushes back the relevant times for IA 1986, ss. 239–45)

presentation of the winding up petition,[5] unless the court validates the disposition. The court will normally approve bona fide payments in the ordinary course of business where the parties were unaware of the petition and the payment does not seek to prefer the creditor: *Re Gray's Inn Construction Ltd* **[1980] 1 WLR 711**, but it remains a matter for the court's discretion.

Liquidators may also avoid transactions at an undervalue occurring within a relevant time: **s. 238**. The relevant time is two years prior to commencement of the winding up provided the company at the time was unable to pay its debts (within **s. 123**, presumed for transactions with connected persons): **s. 240(2)**. A company enters into a transaction at an undervalue if it makes a gift, receives no consideration, or receives consideration significantly less than the value of the consideration supplied by the company (**IA 1986, s. 238(4)**). The last of these requires the balancing of consideration received and given and the liquidator must usually establish the value of any consideration (*Phillips v Brewin Dolphin* **[2001] 1 WLR 143**). The transaction will not be avoided if the company entered into the transaction in good faith with reasonable grounds for believing it would benefit the company: **s. 238(5)**, but this defence must be established by the person relying on it (*Re Barton Manufacturing Ltd* **[1999] 1 BCLC 740**).

Liquidators can also challenge preferences under **IA 1986, s. 239**—where the company does something within the relevant time that puts creditors (or guarantors or sureties) into a better position in the event of the company's insolvent liquidation than they would otherwise have been. The relevant time is two years for connected persons and six months for outsiders (**s. 240(1)(a)–(b)**), and the company must have been unable to pay its debts. Preferences are only voidable where the company was motivated by a desire to prefer the individual (**s. 239(5)**), which requires a positive wish to improve their position (**Re MC Bacon Ltd [1990] BCLC 324**) but this desire to prefer is presumed for connected persons: **s. 239(6)**.

In respect of transactions at an undervalue and preferences, the court may make a variety of orders, including a retransfer of property, repayment to the liquidator, or revival of guarantees: **s. 241**.[6] Third parties who are bona fide purchasers for value are protected: **s. 241(2) and (2A)**. Proceeds of a successful claim are held for the unsecured creditors: **Re Yagerphone Ltd [1935] 1 Ch 392**.

As mentioned earlier, liquidators can use **IA 1986, s. 245** to invalidate floating charges created other than in relation to money paid, goods or services supplied, or discharge or reduction of the company's debts at the same time or after creation of the charge. The relevant time for creation is one year for non-connected persons provided the company was unable to pay its debts: **s. 245(4)**. For connected persons, the period is two years and is not conditional upon the company being unable to pay its debts. The effect of **s. 245** can be seen in **Re Shoe Lace Ltd [1994] 1 BCLC 111**, where a charge executed in July, relating to loans made between April and early July, was invalidated. Banks operating a current account have some protection from **s. 245**. **Re Yeovil Glove Co Ltd [1965] Ch 148** held (thanks to the rule in **Clayton's Case (1816) 1 Mer 572**, whereby credits to a current account discharge debts in the order in which they were incurred) the honouring of cheques after the creation of a charge were new advances even when the overdraft remained virtually unchanged. When **s. 245** does apply, assets otherwise subject to security are instead available for distribution to general creditors.[7]

Liquidators may also apply to set aside extortionate credit transactions within the three years prior to the making of the winding up order: **IA 1986, s. 244**. The court has a range of possible orders including setting aside or varying the transaction, refunding sums paid by the company, and surrendering security.

Liquidators (and victims) can also challenge transactions defrauding creditors made at any time—transactions at an undervalue made with the aim of putting assets beyond the reach of a creditor or otherwise prejudicing their interests: **IA 1986, s. 423(3)**. Possible court orders are similar to those in **s. 241**: **s. 425**.[8] Liquidators may also seek to reclaim property under the anti-deprivation principle, if a main purpose of the arrangement was to deprive the company of valuable property in the event of its insolvency: **Belmont Park Investments Pty Ltd v BNY Corporate Trustee Services Ltd [2012] 1 AC 383**.

[6] This is crucial to link to the focus of the essay ie the assets available to creditors

[7] Again, this makes the link to the essay focus and guards against this paragraph just describing s. 245 without explaining its relevance to the question

[8] There isn't any point in setting out the possible orders again here

Conclusion

A company's assets at the commencement of liquidation may be much smaller than might first appear because of security interests, and devices such as trusts and retention of title clauses. This is balanced to some extent by the ability of liquidators to seek to recover assets disposed of both before and after presentation of the winding up petition. In addition the liquidator may be able to claim contributions from company directors, for example by using misfeasance proceedings (**s. 212**) or fraudulent or wrongful trading (**ss. 213–14**) to further swell the assets available for creditors. The ability to assign a liquidator's statutory rights of action (**IA 1986, s. 246ZD**, introduced in 2015) may make at least some financial recovery more likely,[9] to the benefit of creditors.

[9] This shows you have a broader understanding of the liquidator's position

LOOKING FOR EXTRA MARKS?

- Explore more complex and controversial areas such as the anti-deprivation principle or retention of title clauses in more detail

- Explore which of a liquidator's claims relate to property of a company existing at the time of liquidation, and which claims are subsequently acquired, and the difference this makes to which creditors primarily benefit from the recovery. See eg *Re Oasis Merchandising* [1995] 2 BCLC 493

QUESTION | 5

Frank, and his wife Chelsey, are the shareholders and directors of Stamford Ltd, a company that owns and manages several health spas. The day-to-day running of the business is undertaken by Frank, and although Chelsey undertakes clerical and administrative tasks, she leaves management decisions to Frank and simply signs documents as and when directed by him to do so. The company pays them each an annual salary of £65,000.

Stamford Ltd was incorporated in 2012 and was profitable initially, but began making losses from early 2015. Although the losses were apparent from the company's financial documents, Frank continued to believe that the problems were temporary and Chelsey was happy to believe him. In 2017 one of the company's spas was forced to close and no buyer could be found for the property, although Frank continued to include the property at full value in the company's accounts. Pressure from unpaid creditors continued through 2017 and 2018, but Frank continually assured Chelsey that the problem was simply a short-term cash flow issue that would be resolved as the economy improved, which Frank believed would be very soon. In the meantime Frank only paid those creditors who actively demanded payment, while creditors who did not demand payment were left unpaid. The business continued to decline and in March 2019 a winding up order was made against Stamford Ltd. Lewis has been appointed liquidator.

Advise Lewis in relation to both wrongful trading and disqualification proceedings against Frank and Chelsey.

CAUTION!

■ You must consider both wrongful trading and disqualification: deal with wrongful trading first, and then go on to consider how the facts might relate to disqualification

■ Make sure you explain the law and then apply each element to the facts of the question. Don't be tempted simply to recite the problem facts—show explicitly how they are relevant

■ As the question expressly instructs you to consider particular areas of law, keep your focus on these rather than considering other provisions

DIAGRAM ANSWER PLAN

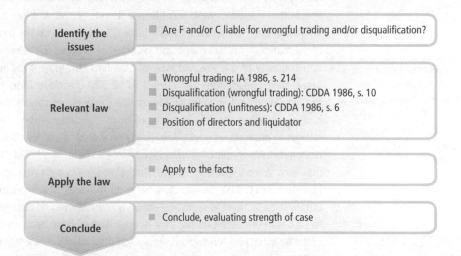

Identify the issues	■ Are F and/or C liable for wrongful trading and/or disqualification?
Relevant law	■ Wrongful trading: IA 1986, s. 214 ■ Disqualification (wrongful trading): CDDA 1986, s. 10 ■ Disqualification (unfitness): CDDA 1986, s. 6 ■ Position of directors and liquidator
Apply the law	■ Apply to the facts
Conclude	■ Conclude, evaluating strength of case

SUGGESTED ANSWER

Lewis specifically seeks advice regarding wrongful trading proceedings (**Insolvency Act 1986 (IA 1986), s. 214**) and disqualification (**Company Directors Disqualification Act 1986 (CDDA 1986)**). Accordingly this answer will not consider other possibilities such as misfeasance (**IA 1986, s. 212**) or fraudulent trading (**s. 213**).[1]

[1] This demonstrates that you know there are other possibilities for a liquidator to consider, but that you are following instructions in not dealing with them

Wrongful Trading

Wrongful trading proceedings would be brought by Lewis, as the liquidator. A director of a company in insolvent liquidation is liable for wrongful trading if, prior to the commencement of winding up, he knew or should have realized that there was no reasonable prospect of the company avoiding insolvent liquidation (**s. 214(2)**) unless he took every step to minimize loss to creditors (**s. 214(3)**). Stamford Ltd is in insolvent liquidation and Frank and Chelsey are directors of the company[2] so both are potentially liable.

[2] You are told in the question that they are directors, so you don't need to spend time considering de facto and shadow directors

The issue is thus whether Frank and/or Chelsey knew or ought to have known, before liquidation commenced, that the company could not reasonably avoid insolvent liquidation. The facts they knew, or should have known, and the conclusions they should have reached are those known or reached by a 'reasonably diligent person' with (a) the general knowledge, skill, and experience of someone carrying out the functions of that director (including the functions that should have been carried out but weren't: **s. 214(5)**) and (b) the general knowledge, skill, and experience that the director has (**s. 214(4)**). Thus, part (a) imposes a minimum objective standard (*Re DKG Contractors Ltd* **[1990] BCC 903**) varying according to the type of company and role, while (b) is subjective, imposing additional expectations on someone with greater skills, knowledge, or experience than expected of someone in that position. Frank and Chelsey do not appear to have any additional skills, etc so their knowledge will be assessed on the basis of the minimum objective standard expected of directors in their roles in a company of the size and type of Stamford Ltd. In *Re Produce Marketing Consortium Ltd* **[1989] BCLC 520** (*Produce Marketing*), the court took account of information the directors should have had, even though they did not actually have it because of their own failures to draw up accounts. So reliance on inaccurate accounts will not protect Frank and Chelsey, nor will Frank's continuing belief that problems were temporary.[3] In *Re Rod Gunner Organisation Ltd* **[2004] 2 BCLC 110**, the directors hung on to hopes of refinancing, but these hopes were unrealistic—similarly Frank's hopes do not seem to be based on facts. Chelsey, as a director, should have been aware of the financial position and not simply accepted Frank's reassurances.

Although the company started making losses in 2015, making losses does not make insolvent liquidation inevitable—even knowledge of insolvency is not sufficient in itself (*Re Hawkes Hill Publishing Ltd* **[2007] BCC 937**)—but by 2017 as losses continued, the property could not be sold and creditor pressure mounted, the directors should have realized liquidation was inevitable. In *Re Brian D Pierson Ltd* **[1999] BCC 26** (*Pierson*), a husband and wife were both liable where they refused to face facts and made only superficial judgments as to the company's financial state—this is similar to Frank and Chelsey's position.

Directors can avoid liability if they took 'every step' they ought to have taken to minimize loss to creditors (**IA 1986, s. 214(3)**), assessed using the **s. 214(4)** dual objective/subjective standard. The onus is on the director to establish such a defence: *Brooks v Armstrong* **[2015] EWHC 2289**. *Pierson* indicates directors should show specific steps to preserve or realize assets for creditors—Frank and Chelsey have taken no such steps. Chelsey might claim in relying on Frank she acted 'honestly, reasonably and ought fairly to be excused' and so should be relieved from liability under **Companies Act 2006, s. 1127** but even

[3] The relevant case facts are indicated (which also identifies the issue) and then expressly applied to the problem facts; the same technique is used in the next sentence. This is in essence a condensed version of IRAC

[4] Not an essential point but the examiner will be pleased to see you recognize it, while still relating it to the facts of the question

if a court thought this reasonable, *Produce Marketing* indicated **s. 1127** does not apply to wrongful trading.[4]

If Frank and Chelsey were found liable for wrongful trading the court can order them to make such contribution to the company's assets as it thinks proper (**s. 214(1)**). The measure of liability is compensatory—the amount the company's assets were depleted by the director's actions (*Produce Marketing*)—ie the losses incurred after Frank and Chelsey should have realized the company was unlikely to avoid insolvent liquidation. Accordingly, provided Frank and Chelsey have sufficient private resources to meet the claim[5] Lewis should seriously consider bringing proceedings against them.

[5] This is a practical observation—there would be no point in bringing proceedings if the directors don't have the money to meet the claim—and shows you are thinking about the situation

Disqualification

The primary purpose of **CDDA 1986** is to protect the public from those who are unfit to be directors (*Re Sevenoaks Stationers (Retail) Ltd* **[1991] Ch 164** (*Sevenoaks*)).[6] A disqualification order prohibits that person, for a period of time, from being a director, receiver, or taking part in the promotion, formation, or management of a company or acting as an insolvency practitioner.

[6] A basic introductory point: it can be useful to set the scene but don't get distracted into a more general discussion of disqualification

If Lewis successfully brings wrongful trading proceedings against Frank and Chelsey, the court can disqualify the directors under **CDDA 1986, s. 10**.[7] However, the more common ground for disqualification is 'unfitness' where a company has gone into insolvent liquidation (**s. 6**). Under **s. 7A** Lewis has an obligation to make a report on the directors' conduct to the Secretary of State, who then decides whether to bring proceedings under **s. 6**.

[7] This is a commonly overlooked point

In assessing unfitness **CDDA 1986, s. 12C** directs the court to **Sch 1**. This is a non-exhaustive list of factors for consideration, based (since reform in 2015)[8] on fairly general concepts, such as breach of duty, material contravention of obligations, and responsibility for the causes of insolvency. The courts have held that unfitness does not require deliberate wrongdoing or dishonesty: negligence (or even marked incompetence) can amount to unfitness (*Sevenoaks*).

[8] The Small Business, Enterprise and Employment Act 2015 made a number of significant changes to CDDA 1986

A common ground for disqualification is trading at creditors' risk. This is similar to wrongful trading, although it is not necessary to establish breach of **IA 1986, s. 214**. It is unfit to continue to trade and build up further debts with little prospect of creditors being paid: *Re Living Images Ltd* **[1996] 1 BCLC 348**. A policy of paying only pressing creditors, as in this case, is clear evidence of unfitness (*Sevenoaks*). While paying directors' salaries is not in itself unfitness, this may be unfit if it is more than the company can afford (*Secretary of State v Van Hengel* **[1995] 1 BCLC 545**) which seems to be the case here.

Chelsey's failings lie in inactivity which can amount to unfitness. Directors can delegate but cannot abrogate their responsibilities or allow themselves to be dominated by a board member (*Re Westmid Packing Services Ltd* [1998] 2 All ER 124). *Re Barings plc (No. 5)* [2000] 1 BCLC 523 makes clear that each individual director has inescapable minimum obligations and Chelsey seems to have failed to meet these.

If unfitness under **s. 6** is established—there is evidence of unfitness for both—the court must make a disqualification order of at least two years (maximum 15 years). *Sevenoaks* established three brackets: 2–5 years for relatively not very serious cases, 6–10 years for serious cases not meriting the top bracket, and 11–15 years for particularly serious cases. Here Chelsey's behaviour would put her in the lower end of the bottom bracket, while Frank's behaviour warrants a higher tariff, although still not a particularly serious case.[9] While the period may be reduced by mitigating factors (including the age and health of the director and his/her general conduct before and after the liquidation), there are no particular mitigating factors mentioned here.

Since 2015 there is the possibility of a direct financial penalty for unfit directors; **CDDA s. 15A** allows the Secretary of State to apply for a compensation order[10] against Frank and Chelsey, if disqualified, requiring them to pay an amount for the benefit of a specified creditor, creditors, or class of creditor, or contribute to the assets of Stamford Ltd (**s. 15B**). So far only one compensation order has been made: *Secretary of State v Eagling* [2019] EWHC 2806, where the director misappropriated company assets for his own benefit and was disqualified for the maximum period. A relevant factor is whether the director(s) have already made (or are at risk of making) a financial contribution in separate proceedings, so Stamford Ltd's creditors would not get double recovery from disqualification and wrongful trading.

Conclusion

Lewis has a good case against Frank and Chelsey for wrongful trading in continuing to trade for over a year after they should have realized there was no reasonable prospect of the company avoiding insolvent liquidation; if successful the creditors will benefit from the recovery of losses made after that point. The directors could also be disqualified under **CDDA 1986, s. 10**. In any event Lewis must make a report on their conduct, and the case under **s. 6** against them appears strong. The directors may wish to offer a 'disqualification undertaking' (**CDDA 1986, s. 1A; s. 7(2A)**), which operates just like a disqualification order, to avoid the cost of proceedings. If subject to a disqualification order or undertaking, the court may make a compensation order against them (or they could give a compensation undertaking: **s. 15A(2)**).

[9] Even without extensive knowledge of likely disqualification periods, you can still have a go at applying the facts to the *Sevenoaks* brackets based on the kind of behaviour you've seen in other cases. Of course the period of disqualification is not up to Lewis, and you could make that point

[10] Another important recent development

LOOKING FOR EXTRA MARKS?

■ Explain and assess further the relevant changes made in this area by the 2015 reforms

■ Explore some of the facts of the key cases to highlight similarities or differences with the facts of the problem question

■ Consider the factors that may encourage or discourage Lewis from taking action against the directors for wrongful trading, such as funding, and the possibility of assigning this right of action

TAKING THINGS FURTHER

■ Adebola, B., 'The case for mandatory referrals to the pre-pack pool' (2019) 32 Insolv Int 71

Makes the case, in light of the very limited use of the pre-pack pool and criticisms of pre-packs more generally, that referrals should be mandatory in order to ensure appropriate oversight and provide broader reassurance. See also Vaccari, E., 'The pre-pack pool: is it worth it?' (2018) 29 ICCLR 697.

■ Akintola, K., 'The proposed preferential prepaying consumers: a fair pack of insolvency recommendations?' [2018] JBL 1

Examines Law Commission proposals ('Consumer Prepayments on Retailer Insolvencies' (2016) Law Com No 368) for prepaying consumers to have preferential status in retail insolvencies, arguing instead for reform of the prescribed part.

■ Astle, T., 'Pack up your troubles: addressing the negative image of pre-packs' (2015) 28 Insolv Int 72

A concise review of the main criticisms of pre-packs and the recommendations of the Graham Review. See also Kastrinou, A., 'An analysis of the pre-pack technique and recent developments in the area' (2008) 29 Co Law 259 on the practice and legality of pre-pack administrations.

■ Dabor, I., 'The directors' disqualification compensation order regime: the panacea for preventing corporate abuse' (2018) 39 Co Law 243

Discussion of the introduction of the disqualification compensation order, viewing it as a 'welcome development'. Worth considering alongside some of the concerns expressed; see for example Secretary of State v Eagling.

■ Finch, V., 'Corporate rescue: who is interested?' [2012] JBL 190

An examination of corporate rescue processes, focusing in particular on whose interests are and should be the focus of these processes.

■ Frieze, S., 'The company in financial difficulties: the alternatives' (2008) 21 Insolv Int 124

A brief consideration of options open to a company approaching insolvency.

■ Hicks, A., 'Director disqualification: can it deliver?' [2001] JBL 433

Based on some empirical studies, this article considers how effective the CDDA 1986 is in removing 'rogue' directors and protecting creditors. Suggestions for reform and alternative approaches are also discussed. See also Williams, R., 'Disqualifying directors: a remedy worse

than the disease' (2007) 7 J Corp Law Studies 213 for a critical view of the disqualification regime, arguing that it fails to meet its stated aims.

■ Keay, A., 'Disputing debts relied on by petitioning creditors seeking winding up orders' (2001) 22 Co Law 40

A helpful examination of the law on disputed debts and cross-claims.

■ Keay, A., 'Wrongful trading: problems and proposals' (2014) 65 NILQ 63

Considers the principal difficulties facing liquidators in bringing wrongful trading claims and makes proposals for reform. See also Werdnik, R., 'Wrongful trading provision—is it efficient?' (2012) 25 Insolv Int 81.

■ McCormack, G., 'Swelling corporate assets: changing what is on the menu?' (2006) 6 JCLS 39

A wide-ranging examination of the transaction avoidance provisions.

■ Milman, D., 'Personal liability and disqualification of company directors: something old, something new' (1992) 43 NILQ 1

Explores the trend towards imposing personal liability on directors of collapsed companies, examining the circumstances in which this might arise. There has been significant case law and statutory development since this article, but many of the points it makes remain valid.

■ Umfreville, C., 'Pre-packaged administrations and company voluntary arrangements: the case for a holistic approach to reform' (2019) 30 ICCLR 581

Analyses the use and effectiveness of CVAs and pre-packs, and considers how both might be reformed, calling for a move from a 'reactive, piecemeal and disjointed approach' to a 'proactive, strategic and aligned' process. See also Ellina, S., 'Administration and CVA in corporate insolvency law: pursuing the optimum outcome' (2019) 30 ICCLR 180.

■ Williams, R., 'What can we expect to gain from reforming the insolvent trading remedy?' (2015) 78 MLR 55

Argues that even when reformed the wrongful trading provision will fail to bring significant recoveries for creditors as it has inherent limitations. Includes a helpful account of the origins, objectives, and use of the remedy. See also Williams, R., 'Civil recovery from delinquent directors' (2015) 15 JCLS 311.

Online Resources

www.oup.com/uk/qanda/

For extra essay and problem questions on this topic, as well as advice on revision and exam technique, please visit the online resources.

Mixed Topic Questions

12

ARE YOU READY?

Lots of topics in company law interlink so there is plenty of scope for mixed questions in company law exams. (You'll already have noticed some overlapping of topics in some questions in previous chapters.) While mixed topic questions are often problem questions, essay questions can also require you to stretch over two (or more) topics. Some examiners make more use of mixed questions than others so check your own course to see whether there is any particular approach to setting mixed questions— look at past papers, attend revision sessions, ask your tutor what the practice is (they may or may not tell you). Just about any topics in company law can be connected in a question, but be particularly aware of any connections your lecturer explicitly highlights in class. Some common connections are:

- Directors' duties and shareholder remedies
- Corporate personality and insolvency
- Articles of association, shareholders, and shareholder remedies
- Directors' duties and insolvency
- Share capital and loan capital; loan capital and insolvency
- Corporate contracts and pre-incorporation contracts; contracts and directors' duties
- Corporate personality and corporate liability

 QUESTION | **1**

In October 2019 Stella decided to turn her hobby of craft-making into two businesses. She planned to incorporate two companies, Beadie Ltd (through which she would run a jewellery-making business) and Craftie Ltd (which would run craft-making courses). Accordingly, on 4 November 2019 Stella entered into a contract with Alexis for a large supply of glass beads for making jewellery.

(>)

She signed the contract 'Stella, director, Beadie Ltd' and put her initials beneath it. On the same day she entered into a contract with Indira for fabrics for her craft courses, signing the contract 'Craftie Ltd'.

The following week Stella decided she would run both businesses through a single company to save on registration costs and so incorporated Craftie Ltd, with Stella as sole shareholder (holding one £1 share) and director. Craftie Ltd's certificate of incorporation is dated 15 November 2019. On 20 November 2019 Stella purchased £1,000 worth of office supplies (in the name of Craftie Ltd) from Paperco plc.

It is now clear that Stella has sold all the jewellery she had made at a loss and has failed to get any customers for the craft-making courses. All the stock and supplies have been used and Craftie Ltd has no assets of any value. Alexis is owed £500 for the beads, Indira is owed £800 for the fabrics, and Paperco is owed £1,000.

Advise Alexis, Indira, and Paperco.

CAUTION!

- Focus on what the individuals want to achieve, and think of the routes by which this might be possible. Start with the facts, and use these to direct you to the right areas of law, rather than searching for particular topics

- Remember that personal liability is not just about piercing the veil of incorporation. Think about the other ways in which personal liability might attach to a shareholder or director, particularly when a company is insolvent

- If dates are given, they are probably there for a reason, so considering their significance might give you a clue as to the relevant topic

DIAGRAM ANSWER PLAN

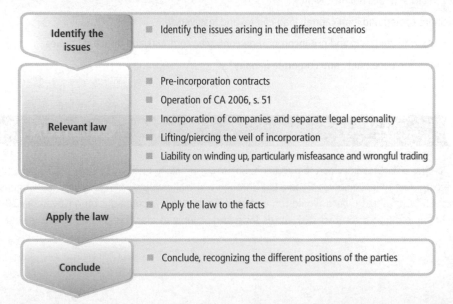

Identify the issues	■ Identify the issues arising in the different scenarios
Relevant law	■ Pre-incorporation contracts ■ Operation of CA 2006, s. 51 ■ Incorporation of companies and separate legal personality ■ Lifting/piercing the veil of incorporation ■ Liability on winding up, particularly misfeasance and wrongful trading
Apply the law	■ Apply the law to the facts
Conclude	■ Conclude, recognizing the different positions of the parties

SUGGESTED ANSWER

[1] Identify what the individuals want to achieve, and why, to show the examiner you understand the basic premise of the question

As Craftie Ltd has no assets, Alexis, Indira, and Paperco will be looking to establish personal liability on the part of Stella.[1] At first sight this is not easy: *Salomon v A. Salomon & Co Ltd* [1897] AC 22 (*'Salomon'*) shows a company is a separate legal person from its shareholders (and directors); even in a 'one-man company' (like Craftie Ltd), the individual behind the corporate veil is not normally liable for the company's obligations.

However, the positions of Alexis and Indira, and of Paperco are distinct because the contracts with Alexis and Indira were entered into prior to incorporation, while Paperco's contract was entered into after Craftie Ltd was incorporated. It will be necessary to consider the law on pre-incorporation contracts for Alexis and Indira, and to consider more generally the liability of those behind the corporate veil in relation to Paperco.

[2] You could deal with these two contracts separately, to ensure you deal with their different features

Alexis and Indira[2]

A company comes into existence on incorporation (**Companies Act 2006 (CA 2006), s. 16**), the date of its certificate of incorporation. This is 15 November for Craftie Ltd, while Beadie Ltd was never actually formed. Accordingly, on 4 November when the contracts were entered into, the companies did not exist and could not be bound.

Liability under a pre-incorporation contract is now governed by **CA 2006, s. 51**. This makes the person purporting to act for a company (or as agent for it) before it is formed, personally liable on the contract.

[3] This shows a bit of further analysis about what is happening, and links implicitly to the wider context of the question

Although it might be tempting to view **s. 51** as piercing the veil of incorporation by imposing liability for 'the company's contract' on someone behind the veil, this isn't so, as the company was never itself liable. At most the veil is glanced behind to check the date of incorporation,[3] like checking an individual's birthdate.

Section 51 makes Stella personally liable on both contracts; it is irrelevant how they were signed. At common law the form of signature could be crucial: in *Kelner v Baxter* (1866) **LR 2CP 174** (*Kelner*) where the contract was signed by the promoter on behalf of the company, the promoter was bound, but in *Newborne v Sensolid (GB) Ltd* [1954] **1 QB 45** (*Newborne*) where the contract was signed purportedly by the company (authenticated by the individual) the contract was void (as with a non-existent principal).

[4] Always try to link the law to the facts of the question

This would have led to different results for Alexis (akin to *Kelner*) and Indira (akin to *Newborne*)[4] but **s. 51** removes the distinction: Stella is bound by both the contracts, notwithstanding the difference in signature. Although **s. 51** allows an individual to exclude personal liability, this must be explicit, and signing in the company's name (as in Indira's contract) is not sufficient to exclude liability: *Phonogram Ltd v Lane* [1982] **QB 938** (*Phonogram*).

[5] If dealing with the two contracts within the same part of the essay as here, make sure you expressly recognize (and deal with) their different features

Another difference between Alexis and Indira's contracts is that while Craftie Ltd was subsequently incorporated, Beadie Ltd was not in fact formed.[5] But this does not prevent **s. 51** operating. In *Phonogram*, the court held the section applied wherever a company was in contemplation of formation, it didn't matter that the company was never actually incorporated.

Alexis and Indira can therefore be advised that Stella is personally liable on the contracts with them. Stella could have avoided liability by expressly excluding personal liability in the contract (**s. 51**; *Phonogram*) but it is highly unlikely she has done so. She could also avoid liability if the contracts had been novated after Craftie Ltd's formation, although simple adoption or ratification of the contract by the company would not be effective (*Natal Land Co & Colonization Ltd v Pauline Colliery and Development Syndicate Ltd* **[1904] AC 120**). However, novation requires the company to make a new contract on the terms of the old one; simply acting in the belief the old contract is binding is not sufficient (*Re Northumberland Avenue Hotel Co* **(1886) 33 ChD 16**). Novation does not appear to have happened here; Stella remains personally liable on both contracts.

Paperco

Paperco's contract was entered into after incorporation of Craftie Ltd. The contract appears valid (as director, Stella had authority to enter into it on the company's behalf); the problem is that Craftie Ltd does not have the resources to meet its obligations.

[6] It is tempting to provide a lot of information about *Salomon* and the veil of incorporation more generally but this would be very descriptive; make sure you concentrate on points that are really relevant to the problem question

The starting point is *Salomon*: as the company is a separate legal person, Stella is not personally liable for debts incurred by the company.[6] However there are exceptions: the court may pierce the veil of incorporation, or Stella could be personally liable through other legal routes or statutory provisions.

Unfortunately for Paperco, the jurisdiction to pierce the veil of incorporation, to make Stella liable for Craftie's debt, is very limited. In *Prest v Petrodel Resources Ltd* **[2013] UKSC 34**, the Supreme Court held it could be used only as a last resort (when no other remedy was available) and only where the corporate form had been used to evade or frustrate an existing legal right or remedy. That is clearly not the case here; there is no 'relevant impropriety' to trigger the jurisdiction. Stella was using the company legitimately to run her business, not evade existing liabilities: choosing the corporate form in order to avoid personal liability is not impropriety, but a legitimate reason for incorporation (*Salomon*; *Adams v Cape Industries plc* **[1990] Ch 433**).[7]

[7] This passage deals with the fundamental points concisely; if you had time you could expand this a bit more and provide additional authority

Liability could fall on Stella ('lifting the veil' in a wide sense) if Craftie Ltd were acting as her agent—Stella would therefore be liable as principal. But that argument is highly unlikely to succeed; it failed in *Salomon* and very few cases have found agency on the facts (eg *Smith, Stone & Knight v Birmingham Corpn* [1939] 4 All ER 116). More recent cases indicate clear evidence of an agency relationship will be needed (*Adams v Cape Industries plc; Yukong Line Ltd of Korea v Rendsburg Investments Corpn of Liberia (No. 2)* [1998] 1 WLR 294). It is highly improbable an agency relationship would be found here. Other ways in which the courts have effectively avoided the veil, for example through imposing direct liability on an individual through tort law, do not apply here.[8]

[8] This shows you understand there are other ways around the veil, but without wasting time

Relevant statutory provisions that might impose personal liability on Stella are triggered by the company going into liquidation and Paperco, as a creditor owed more than £750, could present a winding up petition under **Insolvency Act 1986 (IA 1986), s. 122(1)(f)**.[9] The liquidator can seek a contribution to the company's assets from Stella under **IA 1986, ss. 213–14** for fraudulent or wrongful trading. Fraudulent trading (**s. 213**) seems unlikely as there is no suggestion of intent to defraud creditors or a fraudulent purpose. Wrongful trading (**s. 214**) is where a director continues to trade beyond the point s/he should have concluded there was no reasonable prospect of the company avoiding insolvent liquidation. Arguably Stella should have realized at an earlier stage (it is not clear how long she has been making losses and failing to fill her courses) that failure was inevitable. If found liable the measure is compensatory, ie the losses arising after the point of 'no return' (*Re Produce Marketing Consortium Ltd* [1989] BCLC 520). This would swell the company's assets and make it more likely Paperco could recoup some of its loss.

[9] A minor point, but one that shows the examiner your knowledge and understanding stretches beyond the key topics raised in the question

As director, Stella may have breached her duties to the company, eg the duty of care, skill, and diligence, **CA 2006, s. 174**, although more facts would be needed to conclude on this. If in breach, the liquidator can recover using the misfeasance procedure under **IA 1986, s. 212**. A creditor such as Paperco can also apply under **s. 212**. The liquidator could also make use of other insolvency provisions, such as transactions at an undervalue (**IA 1986, s. 238**) if there were evidence of disposal of Craftie Ltd's assets, but the current facts do not indicate this.

A problem with **IA 1986, s. 214** (and most other relevant **IA 1986** provisions including, in practice, **s. 212** as creditors rarely have the information to start proceedings), is that action is taken by the liquidator. This depends on having sufficient assets in the liquidation to meet expenses, and creditors may be reluctant to fund quite speculative proceedings.[10] A further possibility (which is not in the hands of the liquidator) is disqualification for unfitness under the **Company Directors Disqualification Act 1986 (CDDA 1986), s. 6** as if Stella

[10] Show you recognize practical as well as legal difficulties in bringing claims

is disqualified the Secretary of State may now seek a contribution order from her (**CDDA 1986, s. 15A**), which could benefit Paperco. However disqualification proceedings against Stella are not inevitable, would take some time to conclude, and might not result in a compensation order.

Conclusion

The position of Alexis and Indira is strong. **CA 2006, s. 51** operates to protect them by making the contracts enforceable against Stella personally. The position is very different for Paperco: the courts are reluctant to pierce or lift the veil of incorporation, and its only hope is for some recovery from Stella through the insolvency process if and when the company is wound up—but this is both uncertain and quite unlikely to result in full recovery.

LOOKING FOR EXTRA MARKS?

- Don't just explain the possible routes; evaluate their chances of success. As part of this, recognize more practical issues, such as the likelihood of action actually being taken

- Consider more generally the issue of creditors, risk, and limited liability, linking the discussion to the facts of the problem

QUESTION | 2

'Despite the contractual effect of the articles of association, minority shareholders are greatly in need of the additional remedies provided for them by statute.'

Discuss.

CAUTION!

- Mixed essay questions can be tricky as you need to balance the topics appropriately, and draw the connections between them, so plan your essay carefully before starting to write

- Don't be tempted to provide a standard consideration of the articles of association in answer to this question; it is clear that a more wide-ranging response is required

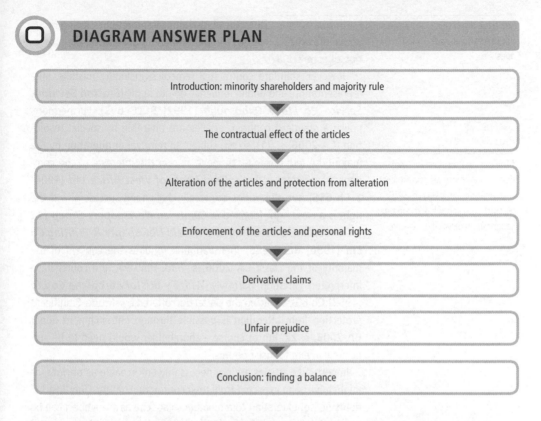

○ DIAGRAM ANSWER PLAN

Introduction: minority shareholders and majority rule

▼

The contractual effect of the articles

▼

Alteration of the articles and protection from alteration

▼

Enforcement of the articles and personal rights

▼

Derivative claims

▼

Unfair prejudice

▼

Conclusion: finding a balance

SUGGESTED ANSWER

A company is an association of members, operating on the principle of majority rule. This doesn't mean a minority shareholder should have no rights, only that these must be considered within the wider framework of an effective corporate structure, taking into account the courts' reluctance to get involved in internal affairs (***Carlen v Drury*** **(1812) 35 ER 63**). The law attempts to balance the interests of the company, the majority, and the minority, but this can be complicated.

This essay will first explain[1] the contractual nature of the articles of association and explore the extent to which this 'contract' provides secure and enforceable rights, to assess whether minority shareholders need further assistance. Secondly, the essay will examine the statutory remedies available to minority shareholders, considering how these improve a minority shareholder's position. The essay will conclude that[2] although the statutory remedies are of undoubted value, the position of a minority shareholder remains a vulnerable one.

The Articles as a Contract

By virtue of **Companies Act 2006 (CA 2006), s. 33**, the articles (the internal rules of the company) bind the company and members as if

[1] With a question like this, it is important to set out what you will be discussing and, in particular, how it relates to the question. This also helps to balance the context-setting first paragraph to reassure the examiner you haven't lost sight of the question itself

[2] It isn't necessary to indicate your conclusion from the start, but it can be quite effective if you know where you are heading

³ Link the discussion of the articles
to the particular issues raised in the
question

terms of a contract. It might be thought therefore that placing rights within the articles provides a minority shareholder with all the protection of contract law.³

However, standard contractual remedies, including mistake, misrepresentation, and undue influence do not apply (*Bratton Seymour Service Co Ltd v Oxborough* [1992] BCLC 693). Furthermore, unlike a standard contract, articles are alterable by special resolution (**CA 2006, s. 21**), so are subject to removal or alteration by the majority. Alteration must be bona fide in the interests of the company as a whole⁴ (*Allen v Gold Reefs of West Africa Ltd* [1900] 1 Ch 656) but alterations are rarely challenged successfully. If the right is a class right (defined in *Cumbrian Newspapers Group Ltd v Cumberland & Westmorland Herald Newspaper & Printing Co Ltd* [1986] BCLC 286) then variation requires the consent of the majority of the class: **CA 2006, s. 630**. However, the courts have interpreted 'variation' narrowly (*White v Bristol Aeroplane Co Ltd* [1953] Ch 65), reducing the protection offered by statute. Significant protection from alteration is possible through entrenchment under **CA 2006, s. 22**, but of course a shareholder would need to be sufficiently aware to insist on this.

⁴ The passage on alteration, variation, and entrenchment has to deal with a lot of points very concisely; be strict with yourself and don't get caught up in detailed discussion

Importantly, articles are not necessarily enforceable as of right, as might have been expected from their contractual nature. Only 'insider' rights (ie rights relating to a member's capacity as a member) can be enforced, while 'outsider' rights (rights relating to another capacity) are not directly enforceable: *Hickman v Kent or Romney Marsh Sheep-Breeders' Association* [1915] 1 Ch 881. However, outsider rights may be indirectly enforced through a member suing qua member (*Quin & Axtens Ltd v Salmon* [1909] AC 442; Wedderburn, 'Shareholder rights and the rule in *Foss v Harbottle*' [1957] CLJ 194), or through a contract extrinsic to the articles (*Re New British Iron Co* [1898] 1 Ch 324). There remain fundamental questions about which articles are directly enforceable, by whom, and in what circumstances, despite determined academic attempts to reconcile the cases⁵ (summarized by Drury, 'The relative nature of the shareholder's right to enforce the company contract' [1986] CLJ 219).

⁵ If you had time you could expand this discussion a bit

Enforcement of the articles is particularly complex because of the courts' desire not to undermine the rule in *Foss v Harbottle* (1843) 2 Hare 461.⁶ This consists of two principles: the 'proper claimant' principle, preventing members bringing action in respect of wrongs done to the company; and the 'majority rule' principle, preventing action about internal matters that can be regularized by the majority.

⁶ This is an important link between the two key elements of the question—the articles and shareholder remedies

The proper claimant principle does not prevent a shareholder bringing a personal claim relating to his personal rights, rather than rights of the company. However, as previously discussed, not all rights contained in the articles can be enforced directly by a shareholder. Members' claims in relation to matters of internal management of the company may fall foul of the majority rule principle. Quite what amounts to a directly enforceable personal right remains uncertain: the cases are inconsistent, and the opportunity to clarify the position in **CA 2006** was not taken. While a shareholder has a personal right to have his vote recorded in accordance with the articles (*Pender v Lushington* (1877) **6 Ch D 70**), in *MacDougall v Gardiner* (1875) **1 Ch D 13** the court held a failure to call a poll in accordance with the articles was a matter of internal management. Sometimes courts will prevent a company from acting contrary to the articles (eg *Quin & Axtens Ltd v Salmon*); sometimes not (eg *Irvine v Union Bank of Australia* (1877) **2 App Cas 366**). A shareholder may bring a personal claim to restrain an illegal or ultra vires act of the company (*Simpson v Westminster Palace Hotel Co* (1860) **8 HL Cas 712**) but this is clearly of very limited scope.

It can be seen that despite the articles being of a 'contractual nature', this does not provide a minority shareholder with secure, absolute, and enforceable rights. Even if the terms of the articles were unalterable and fully enforceable by a shareholder, a shareholder might still suffer from wrongdoing or oppression, as actions of the directors or majority could be within the terms of the articles but still harmful.[7]

7 This paragraph highlights the relevance of the points made, and links forward to the next point. It reduces the risk of the answer appearing to be two separate essays

Statutory Remedies

The true exception to the rule in *Foss v Harbottle* is a derivative claim, originally a common law remedy based on 'fraud on the minority', but now in **CA 2006, ss. 260–4**. This allows a shareholder to bring proceedings in relation to the company's cause of action relating to a breach of duty by a director (**s. 260(3)**), recognizing directors are unlikely to commence action against themselves. However, strict boundaries are placed on claims to ensure the company is protected from undue interference from shareholders. This means minority shareholders can find it very difficult to bring derivative claims, as a range of factors (**s. 263**) must be considered by the court before granting permission to continue the claim. With a risk of costs (unless an indemnity is granted by the court) and any eventual recovery benefiting the company rather than the shareholder directly, derivative claims are unsurprisingly uncommon. Attempts to outflank the rule in *Foss v Harbottle* by alleging 'personal' loss, through a diminution in the value of shares because of wrongdoing, have been rejected as merely 'reflective' of the company's loss: *Johnson v Gore Wood and Co* [2002] **2 AC 1**.

Given the difficulties shareholders have in enforcing the articles, or pursuing a derivative claim, the statutory 'unfair prejudice' remedy (**CA 2006, s. 994**) has become very important. (Shareholders could also seek to wind up the company on the just and equitable ground (**Insolvency Act 1986, s. 122(1)(g)**) in some cases but its restricted scope and fatal consequences for the company rarely make it the best option for a minority shareholder.)[8]

8 There isn't time to look at s. 122(1)(g) in any depth, and it is clearly much less relevant to the issues in the question, so this simply indicates it has been considered

Under **s. 994** a member may petition the court where the conduct of the company's affairs has been unfairly prejudicial to his interests as a member. This is wide enough to encompass non-compliance with the articles, ignoring or removing a shareholder's rights, and wrong-doing that harms the company as well as the individual.[9] 'Interests as a member' is interpreted generously, and not limited to strictly 'membership rights': *Gamlestaden Fastigheter AB v Baltic Partners Ltd* **[2007] 4 All ER 164**.

Nonetheless, although it is a wide remedy it is not 'unbounded' (*Re Tobian Properties Ltd* [2012] EWCA Civ 998). Complaints must relate to the conduct of the company's affairs, which is interpreted widely but would not cover, for example, arrangements between members for the sale of shares: *Re Leeds United Holdings plc* [1996] 2 BCLC 545. More significantly the conduct must be 'unfair' as well as prejudicial. In *O'Neill v Phillips* [1999] 1 WLR 1092, the House of Lords held this does not encompass all failures to meet a shareholder's 'legitimate expectations', but requires some breach of the terms on which the association was formed or continued, other than a 'trivial' breach, or use of legal powers in a manner contrary to equity, typically where the company is a quasi-partnership (per *Ebrahimi v Westbourne Galleries Ltd* [1973] AC 360). Not all shareholder complaints will therefore fall within **s. 994**.

[9] Bring together the complaints considered in the earlier paragraphs, to show how s. 994 is relevant and so of assistance to a minority shareholder

[10] In a mixed topic essay question it is particularly important that your conclusion brings together the different topics to show how they interrelate

Conclusion[10]

The articles have contractual effect but this does not mean a shareholder can enforce terms of the articles exactly as if they were contractual terms. A shareholder is a member of an association, where individual rights cannot be absolute and majority rule normally prevails, which can lead to complexity and result in harsh or apparently inconsistent outcomes. Because of the vulnerability of minority shareholders to oppression or wrongdoing, it is right that statute provides some additional remedies, but equally important that these are not so wide as to undermine fundamental principles underlying company law. By restricting access to derivative claims and providing limits to the notion of 'unfair prejudice', the law maintains a balance between individual rights, majority rule, and the separation of powers.

LOOKING FOR EXTRA MARKS?

- Make sure you spread your time sensibly across the various elements within the question, rather than going too deeply into one part only: it is by dealing with all the elements and making the connections that you will get the most marks here

- Recognize the link between enforcement of the articles, personal rights, and the rule in *Foss v Harbottle*, engaging with the academic discussion if you have time

Jaime is a shareholder in Winterfell Ltd, which has three directors, Arya, Sansa, and Ramsay. Although Arya, Sansa, and Ramsay run the business on a day-to-day basis, it is well known that they refer all major issues to Tyrion for a final decision. Tyrion was managing director of Winterfell Ltd for many years but resigned in 2018 following a local scandal.

Jaime has recently learned that Arya and Tyrion have set up a new business, developing a product Jaime knows the designer originally offered to Winterfell Ltd. Jaime believes this business would have been highly profitable for Winterfell Ltd, and therefore financially beneficial to him. Jaime owns 50 of Winterfell Ltd's 500 issued shares, 25 of which were allotted to him in return for his help updating Winterfell Ltd's computer systems. The board has recently demanded that Jaime either pay for or forfeit those shares, which Jaime suspects is because he had asked questions about Arya and Tyrion's new business.

Advise Jaime.

 CAUTION!

- Duties and shareholder remedies are a common combination so be prepared to deal with both in a question but always check the question instruction to see if you are advising the company, a shareholder, or some other party, so you can direct your discussion accordingly

- Think about how the issues in a problem interrelate when planning your answer; sometimes it is more efficient to deal with issues in a different order to how they appear in the question

DIAGRAM ANSWER PLAN

Identify the issues	■ Share issue to J ■ New business set up by A and T ■ Options available to J

Relevant law	■ Issue of shares for non-cash consideration ■ Forfeiture of shares ■ Proper purposes doctrine ■ De facto and shadow directors and their duties ■ No conflict/no profit rule; the corporate opportunity doctrine ■ Rule in *Foss v Harbottle* ■ Derivative claims ■ Unfair prejudice

Apply the law	■ Apply the law to the various scenarios

Conclude	■ Consequences of actions ■ What can J do about them?

SUGGESTED ANSWER

[1] Indicate that you've spotted there is more than one topic in this question

This question raises several connected issues concerning directors' duties, shareholder remedies, and issue of shares.[1] After examining the share issue and threat of forfeiture, the answer will discuss Arya and Tyrion's situation and consider what action Jaime could take.

Jaime's Shares

A private company can issue shares for non-cash consideration (**Companies Act 2006 (CA 2006), s. 582(1)**), without need for formal valuation (unlike public companies: **s. 593**). The courts will not question the value of consideration received (**Re Wragg Ltd [1897] 1 Ch 796**), provided it is not clearly illusory (**Hong Kong and China Gas Co Ltd v Glen [1914] 1 Ch 527**). Accordingly Jaime's services can be valid consideration for the shares, which would indicate no further liability on his part.

[2] If the facts are ambiguous, that is almost certainly deliberate

However, the facts are not entirely clear[2] whether the services were intended as consideration for shares, or the shares were subsequently given to Jaime as a thank you for his help. If the latter then the consideration would be past, and so invalid: *Re Eddystone Marine Insurance Co* **[1893] 3 Ch 9**, meaning Jaime would remain liable to pay for those shares, and potentially at risk of forfeiture.

To forfeit unpaid shares the company would need the power to do this in its articles (it is not within the current private company model articles: **Companies (Model Articles) Regulations 2008, Sch 1**).[3] Exercising a power to forfeit shares does not breach the prohibition on a company acquiring its own shares (**CA 2006, s. 658**): **s. 659(2) (c)**.[4] However, if the directors sought to exercise the power here, it could be challenged for breaching their duty to exercise powers only for the purposes for which they are conferred: **s. 171(b)**. Here the primary motivation of the directors seems to be to stifle discussion of their activities, rather than to secure payment for the company. If the 'substantial' purpose for which a power is exercised is not within the proper boundaries of the power, its exercise is void: *Howard Smith Ltd v Ampol Petroleum Ltd* **[1974] AC 821**; *Eclairs Group Ltd v JKX Oil plc* **[2015] UKSC 71**. This is so even if the directors genuinely believed their action would benefit the company: *Lee Panavision Ltd v Lee Lighting Ltd* **[1992] BCLC 22**. However, as directors' duties are owed to the company (**CA 2006, s. 170(1)**) Jaime may have difficulty remedying breaches—this will be considered later.

Arya and Tyrion

Arya is a de jure director, as are Sansa and Ramsay, and therefore undoubtedly owes duties to the company. Tyrion is not formally appointed director but may be a de facto or shadow director[5] (and these concepts may overlap: *Re Paycheck Services Ltd* **[2010] 1 WLR 2793**). It is unlikely that Tyrion is a de facto director: this is someone assuming the status and functions of a director (*Re Kaytech International plc* **[1999] BCC 390**). However, on the facts he may well be a shadow director: someone in accordance with whose directions or instructions the directors are accustomed to act (**CA 2006, s. 251**). Tyrion's involvement does not need to be hidden for him to be a shadow director, nor need he be followed on every matter (*Secretary of State for Trade and Industry v Deverell* **[2001] Ch 340**). Shadow directors can be subject to directors' duties where appropriate (**CA 2006, s. 170(5)**; *Vivendi SA v Richards* **[2013] EWHC 3006**; *Standish v Royal Bank of Scotland plc* **[2019] EWHC 3116**). Given the extent of Tyrion's involvement it can be argued he should owe the same duties to Winterfell as Arya in this situation.[6]

By taking up the product offered to Winterfell, it seems likely Arya and Tyrion are in breach of **CA 2006, s. 175**: a director must not allow a conflict between his interest and his duty. This applies in particular to the exploitation of any property, information, or opportunity: **s. 175(2)**. Pre-2006 cases remain relevant to the interpretation and application of the statutory duty (**s. 170(4)**).[7] They show a generally

---

[3] Most examiners would not expect you to know this; it is fine simply to state you are assuming the company has power to forfeit in its articles

[4] Not an essential point, but if you can show off connected knowledge concisely, then take the opportunity

[5] If you are told individuals are directors you can assume they are properly appointed (don't speculate further). If not then consider the possibility of de facto or shadow directorship

[6] Remember to consider whether shadow directors owe duties to the company

[7] This section avoids a historical account of the duty by starting with the statutory formulation, and then explaining why earlier cases are relevant, before considering those cases

strict approach to the duty, with liability even if the company was unable to take up the opportunity itself (*Regal (Hastings) Ltd v Gulliver* [1942] 1 All ER 378; *Industrial Development Consultants Ltd v Cooley* [1972] 1 WLR 443).

Sometimes directors have been permitted to take on opportunities, if rejected by the company in good faith (*Peso Silver Mines Ltd v Cropper* [1966] SCR 673) while other cases impose liability only when there was a 'maturing business opportunity' (*Canadian Aero Service Ltd v O'Malley* (1973) 40 DLR (3d) 371; *Island Export Finance Ltd v Umunna* [1986] BCLC 460). However, on the facts the opportunity appears to have been 'live' and the directors still in post (and recent cases indicate a strict approach: *O'Donnell v Shanahan* [2009] 2 BCLC 666), making it more likely than not that Arya and Tyrion would be in breach. As far as the facts reveal, the conflict has not been authorized by the other directors, but if it had been there is no breach (s. 175(4)). Authorization is clearly a possibility as the directors' actions indicate they do not want Arya and Tyrion's actions challenged. If the directors did authorize Arya and Tyrion's actions, but this was patently not in the interests of the company, then all the directors might be in breach of both s. 171(b) and s. 172 (duty to promote the success of the company).

What Can Jaime Do?

The general duties of directors are owed to the company (s. 170(1)) and the rule in *Foss v Harbottle* (1843) 2 Ha 461 means shareholders cannot usually bring proceedings on the company's behalf. However derivative claims (now in statutory form: CA 2006, ss. 260–4) are an exception to this rule. Jaime has the basis of a derivative claim as this is a cause of action vested in the company (s. 260(1)(a)), relating to a breach of duty by a director (s. 260(3)), and would be seeking relief for the company (s. 260(1)(b)).

Under s. 261 Jaime would have to apply to court for permission to continue a derivative claim, first showing a prima facie case (s. 261(2)). Permission will be refused if a person subject to the s. 172 duty (often called 'the hypothetical director') would not seek to continue the claim, or if the breach has been authorized or ratified by the company (s. 263(2)). Assuming this stage is passed (as seems likely), the court then must consider various factors in the exercise of its discretion. Key among these factors are the good faith of the claimant (ie Jaime), the importance the hypothetical director would attach to continuing the claim, and whether Jaime would have a claim in his own right (s. 263(3)).[8] The court should take particular account of the views of any independent shareholders (s. 263(4)). Accordingly, it would be necessary to consider the circumstances surrounding Jaime's concerns to evaluate whether permission is likely

[8] You are unlikely to have time to set out all the factors and consider each in turn (at least not in a question like this), but the examiner will want to see that you have some knowledge of them

to be granted. If permission is given Jaime is likely to be granted an indemnity against his costs (***Wallersteiner v Moir (No. 2)* [1975] 1 QB 373**), and if successful the benefit will accrue to the company, not him personally.

An alternative to a derivative claim would be for Jaime to petition on the ground that the conduct of the company's affairs has been unfairly prejudicial to his interests as a member (**CA 2006, s. 994**). Given the apparent breach(es) of duty and hostile attitude of the directors, there seem to be grounds for establishing both unfairness and prejudice (***Re Saul D Harrison & Sons plc* [1995] 1 BCLC 14**; ***O'Neill v Phillips* [1999] 1 WLR 1092**). If Jaime were to succeed, the court has a wide discretion as to the order it makes (**s. 996**), but by far the most common order is for the purchase of the petitioner's shares. Accordingly, assuming Jaime wants to remain in the company, this remedy may not be as attractive as pursuing a derivative claim.[9]

⁹ This implicitly justifies dealing with the remedy only briefly

Conclusion

It seems probable that Jaime has no liability to pay for his shares, and so there is no risk of forfeiture. Even if Jaime was liable to pay for the shares, and the articles contained a power of forfeiture in these circumstances, any exercise of that power might well be void because of breach of **CA 2006, s. 171(b)**. Tyrion appears to be a shadow director, and it is probable he therefore owes duties to Winterfell. In taking up the opportunity offered to Winterfell, it seems likely that both Arya and Tyrion have breached their duty to the company under **s. 175**, and there could be further connected breaches of other duties (eg **s. 172**) as more than one duty can apply at one time (**s. 179**).[10] To remedy this Jaime would have to bring a derivative claim under **s. 260**, and appears to have reasonable prospects of success. Alternatively, if Jaime sought a personal rather than corporate remedy, he could consider a petition for unfair prejudice under **s. 994**.

¹⁰ This takes the opportunity to make a minor additional point that was not included earlier on

LOOKING FOR EXTRA MARKS?

■ Explore the requirements of the relevant shareholder remedies in more depth, including the relationship between the different remedies

■ Indicate where facts are not clear or where more facts are necessary and why this matters for a particular issue. If you need to take alternative paths (or make a sensible assumption based on the available facts), then do so, explaining what you are doing and why

Q

Beacho Ltd, a provider of health supplements, is in financial difficulty and is currently not able to meet its debts in full each month, although it is managing to keep trading for the moment, relying to a great extent on the forbearance of its creditors. The company has three directors, Sandy, Ceecee, and Lilo. Angelo (Ceecee's husband) also attends all board meetings and generally helps out in running the business, and calls himself director when dealing with customers. Together, Sandy, Ceecee, Lilo, and Angelo have concluded that the company should continue trading as they believe that there is a chance that they will manage to pull the company through its current difficulties and so this course of action will be the best for the company's shareholders.

Advise the directors whether this course of action risks breaching their duties to the company, and whether there would be any consequences for them should the company ultimately be placed into insolvent liquidation.

CAUTION!

- This question requires you to explore both directors' duties when the company is a going concern, and directors' liability on insolvency. Make sure you are confident on both topics, and the overlap between them

- Don't forget to consider who 'the directors' are in this scenario

DIAGRAM ANSWER PLAN

Identify the issues
- Who could be liable?
- Duties when company is a going concern
- Position on insolvency

Relevant law
- Directors: de jure and de facto
- Directors' duties: owed to the company
- Duty to promote the success of the company: CA 2006, s. 172
- Position of creditors when company is insolvent
- Misfeasance: IA 1986, s. 212
- Wrongful trading: IA 1986, s. 214
- Disqualification: CDDA 1986, s. 6

Apply the law
- Apply to the facts

Conclude
- Conclude, advising the directors

SUGGESTED ANSWER

The directors face a common dilemma: whether to keep going hoping Beacho Ltd will pull through, or admit defeat. We are told they have chosen to continue trading. If successful this would benefit shareholders (who will not lose their investment, and may get dividends later), employees (who keep their jobs), and creditors (who will eventually receive payment). But if unsuccessful, further debt will have been incurred by the time Beacho Ltd fails—additional creditor losses.[1]

The essay will first assess whether Angelo (as well as Sandy, Ceecee, and Lilo) is a director, and then advise whether their decision risks breaching their duties to the company (particularly **Companies Act 2006 (CA 2006), s. 172**) and the consequences for them should Beacho Ltd go into insolvent liquidation.

Directors

Sandy, Ceecee, and Lilo are de jure directors of Beacho Ltd. Angelo may be a de facto director. If so he would also owe duties to the company and be subject to post-liquidation consequences such as wrongful trading and disqualification.[2]

Re Hydrodam (Corby) Ltd **[1994] BCC 161** (*'Hydrodam'*) held that a de facto director assumes to act as director and is held out as such by the company. Later cases, notably *Re Kaytech International plc* **[1999] BCC 390**, emphasized all relevant factors should be considered; the *Hydrodam* points are not determinative. Relevant factors include holding out and using the title of director, but also access to proper information and making major decisions: was the individual part of the corporate governing structure? (*Secretary of State for Trade and Industry v Tjolle* **[1998] BCC 282**.) In *Secretary of State for Trade and Industry v Hollier* **[2007] BCC 11**, Etherton J indicated that a de facto director participates in collective decision-making, which Angelo clearly does (board meetings, deciding to continue trading). As he also calls himself director and helps to run the business,[3] it seems probable Angelo is a de facto director.

Breach of Duty

Directors owe their duties to the company (**CA 2006, s. 170(1)**), normally meaning the shareholders as a body. Under **CA 2006, s. 172** directors must act in the way they consider, in good faith, 'would be most likely to promote the success of the company for the benefit of its members as a whole'. In doing so directors must have regard to a range of matters, including likely long-term consequences and interests of employees (**s. 172(1)(a)–(f)**). This 'enlightened shareholder value' approach[4] requires directors to have regard

---

[1] Starting the essay in this way shows that you understand the significance of the decision the directors are making, and also sets the scene for the later discussion on s. 172 and wrongful trading

[2] There is too much else to pack into this question to spend time also explaining shadow directors, or to delve further into why the law imposes obligations on de facto or shadow directors

[3] Identify the relevant problem facts and link these to the authorities

[4] Show you know the basis for s. 172, albeit only in passing

to other stakeholder interests in order to achieve corporate success for the benefit of members.

'Creditors' are not a separate category within **s. 172(1)(a)–(f)**. In any event **s. 172** does not impose duties directly owed to stakeholders. This might indicate the directors' actions do not risk breach of duty, as continuing to trade would benefit shareholders.[5] However **s. 172** is subject to any 'rule of law requiring directors, in certain circumstances, to consider or act in the interests of creditors of the company' (**s. 172(3)**). This relates to an important common law qualification (and to wrongful trading (**Insolvency Act 1986 (IA 1986), s. 214**), considered later).

In *West Mercia Safetywear Ltd v Dodd* [1988] BCLC 250, the court adopted the approach of *Kinsela v Russell Kinsela Pty Ltd* [1986] 4 NSWR 722: while shareholders could be regarded 'as' the company while the company is solvent, 'where a company is insolvent the interests of the creditors intrude' as it is the creditors who will lose or gain from directors' decisions. Once a company is insolvent (or directors know or should know it is likely to become insolvent: *BTI 2014 LLC v Sequana SA* [2019] EWCA Civ 112), it is the creditors' interests the directors should be considering, although that does not mean directors owe duties to individual creditors.[6]

[6] If you had time you could expand this consideration and reflect on the Company Law Review's decision not to bring creditor interests explicitly into s. 172(1)

Accordingly, as Beacho Ltd is insolvent (unable to pay its debts), the directors should be considering the position of creditors rather than shareholders in deciding whether to continue. They could still conclude it is right to continue trading, but that would depend on how realistic the 'chance' of success is. Although acting in good faith, by not considering creditor interests at all, the directors are prima facie in breach of **s. 172.** Where directors have not considered the issue at all the courts have looked at whether an 'intelligent and honest' director could reasonably have believed the action to benefit the company: *Charterbridge Corporation Ltd v Lloyds Bank Ltd* [1970] Ch 62.[7] That would depend on Beacho Ltd's financial position and prospects.

[7] How the courts should assess breach when directors have failed to consider the question at all is an interesting issue: see further Teele, Langford, & Ramsay, 'Directors' duties to act in the interests of the company—subjective or objective?' [2015] JBL 173

The directors could also be in breach of their duty of care, skill, and diligence: **CA 2006, s. 174**, which is measured objectively in relation to a reasonably diligent director, with additional expectations on directors with particular knowledge, skill, or experience. Completely failing to consider the interests of creditors when the company is insolvent would seem to breach this duty (*Madoff Securities International Ltd v Raven* [2013] EWHC 3147).

[8] This recognizes the practical point about enforcement while also linking to the next section

The directors are unlikely at present to face any threat of action in respect of breaches of duty—there is little risk of a derivative claim in these circumstances. However, the position changes if the company subsequently fails.[8]

Insolvent Liquidation—Consequences for Directors

If directors breach their duties and Beacho Ltd goes into insolvent liquidation, the liquidator (or creditor or contributory) can take action using the misfeasance procedure: **Insolvency Act 1986 (IA 1986), s. 212**. This does not create new rights or obligations, it just provides a summary procedure (*Bentinck v Fenn* **(1887) 12 App Cas 652**; *Cohen v Selby* **[2001] 1 BCLC 176**). Any defences the directors had would remain available, as would relief under **CA 2006, s. 1157**: *Re DKG Contractors Ltd* **[1990] BCC 903**.

Probably more significant is the potential for the liquidator to bring wrongful trading proceedings against them: **IA 1986, s. 214**. Section 214 is designed to ensure directors stop trading when a company is inexorably moving towards insolvent liquidation, the circumstance Beacho Ltd may be in.[9] A director can be ordered to contribute to the company's assets if the company continues to trade beyond the point he 'knew or ought to have concluded' (evaluated using the dual objective/subjective test in **s. 214(4)**) that there was 'no reasonable prospect' of the company avoiding insolvent liquidation. Given the directors are already relying on the forbearance of creditors, if the financial position is not improving it seems likely they ought to conclude insolvent liquidation is all but inevitable. Realistic prospects of a change in fortune would change the position, but a blind hope of improvement is not enough (*Roberts v Frohlich* **[2011] 2 BCLC 625**). Directors are not liable if they 'took every step with a view to minimising potential loss' to creditors that they 'ought to have taken' (**s. 214(3)**), but relying on 'a chance' of recovery would not meet that test. On the (limited) given facts, there is a serious risk of wrongful trading by the directors. Contribution 'as the court thinks proper' (**s. 214(1)**) is a compensatory measure, the amount by which the company's assets were further depleted by the wrongful trading (*Re Produce Marketing Consortium Ltd* **[1989] BCLC 520**).

The directors could potentially face liability for fraudulent trading under **IA 1986, s. 213**, but the facts do not indicate intent to defraud creditors, which requires 'actual dishonesty' (*Re Patrick and Lyon Ltd* **[1933] Ch 786**). While fraudulent trading includes incurring debts in the knowledge they cannot be repaid (*Re William C Leitch Bros* **[1932] 2 Ch 71**), this is more than suggested here.

Another important consequence of the directors' continuation of trading is potential disqualification for 2–15 years under the **Company Directors Disqualification Act 1986 (CDDA 1986), s. 6** as unfit to be concerned in the management of a company. (They could also face disqualification if liable for wrongful trading: **CDDA 1986, s. 10**.) Although mere errors of judgment do not amount to unfitness (*Re Lo-Line Electric Motors Ltd* **[1988] Ch 447**), trading at risk of creditors is a very common factor in disqualification. This means

[9] Show you understand what wrongful trading is all about and so why it is relevant to the problem

accumulating further debt when there is no realistic prospect of repayment, often relying on the forbearance of creditors, as here: *Re*

[10] It is important to recognize that 'trading at creditors' risk' is not satisfied just because the company continues trading while insolvent

Sevenoaks Stationers (Retail) Ltd [1991] Ch 164. Trading while insolvent is not unfit in itself[10] (*Secretary of State for Trade and Industry v Taylor* [1997] 1 WLR 407), provided directors have properly taken the view the company has a sound future. Much therefore depends on the decision to continue trading, and whether this is objectively reasonable.

Conclusion

The directors of Beacho Ltd (including Angelo, as a de facto director) are at risk of breaching their duties to the company (particularly **CA 2006, s. 172**) if they continue to trade, unless they carefully consider the position of creditors. With only a chance of the company surviving, then unless this chance is realistic and substantial, the directors should be considering liquidation or a rescue process such as administration. If they continue to trade and Beacho Ltd does enter into insolvent liquidation, there are real risks they would face personal liability under **IA 1986, s. 214**, and/or disqualification for unfitness under **CDDA 1986, s. 6**.

LOOKING FOR EXTRA MARKS?

■ Engage with and critique the academic work relating to when duties are owed to creditors

■ Explore the connections between directors' duties and liability on insolvency, not just through the misfeasance procedure, but through the development of both sets of obligations

■ Use your time carefully to ensure you cover both halves of the question in sufficient depth

Online Resources   www.oup.com/uk/qanda/

Go online for extra essay and problem questions and a podcast with advice on revision and exam technique.

Skills for Success in Coursework Assessments

Some company law courses are assessed by exam only, but many will include at least some element of coursework. Coursework is simply an assessment, other than an exam, where the mark counts towards the final course grade. Preparing coursework shares some features with writing exam answers—the importance of relevance, structure, and answering the question, for example—but there are differences too. Because requirements for coursework can differ so widely between institutions in terms of length, preparation time, etc, this chapter does not provide sample answers but instead provides general guidance, and then discusses a sample essay question and problem question to give pointers as to how you might approach them.

Why Coursework?

To understand how to do well in coursework it is worth thinking about why it has been included as one of your company law assessments. First, it provides a different way to demonstrate knowledge and skills, recognizing that different people excel in different forms of assessment. Secondly, it provides more than one chance to gain some marks, providing some cushion against the risk of having an 'off day' on exam day.

But the most important reason for assessing by coursework is to test slightly different skills and abilities than an exam: research skills, extended argument, presentational and referencing skills, communication, and so on. Remembering that a coursework assessment is designed to test slightly different skills (or to test skills and abilities in different ways) can be helpful when thinking about what you should be aiming to demonstrate in your coursework. It should also remind you that simply producing what you would produce in an exam is unlikely to achieve great marks.

Types of Coursework

In company law, coursework can take a variety of forms, depending on the inventiveness, interests, or habits of the question-setter, and the learning outcomes of your course. The most common form is an essay, often of extended length. Examiners like setting essays as they give the opportunity to explore a particular issue or issues in more depth. Almost as popular are problem questions, usually involving several different points and rather grey areas of law, to test your ability to identify issues and apply the law.

But company law coursework can encompass a wide range of other tasks. For example, advising a body (such as a government department) on a particular area of law, perhaps including suggestions for reform. Or drafting a briefing document for a law firm or business, preparing slides or a script for a presentation, or creating a poster for a research conference. Other exercises might be more ongoing or reflective, requiring you perhaps to engage with online discussion, contribute to a blog, or engage with topical news stories, and perhaps reflect on your learning journey as part of this. Most coursework will be individual, but you may be asked to prepare work in a pair or small group and this of course brings with it a whole range of different issues connected with team-working. While the advice that follows is primarily directed to traditional forms of coursework, such as essays and problem questions, much is equally applicable to other forms of coursework.

Things to Consider in Coursework

Assessment/marking criteria: Check the assessment or marking criteria that apply to your work—these may be generic to your university or department, or specific to your course or the assessment itself. If you don't know what they are, then ask. Keep the criteria in mind when preparing and reviewing your coursework as these are the things you will be tested against.

Identifying issues in company law: Coursework exercises may cover a range of issues, or make connections between topics, or require you to explore a topic that hasn't been covered in depth in lectures. Don't assume you know what the question is about: think, think, and think some more, and ensure you cover the points you need to. If your lecturer has highlighted particular links, personal research interests, or topical subjects during the course then it is worth considering whether any of these are relevant. To make an obvious, but necessary, point, make sure that your answer responds to the question asked, rather than discusses a topic that you wanted to write about instead.

Research: You are expected to undertake your own research into the topic(s) covered in the assessment—whatever form it takes. Any reading list you've been provided with is a great starting place. But explore more widely—textbooks will have further reading suggestions at the end of chapters or within footnotes, and one article may well refer to another that could be worth following up. Take the opportunity to engage more deeply with the primary material too—examiners love to see you've actually read a case and are not just repeating points from a textbook. Research properly and use appropriate and respected sources (eg academic journals and reform papers, not online encyclopaedias or student essays).

Planning your work: Start work early—if you leave things to the last minute you won't have time to think about the question, develop your ideas, and do your research. Think carefully about the structure of your work, this is a crucial step in creating a thoughtful, analytical argument, and addressing the question. Write a plan, initially in skeleton form, adding more detail as your research and ideas start to flow—modify it as necessary. With a plan in place it is usually helpful to start writing quite early, as this helps to trigger fresh ideas and highlight structural problems. But be prepared to rewrite (or even scrap) these early efforts: your ideas will change as you write, and you need to be flexible in adapting your work.

Length: Coursework is often of a longer length than can be produced in an exam, giving you the chance to show you can maintain and develop an argument. Alternatively you may be set a short piece of coursework that can be just as challenging (if not more so) as you need to pack your brilliance into a very limited space. Use the length of the work as an indication of the depth and breadth of the material you need to cover but remember that just because you've got more words to play with, you still need to be as precise and concise as you possibly can. Don't waste words on waffle. Double check any word limit you are given; many institutions impose extremely strict and severe penalties for breaching these.

Presentation: You will have much longer to prepare your coursework than you have to write an exam answer, and the examiner will therefore expect to see a clearly and professionally presented piece of work. Check whether there are any particular presentational rules that you need to follow: ignoring these will, at best, annoy the examiner, and at worst you may be penalized. Your work should be clearly and neatly presented, using an appropriate font and type size. Include a bibliography unless instructed not to. As part of your professional presentation, make sure your work is written clearly, with a high degree of accuracy, no ambiguity, and only sensible abbreviations.

Referencing and bibliography: Sources must be referenced properly (normally in footnotes), using a consistent format, and following any requirements (or preferences) of your department. This is both a matter of good legal practice (and may well be part of your assessment/marking criteria) and essential to avoid plagiarism. As company law is generally taught later in your legal studies, markers will expect referencing to be of a high standard—both in what you reference and how you reference. If you are not given a specific style to follow, then use OSCOLA (Oxford University Standard for the Citation of Legal Authorities). Don't leave referencing to the last minute, keep good records as you go along. Your bibliography should be prepared sensibly (OSCOLA is helpful here too), ideally with separate sections for different types of sources, and then arranged alphabetically by author surname. A bibliography should include all the material used in the preparation of your coursework, not just sources specifically referenced.

Be critical: As you prepare and write your work, challenge ideas and arguments to develop your analysis and identify other points of view. Try to avoid casual or broad statements that aren't strictly accurate. Read your work with a critical eye, and make sure you have really expressed every point as clearly as you can, remembering that the examiner can't see what is in your head, they can only mark what is on the paper.

Coursework Example 1: Essay

QUESTION

The doctrine laid down in *Salomon v Salomon*[1] has to be watched very carefully. It has often been supposed to cast a veil over the personality of a limited company through which the courts cannot see. But that is not true. The courts can and often do draw aside the veil.[2] They can, and often do, pull off the mask. They look to see what really lies behind. The legislature has shown the way [3] with group[4] accounts and the rest. And the courts should follow suit.[5] Lord Denning, *Littlewoods Mail Order Stores v Inland Revenue Commissioners* [1969] 1 WLR 1241.

Critically discuss the modern[6] approach of the courts to lifting/piercing the veil of incorporation in light of the above statement.

[1] You will need to establish what this means to set the context, but don't spend lots of time explaining the case and principle more generally. And think about its consequences—why is it so important?

[2] This provides you with the focus of your discussion—do the courts watch the veil closely and often 'draw it aside'? And what does that mean? Does it encompass veil-lifting in the broad sense as well as veil-piercing?

[3] Think about the role of statute in lifting/piercing the veil. Is it true, as is implicit in the statement, that statute willingly throws aside the veil?

[4] The mention of corporate groups should remind you that this is a particular area of controversy when it comes to separate corporate personality, limited liability, and lifting the veil. You shouldn't limit your discussion to groups as the statement and instruction are wider than that, but you should engage with the issue.

⁵ This both gives you a focus (the courts) and steers you to deeper analysis. Whatever the position *is*, and you need to explain this, what *should* it be? Even without a clear push from the question itself you should be engaging with these sorts of questions: Why? Why not? Should? How?

⁶ A reminder that, whatever the date of the statement, you need to be focusing on the law as it is now applied by the courts. By all means look back at previous decisions and legal development, this will be an important part of your analysis, but make sure the *current* position is your focus.

ANSWER GUIDANCE

Separate corporate personality is a popular choice for coursework questions—both essays and problems. This is partly because it comes up early in most courses, so enables a question to be set early on. But it is also because it works well either as an almost self-contained topic, or as a topic to interlink with all sorts of others, from corporate structure to directors' duties, and from corporate liability to insolvency, enabling you to show your broader engagement with company law issues. Depending on your course content you may be expected to engage further with corporate law theory, economic analysis and principles of limited liability, corporate social responsibility, and so on. Remember always to view any coursework question you are set through the lens of your own course: if your course or lecturer has a particular focus or interest then take this into account when deciding what to include in your discussion.

With a statement/discuss question such as this, remember to pull apart the statement to find the issues you need to focus on—don't use the statement simply as an indicator of the topic more generally. The more focused and challenging you can be, the stronger your discussion and analysis is likely to be. In your introduction, show clearly how the points you are going to discuss link to the statement and question.

In any answer it is important to question and challenge, and not simply explain, but this is particularly important in coursework when you have more time to research and engage with the issues. Think about not only what the law is (and whether the statement reflects this accurately) but also why the law is the way it is, whether it should be the way it is, and even what, if anything, would be better. This enables you to broaden your research and deepen your analysis, while staying very much within the confines of the question.

Don't be tempted to use the extra time/space coursework gives you to provide lots of detail on well-known cases such as *Salomon*. Demonstrate your knowledge concisely to leave yourself space for the further discussion and analysis that will get you the higher marks. That doesn't mean you should ignore the basics—too often students are so keen to get to the 'higher value' material that they forget to explain the legal principles or set the context for their discussion and so don't get the marks they are expecting—but don't waste lots of time setting out case facts, for example, unless they are really critical to your argument.

This question requires you to explain and analyse the *Salomon* principle and the notion of lifting or piercing the veil of incorporation. But it isn't just a matter of explaining *Salomon*, even less explaining *Littlewoods* itself. You need to consider what the current approach of the courts is, and whether the courts do, as the statement suggests, fairly freely draw aside the veil (was this even true in 1969?).

To deepen your analysis further you could think about why the veil matters—why should the veil ever be disturbed, or indeed should it ever have been allowed to settle? Think about the relationship between corporate personality and limited liability. You might consider the particular issues of one-person companies and/or corporate groups. Think also about whether Lord Denning's link to statute is valid—is there any indication that statute ignores the veil? Even if there is, would that be an excuse for the courts to do the same? What about the merits of legal certainty, which was clearly an influence in *Prest*? What might be the consequence of a broader discretion to lift/pierce the veil, and would this be better than the current position?

By asking yourself questions about the statement you can encourage broader and deeper engagement with the question. Challenge yourself early on in your preparation so you can jot down ideas, see where points link, work out where you need to focus your research, and develop an argument that gets to the heart of the question.

Coursework Example 2: Problem Question

QUESTION

Robin and Linnet are the directors of Hoopoo Ltd, which owns and runs a small chain of coffee shops in Fetherville. Robin left education immediately after school but has always worked in business, while Linnet has an accounting degree and is a former estate agent.[1] Robin and Linnet each own 40 per cent of the shares; the remaining 20 per cent are owned by Serin.[2] Linnet also owns 30 per cent of the shares in another company,[3] Peanuts Ltd, which runs a gift shop in Fetherville.

Last year Robin was having a drink in the pub[4] in a nearby village when he saw the small café next door was for sale. Robin thought the price was very reasonable at £200,000, so he bought it. He did not think it was suitable for Hoopoo Ltd[5] as it wasn't in Fetherville itself and the company would have had to take out a loan to make the purchase. He told Linnet later; she raised no objections.[6]

Last month Robin and Linnet decided to sell two of the company's less profitable coffee shops located near Fetherville High Street. They had valuations on both properties from only six months earlier, when they had updated their insurance, so didn't bother paying for fresh valuations.[7] The cafés sold very quickly at their asking prices: one was sold to Sunflowers Ltd for £400,000; the other was sold to Peanuts Ltd[8] for £300,000. It is now clear that the sale prices were significantly too low: changes to planning regulations the previous month had caused a significant uplift in property prices around Fetherville High Street, although Robin and Linnet hadn't known about this at the time.[9]

Serin has now heard of the purchase of the café by Robin, and of the sales of the two coffee shops. Advise Serin.[10]

[1] If information is included it is probably relevant—here it relates to the later point about skill and care.

[2] It is important to note that S is a minority shareholder.

[3] Again, think about why this is included. There is no obvious conflict just in the shareholding, so keep an eye out for its relevance.

[4] Make sure you address the fact that R isn't in his 'director' role when he gets this information.

[5] Consider whether it is for R to make that call.

[6] Note that L is only told afterwards, not in advance.

[7] Clearly flagging up a potential lack of care—you've got to decide if it is a breach.

[8] The relevance of L's shareholding in P Ltd now becomes clear—this transaction is one in which the director has an interest.

[9] Should they have done? Something else to fit into the evaluation of care and skill.

[10] This shows you are not just advising on what the directors have done, but what Serin, as a minority shareholder, can do about it.

ANSWER GUIDANCE

Directors' duties and shareholder remedies is a popular combined topic question for coursework (as well as exams) as it requires you to work through the different elements to reach a reasoned conclusion. Don't avoid issues or facts that look a bit tricky—deal with them, and explore 'grey' areas. But remember that you need to advise, not just discuss. You are asked to advise Serin, who is a minority shareholder. So you'll need to think first about what the directors have done, and then what, if anything, Serin can do about it.

Rather than trying to spot areas of law that might be relevant or familiar case facts, start by identifying the issues: what is Serin unhappy about? Use the facts to take you to the relevant law, rather than trying to impose the law onto the facts. This helps you focus on using and applying the law rather than presenting knowledge. Here Serin is concerned about: (a) Robin's purchase of the cafe, and (b) the sale of the coffee shops to (i) Sunflowers Ltd and (ii) Peanuts Ltd. Serin's complaints are clearly not about how he has been treated, but about how the directors have acted vis-à-vis the company, so the relevant law seems to be that of directors' duties.

The facts of Robin's café purchase may bring *Bhullar v Bhullar* to mind. But answering questions just by case-matching tends to mean the law and issues don't get fully explored. Identify the most relevant duty (s. 175) and consider its requirements and the courts' approach. Build up your case, applying and distinguishing cases as appropriate, so *Bhullar* becomes part of a more detailed picture that enables you to reflect on different approaches and criticisms too. And what impact, if any, does disclosing his purchase to L have?

The coffee shop sales have resulted in loss to the company but was that because of a breach of duty? Establish the scope of the duty of care, skill, and diligence (s. 174), drawing on relevant cases, and link the facts to the law. Remember both the objective standard, what would be expected of a director in this position, and then whether Robin and Linnet's skills, experience etc increase that expectation (the subjective element). Now you can evaluate whether their actions lived up to that standard. The sale to Peanuts Ltd raises additional issues, because of Linnet's interest. Remember to consider the facts carefully so you address the correct duty—if s. 177 applies, then s. 175 doesn't. Work through the requirements and whenever you are thinking about s. 177 then also be alert to s. 190 (substantial property transactions).

Other duties may be relevant but it is best to spend most of your time focusing on the most relevant one. Section 172 is often worth a mention, but remember its subjective nature, and so the difficulty in establishing breach unless a director's behaviour seems blatantly not in the company's interest. When considering the breaches of duty you could cover whether the directors could avoid liability in any way, for example ratification or court relief, or you can deal with these in the next part.

The second stage is to consider Serin's options in relation to the wrongs you have identified. You can recognize the rule in *Foss v Harbottle* and separation of powers to show you understand the problems facing a minority shareholder, but don't take long over this.

With breaches of duty involved, clearly a derivative claim should be considered. Work through the statute, incorporating the relevant cases, and linking always to the facts. The first steps (the fundamental requirements and the preliminary stage for permission to continue) can be brief thanks to your previous analysis. The next two stages need to be recognized as distinct but the first can usually be dealt with quickly, with more time taken going through the discretionary stage, focusing on those elements that seem particularly relevant. Link to the facts rather than just presenting the material. Ratification and/or authorization is often an interesting area to explore in these kinds of questions (and remember to consider whether some breaches are even capable of ratification) so if you haven't dealt with it earlier make sure you consider it here. Would Serin be likely to get permission to continue based on the facts and your analysis?

Even with permission, Serin will still need to prove his case. Come back to your analysis of the strength of his claim(s), and also whether the directors could avoid liability (if not previously dealt with). Consider too the risks and benefits S might get from bringing a claim: is it worth it?

Another option for Serin could be unfairly prejudicial conduct. Work through the requirements of s. 994, applying to the facts, but your focus here is unfairness, as will be the case in most problems. Establish the principles (*O'Neill v Phillips*), consider where Serin's case fits within these, and bring in relevant cases—remembering here that Serin's complaints relate to breaches of duty, not exclusion from management or similar complaints. Has he got a strong case, and what would the remedy be? You could also touch on s. 122(1)(g) IA 1986 but, on these facts, probably only to show that you understand why that wouldn't be a great option.

Don't forget to finish off by advising Serin. Follow through your analysis to conclude with what you would advise him to do, and why.

Coursework Checklist

● Have I addressed the question that was set, considering all the issues?

● Have I assessed, applied, and analysed the law and not simply described it?

● Have I given authority for all points of law, and referenced all uses of material, including quotes, paraphrasing, explanations, opinions, views, and ideas?

● Are my references complete, accurate, and in proper form?

● Is the work the correct length?

● Have I expressed myself clearly, precisely, concisely, and unambiguously? Have I checked for typographical errors?

● Have I reviewed my work against the assessment/marking criteria that apply to this assessment and evaluated its strengths and weaknesses?

INDEX

T

U

V